On October 1, 1987, Pat Robertson declared his candidacy for the Republican presidential nomination from the steps of the Bedford-Stuyvesant brownstone where he once lived. At the peak of a successful career and ministry in religious broadcasting, why is Robertson entering politics?

Here is an in-depth look at Pat Robertson's political aspirations. Hubert Morken, university professor of government, provides a critical and fair discussion of Robertson's views. He details the reasons behind his decision to seek public office and examines the strategy of Robertson's 1988 presidential campaign. The candidate's stance on a number of important issues are presented, including:

- *Support to families and the poor*
- *Communism and world peace*
- *The erosion of American freedom*
- *Obedience to the Supreme Court*
- *Public prayer*
- *Federal budget cuts*

Pat Robertson

★★★★
★★★★
★★★★
★★★
★★
WHERE HE STANDS

Hubert Morken

Power Books

FLEMING H. REVELL COMPANY
OLD TAPPAN, NEW JERSEY

ISBN 0-8007-5265-1

To my father and mother

who introduced me to politics and more
by teaching me Samuel, Kings, and Chronicles
and by taking me to China.

"Law is King and the King is not Law."

—*Francis Schaeffer quoting Samuel Rutherford
on the CBN "700 Club"*

Contents

Contents

Contents

Preface

Rumors that Pat Robertson would run for president surfaced in 1985. Agreeing with him on some issues, I objected to his candidacy for three reasons. First, he had little experience in government. In American history, only one candidate, Wendell L. Willkie, had not served in government in a high-ranking military or civilian capacity before being selected as a Republican or Democratic nominee. He lost. Second, it seemed that the Christian Broadcasting Network would be at risk without him. Third, for an ordained minister there was a conflict of interest with a government role.

With these objections in mind but respecting his entry into politics, I wrote a paper on Robertson for a conference at Calvin College, basing it on twenty-five speeches and interviews and one of his books, *The Secret Kingdom*. This paper circulated widely. Here are some of the comments written to me from around the country:

- ◆ He is stirring up anti-Christian feeling.
- ◆ He is dividing Republicans.
- ◆ He is a serious candidate.
- ◆ He is dividing Christians.
- ◆ He will be tempted to compromise principles.
- ◆ He is not understood.
- ◆ He is irreplaceable at CBN.

My own commitment to understand Robertson grew. Teaching government has given me the opportunity to explore religion and politics and their connections. Professors doing careful research at both religious and secular universities enriched my thinking. Some of them encouraged me to study Robertson further.

Preface

In the spring of 1987, I approached the Americans for Robertson organization as an independent author, asking them to make available to me copies of speeches and interviews for a full study of Robertson's political perspective. They granted me access to these materials, and in addition, I received assistance from CBN Television and the CBN University.

Robertson is one of the most unlikely presidential candidates in recent American history. In 1980, political observers, including Reagan's team, were shocked at the presence of the Moral Majority and the new Christian Right. In 1984, about 80 percent of the evangelical, charismatic, fundamentalist, pentecostal, and other born-again Protestants, except for blacks, voted for Ronald Reagan. Circumstances, issues, and a popular incumbent president drew these voters together.

In 1986, Pat Robertson announced that with 3 million supporters signing petitions, he would be a candidate, and clearly he intended to appeal to the broader electorate. He is not the first "born-again" candidate—Jimmy Carter obviously was in 1976. But Robertson *is* the first in recent times to do three things:

1. Attempt to mobilize religious people, especially conservatives.
2. Stand on a platform deliberately connected to biblical principles.
3. Pray publicly for supernatural help in facing real tasks.

He is saying, in effect, that America needs the church, the Bible, and miracles to hold it together. Yet Robertson wants more than Christians to support him, because government is in jeopardy, liberties are at stake, and national politics are at a fork in the road. To say it at its most extreme, it is as though Christians and other people are being called on to vote for him to help save America. To many his candidacy is the threefold scandal of:

1. mobilizing the religious in partisan politics,
2. standing on biblical principles for public policy, and
3. praying for supernatural help.

Any question about Robertson's motives calls for a complex answer. In the Bible, for example, King David killed Goliath for multiple reasons: the honor of God, the welfare of the nation, to rid the neighborhood of a bully, to get a rich reward—including freedom from taxes for life and the king's daughter for a wife. At the outset, let me suggest seven reasons why I believe Robertson is running:

1. He thinks there is no other strong political champion, Christian or otherwise. George Bush seems soft on many social issues. Other candidates appear weak. Even as Ted Kennedy ran in 1980 because he thought Jimmy Carter was not a leader, so today Robertson sees few competitors who are true statesmen.

2. He sees God on the move in religion and in politics, bringing salvation and justice to this earth through powerful social movements. These times cry out for leadership with vision, he feels. " 'There is a tide in the affairs of men,' " says Robertson, quoting Shakespeare, and he wants to catch that tide. His eyes are filled with a sense of that opportunity now, for someone, for him.

3. The candidacy looks possible. Changes in politics and communications allow a former Democrat to appeal directly to voters for their votes and financial support. If he gets enough people active for him during the primaries, he will not need much support from Republican leaders. Computerized petition lists and television give him direct access to donors and voters. Ordinary Christians will provide the core of the support.

4. Robertson is convinced it is God's will for him to run, if sufficiently confirmed and supported by the public.

5. He is sure that politics is falling apart because misguided thinking is leading the nation to destruction. Scholars look at problems in detail and in depth, but ignore basic solutions. Also church leaders are still largely silent, without much influence, ignorant of the wisdom of the Bible and its application to issues. Public authorities are getting America into deeper trouble, and the church gives little or no help.

6. From his perspective, his candidacy is an effort to recover the principles of the Kingdom of God for public affairs. Economic

disaster and worse may await the nation shortly, he says, and this requires bold but reliable answers with strong public support.

7. Perhaps Robertson is bored with his job. He has been the best television social critic he can be. He has developed national counseling and social welfare programs. He has even attacked the literacy problem. He has founded a university, a law school, and a legal foundation. What more can he do with his talents and resources? He is not primarily a preacher. He has thought long and hard about government and wants to see it done better.

The campaign process itself will test Robertson's determination and will reveal more of his character, motives, and potential. It will show just how much support he has in America and whether he can attract voters. However, political debate often degenerates into personal attacks, obscuring issues and making it difficult to discover the thinking of candidates.

The thoughts of Robertson, his most basic understanding of himself and the role of religion and government in America, are the subject of this book. Neither the press nor the public knows much about Robertson's views. Many of his political supporters who have watched him on CBN's "700 Club" program or have attended a campaign rally are just beginning to learn about politics. Neither television nor a campaign speech gives a candidate much time to address any one subject. Yet Robertson has written and spoken about government since 1976, developing answers to difficult questions.

This is a study of Robertson's political ideas and their relationship to his religious faith. Robertson is openly Christian, and he will say when asked that he gets his most important beliefs from the Bible. Long before he planned to be a presidential candidate he spoke out on the economy, foreign affairs, and social concerns, taking positions on issues, explaining and defending them partly on religious grounds. His public activities, like praying to stop a hurricane or asking for Christian support, became political issues.

Robertson is an intelligent religious broadcaster with an unknown political future. Some think that his journey into politics will be short, leading quickly to disillusionment and withdrawal, and that he will return to CBN older and wiser. On closer inspection, however, his decision to enter politics seems permanent and his political support substantial. If circumstances permit, Robertson will likely be involved in national politics for several presidential elections, win or lose.

As I attempted to understand Robertson and to present his views fairly and accurately, I found myself shifting from total opposition to his candidacy to a position of sympathetic neutrality, and by the end to supporting him with reservations. Perhaps after more study and thought, my position on Robertson will change again. Robertson makes mistakes, he is vulnerable, and he is attacked and scorned from time to time, and for this reason, from the start I determined that my task was to respectfully understand him as he understood himself and to present this to the reader.

Where possible, Robertson is quoted directly to give access to his thinking. I have not omitted embarrassing material that has caused him difficulty or avoided controversial issues, but have tried to clearly represent his point of view.

Robertson's policies are geared for troubled times. He believes that America faces economic collapse, foreign policy breakdown, and social upheavals in the near future. He has said this repeatedly since the mid-seventies. The Congress and the president face enormous problems and have had trouble coming up with answers. Leaders disagree or refuse to compromise, leaving the nation without clear guidance. But what will they do if a more serious crisis arises?

Robertson thinks his own political ideas are part of the mainstream of American public opinion. They are neither eccentric nor especially hard to understand. He is confident that he has answers the public will support.

In 1987, a number of books and articles dealt with the same concerns Robertson addresses, but from different perspectives. Where possible, I refer to these to give his opinion context or support. As tempting as it might be to dismiss Robertson's views as religiously biased and therefore peculiar, it is harder to do this when others not sharing his religious beliefs agree with him.

Preface

At the 1987 American Political Science Association meeting in Chicago, one distinguished author asked me about Robertson's opinions on the Supreme Court. He had read reports in the *Washington Post* and wanted further information. As we talked, he discovered that Robertson's position was the one he had taken in a book soon to be published.

As a religious candidate, Robertson will be attacked and misunderstood. Other Christians, whether they support him or not, will be identified with him and suffer too. In view of this, I determined to present Robertson matter-of-factly, believing this would be more useful than any defense or criticism of him that could be made.

A critical and fair understanding of Robertson's views is necessary for intelligent decisions for or against him. I hope this book will contribute to that end. Let him be understood first, and then let the reader judge whether or not his opinions are sound. Even if one determines to oppose him, an informed decision contributes more to the democratic process than a prejudiced reaction.

Based exclusively on what Robertson has said or written publicly over an eleven-year period, this is not an insider's exposure of hidden agendas. What is said repeatedly in broad daylight before many audiences is often more representative of what a person thinks than speculations about concealed opinions. I have presented his views as they have been expressed to many people. Robertson is someone who tries to think through complex subjects and put them in simple terms. That has also been my challenge as a teacher. I will have succeeded in my work if Pat Robertson is clearly understood.

From the very first suggestion of the book to the final finishing touches, I received invaluable help. Corwin Smidt asked me to write the paper on Robertson. My brother Paul and colleague Greg Scott suggested the book. Herbert Titus, Bob Slosser, and Joseph Gray of CBN provided sources. Herb Ellingwood, Connie Snapp, Barbara Gattullo, Mary Ellen Miller, and Marc Nuttle at Americans for Robertson were most helpful. David Ringer read and responded to the manuscript. Pieter and Carol Van Waarde and others

Preface

provided hospitality east and west of home, and Steve Elliott assisted with research. Richard Helm, Lorri Mezanko, and the Rob Jackson family contributed generously. My wife, Mary, and my son David learned to use the word processor, and the whole family gave up a summer vacation.

Colleagues in the Section on Religion and Politics of the American Political Science Association helped me to proceed with confidence in the significance of this work, and Ralph Fagin and David Poteet at Oral Roberts University encouraged me with a welcomed sabbatical.

♦ 19 ♦

·1·
Understanding
the Man

♦ *Who is Pat Robertson?*
♦ *Why is he running?*
♦ *What makes his candidacy possible?*

Reporter: You know you're not gonna be able to do this unless
            you change your first name.
Robertson: You mean Pat?
Reporter: No, I mean Reverend!

Marion Gordon "Pat" Robertson was ordained a Southern
Baptist minister, though he served only briefly as a pastor. The
press frequently calls him a "television evangelist." In fact, he
denies ever being an evangelist, claiming rather to be a religious
broadcaster. For twenty-five years he headed the Christian Broadcasting Network, and on October 1, 1987, from the steps of the
Bedford Stuyvesant (Brooklyn, New York) brownstone where he
lived briefly among the poor, he declared his candidacy for the
Republican presidential nomination.[1]

Why is Robertson, previously engaged in a successful career and
ministry in religious broadcasting, going into politics? Why run for
office when leaders, especially religious leaders, are so vulnerable
to attack? With little government experience, is he even qualified
for the highest office in the land? Can people trust a man in public

office who says he communicates with God and who prays against hurricanes, believing in miracles? What chance does he have to win in 1988 or in 1992? What will happen to CBN now that Robertson is not there? In the year of the "Holy Wars," was he leaving religious broadcasting just when it most needed his leadership?

Many have been surprised by this move, even dismayed. Without much consideration, some dismiss him as a religious eccentric, and others say that he is abandoning his calling. Robertson asks simply to be heard before judgment is passed on him.

Confidently he assumes that he can represent the nation, partly because his own biography contains many of the tensions and conflicts that characterize America. He claims that his personal history prepares him to understand and speak for most Americans, honoring their independence and diversity of culture as a matter of principle.

His father, A. Willis Robertson, a conservative Democrat, served the state of Virginia for thirty-four years as a congressman and senator. Pat Robertson was educated at Washington and Lee University and the Yale University Law School and became more of a political liberal. He supported Adlai Stevenson in 1956, chairing the Elect Stevenson committee on Staten Island. A lifelong Democrat born in the South, he recently became a Republican.

Brought up in a traditional Baptist home, Robertson became somewhat irreverent in college and finally, as a young adult, dramatically returned to a personal faith in Jesus Christ. Following this Christian conversion, he left the firm of W. R. Grace and entered the New York Theological Seminary, graduating in 1959. Shortly after that he moved back to Virginia with his young family and worked briefly in a local church as a Southern Baptist minister of education. In 1960, he started the television ministry for which he is now so well-known with a small investment of less than a hundred dollars.[2]

The "700 Club" show, the flagship program of CBN, is watched by 4.5 million viewers a day and over 19 million viewers a month.

Pat Robertson

The CBN cable network reached 37 million homes by the mid-eighties. Robertson's enterprise employed over three thousand people. He estimated that in the years since 1978, his ministry had helped to distribute $130 million of goods and services to financially deprived people. In the late seventies, he founded a fully accredited graduate research university adjacent to the broadcasting network. Traveling extensively, he had operations in Japan, Hong Kong, Taiwan, Israel, Lebanon, Cyprus, Argentina, Chile, Brazil, and Colombia and participated in joint ventures with Australians and Canadians. Robertson believes that his combined experience of executive responsibility, overseas operations, and television journalism gave him an unrivaled preparation for the larger tasks of government. He said that only Vice-President George Bush has traveled more, and he lacks extensive television experience.

Television presents stringent demands for candidates, and given his daily "700 Club" experiences of almost thirty years, Robertson is confident that he knows both the limits and opportunities presented by that medium. He communicates without a Tele-PrompTer and has an exceptional ability to recall details and comment quickly and with ease on a wide range of topics.[3]

Robertson prefers the label Compassionate Conservative, because some conservatives have no concern for the poor. He integrates his conservative family background with his liberal education and Christian convictions. Not viewing his own thinking as narrow or ideological, partly because the influences on his perspective have been so diverse, he tells of his father's conservatism and its influence:

My father was a man who was a rugged individualist. He loved America. He loved the traditions that had come to us from our founders. Our ancestors went way back to the Jamestown colony, and he would tell me of the traditions of America. He would tell me of my Baptist ancestors who used to be persecuted for their faith, and would be put in jail because of an established religion, and yet would preach through the bars of the jail. He respected the

Constitution. He despised federal budget deficits. And he was a man who believed in individual initiative. I went back and read some of his statements before the Senate Judiciary Committee, and I was amazed to see what he was saying that was almost exactly what I was saying. A reporter for the *Washington Post* did a story on me and went back and found other statements that were exactly what I'd been saying, and yet I can't recall my father ever speaking them to me. And yet, there's something just deep inside of me that says, "You're a conservative, you're for freedom, and speak just like your father."[4]

Perhaps Pat himself does not know all the reasons he has chosen to enter politics. It is more an inner conviction than a logical deduction or pure ambition. He is certainly not playing it safe, and he will have to learn the art of electoral politics. His reputation will not escape criticism and ridicule, and his life may even be endangered. His religion certainly will cost him some votes, but it will also be a source of strength, giving him confidence, direction, and a potential support base.

In 1987, when there were no sure winning candidates for either the Republican or Democratic party, Robertson's entry into the race added one more element of uncertainty to an already unpredictable situation. His own decision is that he will never again be the CBN "700 Club" host. Instead, he plans to burn his bridges behind him, no matter what the outcome of the 1988 election, and complete his remaining years in public service addressing the needs of America as a national leader and a political spokesman.

CBN, meanwhile, is continuing its work of evangelism, overseas missions, family entertainment, public affairs, and its programs for the poor. Robertson's son, Tim, is now the head of CBN and will undoubtedly continue to be influenced by his father's counsel. In fact, there are indications that the television programming may become more explicitly Christian and less political as Robertson and the network go their separate ways. Certainly such a change would be prudent, helping to avoid the charge of using religious television to back his political career.[5]

Yet Robertson knows that it goes against both the religious and political traditions of America for an ordained minister to be a political candidate. The roles of clergy and civil authorities have usually been kept separate. And most Americans feel that this division of authority is healthy.

How has Pat Robertson dealt with the issue of running for president as a minister? During 1985 and 1986, he approached this in two different ways. Sometimes he stressed his secular accomplishments as a broadcaster and a businessman, downplaying his clerical status; at other times he mentioned the names of other ministers in Congress, thereby acknowledging his role as a minister but denying its uniqueness. But in either case he largely avoided the issue of having formal church authority while also being president.[6]

In early 1987, however, Robertson indicated that he would consider surrendering his ordination if elected, arguing that for him his ministry is more a question of where he serves than who he is. Politicians and preachers, he argues, are both ministers:

> The Apostle Paul, in Romans 13, said that the rulers are ministers of God. I think that those who are in public service are serving God, as well as those who are in the pulpit. I believe my calling is to serve God and serve man. It's a question of the arena. The calling is a lifetime matter. But the arena is up to the choosing of God. He chose for me the broadcasting arena. But He could also choose for me the arena of government. It's up to him. But in any case, it is a question of service. If that is the attitude, then it's not an abandoning of one calling for the other. It's a question of how God wants you to serve.[7]

Confident that he was choosing a ministry that God could bless and wishing to avoid confusion or compromise with two roles, Robertson resigned his ordination as a Southern Baptist clergyman and his ties to CBN two days before officially declaring his candidacy.

At least one American president was a minister. James A.

Garfield was well-known for the sermons he delivered while president of Hiram College and as a major general during the Civil War. He baptized, married, and buried people. His journal describes his decision to run for a local office.

> I believe that I can enter political life and retain my integrity, manhood and religion. Circumstances have so far led me into preaching and teaching, a desire to do good in all ways that I could, and an appreciation of the discipline and cultivation of the mind in both callings. I have never intended to devote my life to either, or both, although lately Providence has seemed to be hedging my way and crowding me into the ministry. I have always had inner ambitions to be a lawyer and enter political life, and have studied law for some time. The nomination tendered to me opens the way, I believe, for me to enter the political field. I have made up my mind. Mother is at Jason Robbin's. I will go there and talk with her.[8]

Garfield entered Congress in 1863 and became president in 1881. He successfully made his transition into politics, and while in the White House he continued preaching occasionally on Sundays at the Vermont Avenue Christian Church.[9] Much like President Jimmy Carter who taught a Baptist Sunday school class, Garfield functioned as a private citizen exercising his religious liberty. He was known for consistently respecting the separation of church and state. Robertson made a similar change from ministry to politics.

One person who was not surprised by Pat Robertson's new role was Dede, his wife of over thirty years and the mother of their four children. She comments that his decision to leave religious broadcasting for politics is something that has been developing for quite some time. Fifteen years ago in her "heart of hearts" she knew that this day would come.[10]

Their son Tim recognizes, as perhaps few others can, the consequences of his father's decision to step out to meet a need— a crisis in leadership as he sees it. In Tim's opinion his father is a terrific leader, one who knows well how to handle "all-consuming" jobs and the pressures of constant public attention. A younger son, Gordon, is an attorney working independently in a Virginia law office. He observes that his father is "very decisive and not wishy-washy," and believes that he has the right temperament and character to be president.

Daughters Anne and Elizabeth feel the weight of their father's decision on their personal lives. The loss of privacy will be a particular burden, but they and other family members are strongly supportive. Before going public with his decision, the entire family went on a vacation to discuss the possibility of a political career. Robertson asked them to pray, and all agreed that he should pursue the candidacy and they would help where possible.[11]

Transition Into Politics

April 29 is an important date to Robertson. On a beach twelve miles from his home, the first permanent English settlers stepped ashore on that day in 1607. He visualizes them planting a wooden cross brought from England, kneeling gratefully in the sand to give thanks to God, and dedicating themselves and the land to the work of the Lord.[12] A large oil painting at CBN headquarters commemorates this scene and serves Robertson as a reminder of the diversity and the faith of America at its founding.

> In *The Landing at Cape Henry*, sailors and gentlemen merchants kneel side by side with soldiers in steel armor. Masons and carpenters, farmers, cooks, and deck hands remove their caps and stand or kneel in quiet reverence.[13]

John Woodson, the surgeon of the Virginia Company, is a direct ancestor of Robertson. Robert Hunt, the chaplain who may have led a prayer of dedication that day on the beach, is related to Robertson by marriage. He feels his work is a direct fulfillment of the original dreams and intentions of the founders. If his ancestors could risk their lives and their families crossing the ocean to plant an outpost of liberty and opportunity in the New World, can he do less to continue their work? For Robertson, risking all in pursuit of a noble cause is simply a matter of duty. He quotes from the warning in the original Virginia Charter given by King James I:

> The way to prosper and achieve good success is to make yourselves all of one mind for the good of your country and your own, and to serve and fear God the Giver of all goodness, for every plantation which our Heavenly Father hath not planted shall be rooted out.[14]

On another April 29 in 1980, Robertson stood on the mall in Washington, D.C., and commemorated the landing at Cape Henry, looking out over a peaceful throng of several hundred thousand people gathered to pray for the nation. "Washington for Jesus," cochaired by Bill Bright of Campus Crusade for Christ and by Robertson, pulled together a cross section of Christians young and old, black and white, from the North and South. As the crowd prayed fervently for America, Robertson thought of God's words to King Solomon, "If my people, which are called by my name, shall humble themselves and pray, and seek my face, and turn from their wicked ways; then will I hear from heaven, and will forgive their sin, and will heal their land."[15]

The larger world hardly noticed the "Washington for Jesus" event, and the Cape Henry landing has little significance in historical accounts. For Robertson, however, these are great landmarks, key days that connect America to a providential history ordained by God. Someday, he believes, these prayers offered by Christians in 1607 and 1980 will receive their appropriate recognition.

Before the "Washington for Jesus" gathering, in the fall of 1979, Robertson wrote a proposal entitled "A Christian action plan to heal our land in the 1980s" and sent it to his supporters in anticipation of the 1980 election. His priorities were fighting inflation, resisting communism, promoting spiritual revival, electing strong moral leaders, involving Christians in politics, reversing some Supreme Court decisions, reforming education, and transforming the media. Somewhat pessimistic during the Carter years, Robertson was encouraged by "Washington for Jesus." "The diligent will bear rule," he said, quoting a biblical promise. Evangelical Christians were stirring, waking up to their public responsibility, and although their time had not yet come, he felt sure after this rally that it was coming.[16]

Robertson considered his fellow Christians a people dispossessed, "put to forced labor." Without much security or influence, the religious people of America were beginning to understand their condition. Part of the bondage was self-imposed, according to Robertson, because Christians had been slow to take responsibility for themselves and for America. As a result, they were not prepared for politics or for government. He was also concerned about the rising conflict with public authorities and the danger that conservative and liberal politicians would take advantage of a rising Christian interest in politics.

The example of ancient Rome where Christians merged church and state power should warn the nation away from too cozy an alliance between religion and politics in America, Robertson wrote. "To the Christian, there are dangers in silence, there are dangers in fighting, and there are dangers in winning." The way out of this cruel dilemma, he said, was to seek wisdom and to learn to take responsibility; in time, Christians would be ready to "bear rule." In any event, after being political outcasts for so long, he preferred the dangers of winning.[17]

As the "Decade of Destiny" approached, the "700 Club" format added coverage of public affairs, with news and commentary for the first half hour of the show. He increasingly interviewed public figures, writers, and professionals from many fields. According to one study, the program was 40 percent public affairs, 35 percent entertainment, 16 percent religious, and 9 percent fund raising. The "700 Club" adapted the talk show format to give substantial attention to politics and religion.[18]

As Robertson began to articulate a political agenda on television, some activists in the Republican Party took an interest in him. Robertson had campaigned for a Democrat, G. Conoly Phillips, in an unsuccessful Virginia Senate race in 1978. Following Jimmy Carter's defeat and the election of Ronald Reagan in 1980, Robertson leaned more decisively toward the Republicans. Even before 1984, some conservatives pressed him to enter presidential politics. Critical of Reagan's lack of action on social issues like abortion, they feared the influence of moderate Republican Vice-President George Bush. Robertson represented to them a credible alternative with national drawing power.[19]

Asked why his television program was devoting so much time to public affairs in 1984, Robertson replied that he had had little choice in the matter:

> If all was well, if the government and the church did what they were supposed to do, everything would be fine. But the government is involved in laws that force churches to hire people they don't want to hire. The government is involved in laws that prevent Christian people from praying in certain places and exercising their faith. And what's happening is the government is moving into an arena that it used to stay out of. And, as a result, it isn't that we're getting into politics, they're getting into religion. And all we want to do is get them out. I mean it's that simple.[20]

Using CBN initially to defend religion from secular attacks, Robertson moved quickly to a wider agenda and eventually decided to leave religious broadcasting altogether.

The first media recognition of Robertson's potential shift from broadcasting to politics hit the newsstands in a March 1985 *Saturday Evening Post* cover story. The *Post* claimed that "gentle but persistent" questioning was underway indicating widespread interest in Robertson's possible candidacy. The article, "CBN's Pat Robertson: White House Next?" pictured his life and accomplishments. He was shown addressing CBN University, walking one of his thoroughbred horses, in the Philippines, in

Afghanistan, beside the Berlin wall, in front of the Wailing Wall in Jerusalem, sitting with Billy Graham, and listening to Attorney General Ed Meese. The *Post* article was clearly a political promotion. It included a brief survey of his political ideas, with comments by those who hoped that he would run. The article quoted Paul Weyrich, a well-known Roman Catholic conservative activist:

> I've never seen so much unity among such a wide variety of people who normally don't agree on a candidate. When his name was mentioned, there was just an extraordinary unity, because, first of all, Pat represents the values that I think are shared by a majority of Americans, and he lives those values. Secondly, being the son of a United States senator, he has a good understanding of how things work. Thirdly, he has an extraordinary personality, attractive to millions and millions of people. He presents sound views in a non-threatening manner, which I think is essential. Among potential candidates today, political or non-political, there is no one with a higher rating in education, experience, family background, name recognition, popularity and vigor.[21]

That summer, *Conservative Digest* printed a cover story with comments on Robertson, reprinting part of the *Post* story. The more skeptical press, both religious and secular, picked up the story. *Christianity Today* asked, "Pat Robertson for President?" and *Time* magazine followed with a cover story, "Religion, Politics, and Money." Robertson shared a cover with Chrysler's Lee Iacocca in *U.S. News & World Report*'s article "Wild Cards for the White House." *People* magazine titled its article "Heaven Only Knows." Meanwhile, reaping whatever benefits he could from this mixed reception of a possible candidacy, he traveled extensively across the nation seeking support.[22]

During this early period of 1985 and 1986, Robertson initially appeared at rallies sponsored by the Freedom Council, a nonprofit, nonpolitical civic educational organization that he founded. His use of the Freedom Council and its funding by CBN raised serious questions about the use of charitable contributions for political purposes. Eventually, the partisan nature of his efforts led him to disband the Freedom Council in the fall of 1986. Two years prior to the presidential nominating conventions of 1988, the party nominee selection process was already heating up. Exuberant and expectant Texas and Oklahoma supporters gathered to hear Robertson say:

> What began as a trickle has become a torrent. And in the last few months, tens of thousands of people just like you and those on this platform have been coming to me and standing on their feet cheering and saying, "Go for it!" And those of you who have known me for a long time know very well that's not enough. And you know that a decision of this magnitude, or any decision I would make, is very frankly only dependent on one criteria, what is God's will for me at a time like this? And I want to assure you that as somebody that has known God, and served Him, and served my fellow man for thirty years, that I know deep in my heart what God's will is for me in this crucial decision. And on September the seventeenth of this year, I plan to make a more definitive statement with the precise conditions I'm asking for.[23]

On September 17, 1986, from Constitution Hall in Washington, D.C., before a coast-to-coast closed-circuit television audience, those conditions were announced: 3 million signatures of people promising to pray and work for his candidacy.

The number was picked somewhat arbitrarily, partly to make sure there was enough support to give him credibility. Robertson calculated that in 1984, Walter Mondale won the Democratic nomination on the first ballot after receiving 6 million votes in all the party caucuses and primaries. The 3 million represent 50 percent more than the largest Republican mailing list. He thought that, "If we have three million signatures in the right states, it's tantamount to victory in terms of the Republican nomination." Goals were set for each state, based on size and relative value: for New Hampshire, 50,000 signatures; 300,000 for Florida; 400,000 in Texas; and 1 million in California. He also said that if he could not get the 3 million signatures, that would be a sure indication that

God did not support his decision. This was his way of pouring cold water on the candidacy to test the extent of his support, both popular and divine.[24]

Robertson showed few signs of flinching from the first abuse he received. Speaking to CBN employees, he told of attacks by the press and his growing tolerance for the rough and tumble of politics, which, he said, are more like a street fight than the boxing ring—"None of this Marquis of Queensberry stuff," he exclaimed, referring to the careful restrictions that govern boxing. Obviously he was getting ready to throw his own share of punches.[25]

A former California congressman, Paul N. McCloskey, accused Robertson of getting out of combat duty during the Korean War by using his father's connections. Stung by this accusation of personal cowardice and influence peddling, Robertson sued McCloskey in Federal District Court, Washington, D.C. The court agreed to hear the case after listening to preliminary testimony and evidence, although proving either that McCloskey deliberately lied to defame Robertson or that he spoke the truth would be difficult. U.S. District Judge Joyce Hens Green set a trial date for March 8, 1988, which is "Super Tuesday," the day of the southern primaries, and also advised the litigants to settle out of court. Knowing that anything said and done in the past, true or false, would be used against him did not deter Robertson. However, he may decide to settle out of court as the judge advised.[26]

Asked if he would run simply to influence Republicans or as a symbolic candidacy, he emphatically denied this—his own work at CBN gave him plenty of influence, he said, and nothing would draw him out of his ministry other than the real chance of winning the presidency: "I'll be in it to win." He said that thousands had asked him to be "their champion" and millions more encouraged him to seek public office.

> I want to win. I want to put together a coalition of people, bring a broad base of Americans together in the political process—Hispanics, Blacks, and women, minorities of all kind, the laboring people,

Roman Catholics, Protestants. I believe there are people who love America, want us to be free and strong, and who care about moral family values and traditional values, and that will make a winning coalition for a lot of elections to come. So not only do I want to win the presidency myself, but I want to see America win long range.[27]

Comparing his efforts with those of other Republican politicians, Robertson claims that they have party leaders or wealthy elites behind them, but only his has a grass-roots popular base. "There are thousands and thousands of people praying for me." As he travels, seeking support, he finds "people all over the country standing on their feet and cheering."[28]

When asked in a Jewish Federation meeting why he would want to run for the presidency, Robertson responded that he felt a strong obligation both to his own ancestors who helped to create America, to his grandchildren, and to those who would follow them, to pass on the heritage of liberty "There's a lack of cohesion in our country, and I believe I'm a person who could bring harmony and reconciliation between groups."[29] But Robertson is often accused of being divisive. His national and even world reputation as an articulate spokesman for the Christian faith is well established, and nothing has been more explosive in recent times than combinations of religion and politics. Many ask how he could possibly be good for the nation, given his strong religious convictions.

John Whitehead, founder of the Rutherford Institute and a leading attorney defending the free exercise of religion, phrased the issue:

> The big question with a Christian candidate is, can he be the candidate for all people? You have to be that, especially with the United States Constitution. You have to be the father figure for all the little groups out there. I don't think the American people are going to elect a fellow that is put in the position of being the Christian candidate. I don't think they will elect someone like that. I don't think the non-Christians will vote for him. I don't think a lot of Christians will vote for him because everybody is worried about someone taking the reins of government and pushing religion on somebody.[30]

Whitehead warned that a presidential candidate cannot be the prisoner of a narrow ideology or represent some faction of religious belief. The president must care for all the people and teach the nation to respect what is right and wrong, especially when it comes to the law. Whitehead, speaking in effect for many observers, considered Robertson a viable candidate if he could be broad enough:

> I think it's good that a Christian run for president. The only thing is, Pat's got to be president for all the people. That's the key.[31]

· 2 ·
What Kind of a President?

- ♦ **What qualities does a president need?**
- ♦ **How would Robertson differ from Carter or Reagan?**
- ♦ **Who would he appoint to key government posts?**

Pat Robertson was once asked, "What are the qualities that are needed for president?" He replied:

> Everybody says *leadership*. Some of our surveys have Lee Iacocca running away with it. I mean, absolutely running away with it, because they say here's a tough, candid leader. He turned around a major corporation and he makes hard decisions. What people want more than anything else is leadership. The second thing they want is integrity. They're tired of being lied to by politicians and having politicians play games with them. They want somebody to tell it like it is. Tell it straight. The third thing they want, as you look at the community, they want somebody who can take relatively complex issues, frame them in terms they can understand, that tell what the consequences of policies are, too. And then, mobilizing consensus behind noble goals and objectives for the country. I think those three are primary.[1]

It is clear that Robertson is taking a giant leap from broadcasting to a try for the White House, but to him the leadership task is much the same: to join with like-minded people, to seek and to speak the whole truth, and to give it sensitively and in measured amounts, to avoid overloading people before they can make a genuine commitment to follow his leadership. He calls himself a "persuader."

> I've been in communications for the last twenty-five years and all somebody has to do is sit in an easy chair with what's called a "zapper" and he takes me off the screen. With that type of environment, one hardly forces one's views on anybody. I'm in the business of persuading people and I don't think there's any way in the world—whether it's political or religious or anything else, business wise as well—that in a free country like ours any leader could lead without being able to persuade. That's all we can do is to persuade, set an example, lift up noble goals, and hope to arouse support behind those goals.[2]

A look at his views on recent past presidents will throw light on what he thinks of leadership. When Jimmy Carter was elected president in 1976, Robertson became more interested in national politics. This was his opportunity to observe a confessing, born-again Christian serving the nation in its highest public office. Before the 1976 election, he had interviewed Carter, but he voted for Gerald Ford and was disappointed in Carter's presidency.[3]

Throughout the Carter years and the first year of the Reagan administration, Robertson wrote a political and economic newsletter called "Pat Robertson's Perspective." In it he tried to explain to readers who shared his respect for Carter as a person why Carter had failed to be an effective public leader.

In his first issue of "Perspective" in February 1977, Robertson wrote that he thought Christians were unable to size up the new president. Though he believed Carter was "God's man," he felt that eastern liberal elites had too much influence in the new administration. However, he said, "It is doubtful that some monstrous plot is in operation." Distancing himself from common right-wing conspiracy ideas, Robertson did not hide his personal distrust of elite politics, where a few powerful people without any formal authority helped to rule the nation, as he said they had for the last twenty years and more.[4]

Robertson was especially concerned about David Rockefeller, the New York banker. Subsequent issues of "Perspective" claimed that Rockefeller's influence was so complete over United States foreign policy that, "He or his family have personally controlled the selection of every Secretary of State for years." Eastern bankers were making large bank loans to the Soviet Union and encouraging trade that strengthened Communist powers, and these same bankers all but directed American foreign policy, Robertson felt. He pointed out the conflict of interest between business and government goals.[5] At stake was the future independence and direction of the Carter administration. Partly because of its ties to eastern financial leaders, Robertson was pessimistic about the outcome.

> Consternation centers around the administration of President Carter. Is it able? Inept? Machiavellian? Poorly advised? Captured by trilateralist bankers? Liberal? Conservative? Blessed by God? Some of these things? None of them? Carter watchers abound. Most people tend to like Carter as an individual, yet in the United States and abroad there is a profound sense of uncertainty about his administration.[6]

The loss of Burt Lance in 1977, one of Carter's top advisors, was disastrous according to Robertson because he was the only genuine Christian in the upper levels of that administration, and his departure helped to isolate Carter from "acceptable counsel." By the spring of 1978, with the administration barely underway, Robertson was writing its epitaph. Carter had attempted to do too much, had little support from Congress, and failed to command respect. His appointment of inexperienced Hamilton Jordan to a key White House position was a mistake that further compounded problems, according to Robertson. In March 1979, before the Iran hostage crisis, Robertson wrote that, "Unless a miracle happens, Jimmy Carter seems destined to be a one term President."[7]

Carter later received praise from Robertson for the Camp David agreement signed by Egypt, Israel, and the United States in the spring of 1979.

It is fitting that a born-again Christian was the key ingredient to bring together a religiously inclined Jewish leader and religiously inclined Moslem leader. Perhaps no other world leader could have been more uniquely used as an "honest broker" than a born-again Christian President.[8]

However, Robertson considered this accomplishment too little to help the administration win in 1980. He blamed Carter's failure on a lack of clear vision and public support.

The main task of our President is to conceive reasonable national goals, to present them simply, and to advocate them in such a fashion that the majority consensus will rally to support them. Unless the President has a clear cut program which coincides not only with reason and the good of the country but also with the desires of the majority of the people, he cannot form a working consensus. Perhaps above all else the problem with our incumbent President can be traced to lack of forcibly presented, clear cut, and rational goals which are capable of uniting the American people.[9]

In the middle of the Carter years, Robertson questioned whether anyone could govern effectively in America. The man he called "the weakest President to occupy the White House in the memory of most Americans" was not the whole problem. He pointed out that Carter faced enormous problems: a rebellious Congress, no party discipline, numerous pressure groups, a volatile public opinion, a press out to devour leaders, families breaking down, a public given to private greed, and intellectuals arguing that nothing much could be done.[10]

Looking ahead, Robertson saw little reason to think that the election of 1980 would make a difference. In January 1979, he wrote that George Bush, a leading Republican presidential contender, was no more than the eastern establishment's choice for president.

If Bush were elected, said Robertson, that would "serve for all time to pinpoint the focal point of control in the United States." Bush may have lived in Texas and may have been a Republican, but that made little difference. As for Ronald Reagan, another leading contender, Robertson doubted his depth, and from the start of his administration in 1981, he thought Reagan was a politically compromised president. Though not personally dominated by the eastern leaders, he felt Reagan allowed that group to come into the White House by the back door, through George Bush and his associates. Later, Robertson said Reagan's greatest mistake was his failure to appoint people who were like-minded.[11]

> He left former Carterites in the State Department. He allowed a conflict in the inner echelons of the White House itself between those who believed as he did, the conservative point of view, and those who are the so-called moderates. And they really have been at war for the last six or seven years.[12]

Robertson's view was that Reagan's principal error was to ignore what he called the law of unity. At the core of the administration there were two teams often in opposition with only the president to decide the outcome. This may have kept the president from being the prisoner of any one group, but it also significantly weakened his grip on the executive branch of government. Robertson said that the resulting "vicious friction" within the government was inevitable, given Reagan's personnel appointments.[13]

Robertson has generally been positive in his observations of the Reagan administration. Unlike Carter, Reagan had a clear sense of what to do, he said, and mobilized support behind his programs. According to Robertson, the problem with the Reagan administration is that it has been divided against itself.

Carter and Reagan both promised America a government of the people, not dominated by elites inside or outside of Washington. They each ran as representatives of the people. Robertson now gives the same promise but hopes that he can do better because, if anything, he feels stronger than Carter and Reagan about this issue. He also has hope that new centers of leadership are rising outside of the Northeast, in southern and western states.[14]

Secular Elites

As a Virginian, Robertson is an outsider to Washington, and his religion contributes to his hostility for the eastern establishment. Following his conversion, Robertson was repulsed by the restaurants and bars of Manhattan that he had once so thoroughly enjoyed. He had "no desire to go into those softly lit, upholstered sewers any longer." To reject "happy hour" was to abandon any hope of belonging to the leadership groups that eat and drink together.[15] But Robertson's aversion to social drinking now pales in comparison to his well-developed contempt for secular elitist politics. He says,

> The prophets of our generation are no longer the men of God. The prophets are the psychiatrists, the social scientists, the humanists, if you will, the heads of the learned departments at major universities . . . these men of science are the new religion . . . they are the prophets . . . the priests again are no longer the religious leaders. The priests who have the black robes, the mark of distinction, that sets them apart from the rest of us, are the judges. They are the priests of this new religion we serve, and they rule by the direction of the social scientists.[16]

Half in jest because he is a Yale Law graduate himself, Robertson singles out the Harvard Law School as one power center in America that wants to run everything and assumes the public is ignorant of this. The nation is said to be unenlightened, and the privileged prepare at Harvard and other elite schools to lead the nation in new directions.

Citing the enormous influence of a few university professors, the National Education Association, and a few textbook publishers, whom he calls the false prophets of this generation, Robertson extends this indictment to judges who use their judicial positions to bring political changes that would not be possible if put to a popular vote. Robertson says, "There is a small oligarchy that has been running this country for a long time, and it has centered in the courts."[17] In addition to the Supreme Court, Robertson attacks the Federal Reserve Board, a partly private and partly public agency that regulates the nation's money supply and interest rates:

> In essence, we have two unelected elites which have enormous control over our destiny. One is our court. Five members of the court can make decisions which can radically alter the way we live, do business, educate our children, take care of our children, our prisoners; five members can do that. And the Federal Reserve, four members can do that. They are outside of the political process, except incidentally. That means essentially that nine people can control the economy, control the values of money, bring about inflation, reduce inflation, skyrocket home mortgages, put us into depression, and can radically alter our relationships to one another, and they are outside the political process. I think that is wrong, I think that we are a democracy, and I don't think there is any official that should be above the processes of democracy, of what we would call a republican government.[18]

Education, law, and banking are all beyond popular accountability in his view. In particular, international bankers draw Robertson's fire. Even though he is a cool television communicator, his soft tones do not hide a flaming indignation against any political sellout or subversion. He recalls that bankers opposed the Solidarity movement in Poland because they were afraid that democracy in Poland would imperil their loans to the Communist government. When American bankers oppose democracy in Poland, he says, "There's something inside of me viscerally that is opposed to that kind of greed and hypocrisy."[19] His response was to strike out against the bankers and the Council on Foreign Relations, a private foreign policy advisory association. He said these groups of people are attempting to manage world affairs without either moral or political authority.[20]

Robertson considers secular elites hostile to democracy—the leaders of major universities, publishing houses, educational unions, think tanks, banks, courts, the Federal Reserve, and the national press. He calls himself a Jeffersonian Democrat turned Republican, and this, combined with his biblical faith, is a powerful and even volatile combination. Robertson believes that the president, fully independent of any elite, must give nonsectarian moral leadership.

Even pagan religious celebrations are protected by law and are beyond the authority of government to regulate. This was his response when asked if he would ban the celebration of Halloween if he were in the White House. Asked if he would appoint only Christians to the cabinet, he replied that he would rather be "ruled by a competent Turk than an incompetent Christian," quoting Martin Luther. However, Robertson draws the line at the selection of atheists to top levels of administration.[21]

On his CNN talk show in April of 1987, Larry King asked Robertson if he could vote for an atheist for president. He replied that he would not, saying that since most people in America believe in God, an atheist could not represent them. Such a person would have too little sense of moral constraint and would be missing "a great part of reality." Furthermore, in his own administration Robertson said he would expect all of his official family in the White House and cabinet to at least believe in God. A Robertson administration would be a praying administration even if its members addressed God in different ways. Unity is important to Robertson and this includes some minimum personal commitment to God.[22]

Robertson says that his top appointments would share these views. In speeches, he presented a demanding set of specific criteria for his cabinet selection. His top officials would need to:

1. Believe in the moral principles of the Bible and not be moral relativists.
2. Have a passionate love for liberty, not merely tolerating different views.
3. Be confident of the future demise of communism, not pessimistic.
4. Have a classical view of law, not thinking that law is simply a political game to be manipulated by the strong.

5. Support free enterprise and oppose state socialism.
6. Actively help the poor and dispossessed, not simply be rich and successful captains of industry.
7. Have an international perspective, not just be American nationalists or isolationists.
8. Have a keen appreciation for American history and its ideals, not be only present-minded.
9. Be confident, intelligent, and experienced leaders, not new to responsibility.
10. Be committed to service, not arrogantly ambitious.[23]

When asked which leaders inspired him to excellence, Robertson characteristically responded, "Moses, David, the Apostle Paul, Jesus Christ, George Washington, Abraham Lincoln, and Winston Churchill." Churchill is his favorite contemporary example, he says, because he gave moral leadership, was a gifted communicator, and knew how to balance his time and energy between daily management tasks and grand strategy. No doubt Robertson aspires to similar greatness—he is persuaded that the times may shortly demand leadership of near legendary stature.[24]

Asked who would meet his criteria, Robertson mentioned that he endorsed Reagan's nomination of Judge Robert H. Bork to the Supreme Court, and in fact, long before the nomination, listed him as a candidate that he would support. Repeatedly Robertson praised certain businessmen, like Ross Perot, and scholars, such as Thomas Sowell, as good potential cabinet members. He has also been critical of some of Reagan's appointments because they lack administrative experience or are not philosophically conservative.[25]

Robertson's view of presidential leadership suggests that he would want to avoid the mistakes of Carter and Reagan: Carter was taken up with detail and lost sight of broad goals, and Reagan was too dependent on subordinates. For example, Robertson thinks that the Iran-Contra affair would never have happened if the National Security Council in the White House had stayed out of operations and had remained simply a policy-making vehicle. With the best of intentions, and because President Reagan was not sufficiently in charge, Colonel Oliver North and his immediate superiors exposed the presidency itself to attack.[26]

Robertson has a special concern to see the rift between the president and Congress mended, especially in foreign policy. Recalling how the nation closed ranks under Roosevelt, Truman, and Eisenhower during World War II and the early days of the cold war when his father was a representative and then a senator, Robertson says that America needs unity again. He calls for more respect between the branches of government, with discretion granted to the executive in foreign relations, as the Constitution intended.[27]

Running for president would have been impossible for a person like Pat Robertson a few years ago. Before primary elections and local caucuses brought politics to the people, candidates were screened by party leaders. Robertson has never held a position of public trust in government and has recently changed parties; yet he is evidently able to overcome these liabilities because a personal campaign organization is far more important than the support of party regulars. Changes in campaign finance laws that reward those who can raise large amounts of money from many small donations give Robertson an advantage over less well-known candidates. In addition, television, computers, and changes in both party and state election procedures combine to make this candidacy possible.[28]

Robertson has promised that if elected president he will take a ı ax to the federal budget. He has said that he may get rid of whole departments of government, such as Education and Energy. He thinks that agencies must not only do a good job, but prove that they have a right to exist in the first place. Even successful programs must reassess methods and purposes in the light of results. Expecting hard times for America, Robertson is positioning himself to be part of the national leadership that the people will turn to for guidance.

The old elites have failed, he concludes; lacking wisdom and understanding, they make real troubles worse, hindering President Reagan's best efforts. He is also concerned that the nation is becoming ripe for dictatorship. What happened in Germany before Adolf Hitler came to power could happen to America, given the right circumstances. Calling William Shirer's book *The Rise and Fall of the Third Reich* one of the best books he ever read, he expressed concern that the American people may lose the desire and ability to govern themselves.

> Dictators come to power because self-indulgent people have refused to discipline themselves. When hard times come, a small disciplined elite comes forward to dominate the majority. This cannot happen when the majority is alert, disciplined, and self-controlled.[29]

Understanding the times is critically important to Robertson. He prays for a religious revival to restore good sense to the American public, helping them to choose trustworthy candidates, loyal to the principles that once made America great. In essence, he wants to be an American Winston Churchill called to preserve democracy. Whatever one thinks of his ambition, Robertson's candidacy is a challenge to the American political and religious establishments, a rebuke to government and religion, and an offer of real alternatives.[30]

·3·
The Economy: Barometer of the Presidency

- ♦ *Is the economy a moral issue?*
- ♦ *Will there be a worldwide depression by 1989?*
- ♦ *How would Robertson cut the budget?*

Presidential leadership in America is measured by the health of the economy. If employment is up and inflation down, the public gives credit to the president. In peacetime, no other measure of success is looked at so closely by Americans. In a recent study of public opinion during the Reagan years of 1981 to 1987, the distinguished political scientist Seymour Martin Lipset observed,

> A troubled economy, we have found, significantly affects people's feelings about their leaders and institutions. Their attitudes also influence electoral outcomes.[1]

People were asked, "In general, are you satisfied or dissatisfied with the way things are going in the United States at this time?" In economic hard times, under President Carter, only 26 percent indicated that they were satisfied, and 69 percent expressed dissatisfaction. These figures reversed under Reagan: by 1986, 69 percent approved and only 26 percent did not. President Reagan's personal approval ratings climbed to almost 70 percent by the summer of 1986, the highest rating ever for a president midway in a second term. The Iran-Contra affair sharply reduced the estimation of Reagan and the stock market crash of October 1987 was a further heavy blow, but in recent years the high ratings given to the president and general confidence in the nation were both partly the result of good economic news.[2]

The American people are extremely sensitive about taxes. During the Carter years, 71 percent of the people considered the federal income tax unfair to most people. Almost 75 percent of the middle-income families in 1978 said that they paid too much in taxes. Eight years later under Reagan, 62 percent of the middle-income families complained about their tax load. The generally favorable opinion of the Reagan administration and his tax reforms helped tax resentment diminish.[3]

In the midst of economic good times with a popular president, people felt much better about the country. They did not, however, have high regard for the major public and private institutions in America—the Congress, the Supreme Court, the military, organized religion, banks, newspapers, labor, big business, and television. These basic institutions and their leadership had overall approval ratings of from only 40 to 50 percent.

Approval rose for some parts of the government under Reagan; however, approval for the private sector fell. Business succeeded best, in the public's opinion, in developing new products. However, most thought business charged too much and profits were too high. Trade unions fell most in public esteem—42 percent in 1986 considered unions no longer necessary for the average worker's well-being. After being told that the percentage of workers in unions had declined over the past twenty years, more than half of those polled said this was good for the nation.[4]

Lipset says there is a "confidence gap" in America, partly real and partly manufactured by the press. People are committed to the basics of American life, but are not so sure of the strength of

American institutions and their leaders. Economic recovery may well be temporary; business has yet to prove its ability to meet the competitive challenges ahead, and people do not think that labor unions help the economy. Strong presidential leadership makes a difference, giving hope that the future can be brighter, but neither American business, labor, or other private institutions are trusted.

Lipset argues that the press is largely responsible for informing the nation on the performance of its institutions. The press is down on business, pointing out business fraud and the failure to meet foreign competition. Even when business did well, between 1983 and 1987, the press looked for the bad news that supposedly made a good story. There is always some scandal or failure that can be seized on for negative but entertaining reporting.[5] The press makes it difficult for the public to respect leaders.

In recent years, the American people have turned to Jimmy Carter and Ronald Reagan, people from outside Washington, to help get government and the nation back on track. This makes it difficult to predict how the public will respond to the election of 1988. Will they turn to another outsider, or will they prefer the less charismatic, less forceful politicians of Washington?

Robertson says that America's problems are beyond the reach of any president, and he agrees with one implication of Lipset's study, that the nation must develop a greater sense of unity and confidence in its leaders for it to succeed. The press must reassess its role and begin to give support to government leaders, according to Robertson:

> I was with the black assistant city manager of Philadelphia, driving through slums that he was trying to renovate and bring civic pride to, and I said to him, "What is the number one problem in Philadelphia?" And I thought he would say drugs or crime or illiteracy or something like that. He's a black Democrat, in a big major industrial city. He said, "The press." I said, "What do you mean the press?" He said, "The press is our biggest problem. They set one side of society against another, they cause us to have distrust for our leaders, they have constant contention that is being built up

in our city so that we are not able to move together as a unit and join in as a community to get the job done."[6]

Controversy may sell, but Robertson feels that the time is past for adversarial relationships, setting the press against other institutions. He believes America needs a measure of harmony and cooperation in politics for it to prosper, and he thinks that there are urgent reasons to work for a consensus on economic policy.

In "The Morning After," an article published in the October 1987 *Atlantic Monthly*, Peter G. Peterson, Chairman of the Council on Foreign Relations and former Secretary of Commerce, warns that America must immediately export more products than it imports, or face a global depression. To prosper in the long run, he says, the nation must also reduce government deficits and private consumption to release capital for savings and investment. According to Peterson, there is no other way to avoid economic decline, but "neither the American public nor the nation's politicians have even begun to face this prospect."[7]

The economy suffers, according to Peterson, because people prefer to borrow and spend rather than to work hard and save. Economic stagnation or collapse are fast approaching, he thinks. In 1981, the United States was a world creditor owning $141 billion more than it owed to other nations. In 1986, $143 billion of American assets went to foreign investors. This was caused largely by government deficits and consumer practices. By the end of 1987, the United States will owe foreign investors close to $400 billion. In six years, Peterson claims, the nation "burned up more than 500 billion dollars" of assets, a sum that will take years to recover.[8]

Government debt will shortly reach $1 trillion, and total national savings per year are already smaller than Japan's, a nation half the size of the United States. Today 80 percent of the nondefense budget is spent sending checks to the elderly, to people on pensions, to welfare recipients, and for medical care, but not to projects that increase national wealth. Peterson says,

For Americans to believe that their national balance sheet is in the same shape now as it used to be, they would have to believe that the enduring investments made by the federal government during the past seven years are comparable to all those made during the preceding two centuries—including the taming of the frontier, victories in several wars, the Marshall Plan, miracle vaccines, the Apollo missions, Grand Coulee Dam, and the interstate highway system.[9]

America cannot afford to borrow so much money from foreign nations and then give money to individuals who buy imported cars and other consumables. Sinking his teeth into the problem, Peterson advises that a nation's wealth rests on each generation's ability to produce wealth and to save a portion of it to pass on to their children. But America is neither producing nor saving enough to give the next generation a standard of living equal to their parents, he says.

But if the flow of invested endowments from each generation to the next has ceased—and if each generation instead insists on its "right" to consume all its own product and part of the next generation's as well—then we can count on a meager and strife-torn future. In any summary discussion of America's prospects in the near, the medium, and the long term, there is one theme that must be emphasized above all others: the indissoluble bond between the economic behavior of one decade or generation and the economic well-being of the next decade or generation.[10]

Democrats and Republicans are equally to blame in his view. Democrats set up the programs that drain the national treasury, and President Reagan accelerated the problem with his budgets. Looking ahead, Peterson recommends increased production, reduced federal spending, and increased taxes if the spending cuts are not sufficient to protect savings. While Robertson opposes tax increases, he would agree with this general analysis.

The Economy as a Moral Issue

Robertson is known for his strong views on social issues such as abortion and pornography. What is less well-known is that he is more concerned with economic problems than with any other issue, and partly for religious reasons.

I think the greatest threat we have to our stability is the continuing federal budget deficit. This will put an intolerable burden on the domestic economy and has caused the interest rates to stay higher in order to attract foreign capital. Because of the deficits we will keep things in a "stag-flation" which will ultimately destroy us as a nation. That's a major problem. The second thing is a moral problem having to do with the crisis we have in this country and some of the other moral issues that we are facing. So I think obviously the federal deficit spending itself is a moral issue.[11]

Robertson disagrees with those who would label issues religious and secular, leaving the church to address religious issues only. His understanding of economics is strikingly religious. He believes that one must give in order to receive. This makes prosperity in the long run dependent on respect for other people and their needs. Discussing trading policy with other nations, Robertson says:

Basically, tariffs are not a good idea. And if you beggar your trading partner, then he'll beggar you. It's a spiritual law; I call it the Law of Reciprocity, that says, "Do unto others as you would have them do unto you." And if you want a wealthy trading partner, then you'd better not take all his money away from him because you want him to buy what you're doing. Now that's just long-range best policy.[12]

This understanding leads him to ask for a tough policy on trading partners like Japan, demanding that they open their markets to American goods on fully reciprocal terms. "We're going to hold and insist on it, and I don't think we've gotten near tough enough in this area."[13]

Robertson wants America to be productive, making real products that can be sold worldwide. He holds to a Law of Use that stresses hard work, creative imagination, and risk, all attributes needed in successful manufacturing and trade. He denounces any program or ideology that tends to obscure this truth.

> Despite the New Deal, despite the Fair Deal, despite any other deal that's ever come along, despite the redistributing, the concepts of the Soviets, the Socialists, the Labor Party, or anybody else, there is a fundamental law in human relationships that is enunciated in this. I call it the Law of Use. It says that if you will exercise what you have, it will grow. And if you do not exercise what you have, you will lose it. There's no way a government can revoke that because it's fundamental to human existence [14]

The federal deficit was a moral issue to Robertson, and so now is manufacturing. To be greedy, lazy, or even to allow oneself to be taken advantage of by unfair trading practices is wrong because all lose in the end. Healthy economic relationships are considered the subject of moral as well as pragmatic scrutiny.

Before a group of pastors in Florida, Robertson predicted that the overriding issue of greatest importance in 1988 would be the budget deficit problem and wasteful government spending.[15] The federal deficit is the symbol of evil and foolish policy in his campaign because it cuts America off from a productive future. Unless something is done, Robertson foresees catastrophe, if not for this generation, then certainly for its grandchildren.

> Several weeks ago, my lovely daughter-in-law gave birth to a redheaded, blue-eyed baby boy—my first grandson. As I looked down at the little fellow, I knew we had placed on his tiny shoulders a share of a two-and-one-third-trillion national debt. As I thought more about it, I realized that before he began kindergarten, he would owe a share of three trillion.[16]

This debt burden is especially reprehensible because it cannot be justified by any national crisis or need: "In times of extraordinary prosperity we have become the first generation ever to plunder the patrimony of its children and grandchildren."[17] He cuts through all of the reasons given for the deficit, such as the need for more defense spending or social programs, and calls this unprecedented state of affairs sheer robbery. His sense of the future is very critical here, because his religion leads him to focus on relationships and their long-term as well as immediate consequences. When Americans today damage the future of others, they are responsible, whether they realize it or not. Time is the critical common denominator that reveals the truth and practicality of all his principles.

Robertson's insights into economics have immediate implications, but long-term focus. For example, CBN University does not participate in Federal Student Loan programs because of the debt that would hinder the ministry, careers, and families of graduates. Debt, in his view, leaves people vulnerable, and is to be avoided at almost all costs.[18]

To Robertson, the fact that America, with its vast natural resources, does not have enough money to pay its bills or to help its less fortunate neighbors is a disgrace. The basic problem is the greed of individuals and special interest groups, and the readiness of government, and especially Congress, to meet their demands. Unless citizens recover a readiness to work and save and provide for their own needs without significant government subsidy, they will be forever dependent; and too many dependent people cripple the effectiveness of government to operate efficiently, according to Robertson.[19]

If America recovers some good economic sense, however, he is sure prosperity will come. "Do away with the pork barrel and adopt statesmanlike politics" is his cry. Adopt a national perspective that sees beyond immediate self-interest and the nation will experience economic deliverance; do less and it will go under. This is certainly a religious perspective, linking economics, moral purpose, and human reed to the promise of the future.

Compound Interest and the Exponential Curve

Robertson is concerned about the national debt because of the speed with which interest compounds. He is fond of quoting Baron Rothschild's saying that compound interest is the "eighth wonder of the world." Frequently he tells the story of how the Bank of England started when William Paterson discovered that he could loan money to the King of England and charge interest. He found that he could in a sense create wealth out of nothing and secure his fortune forever—interest multiplies profits over time and governments can be trusted to pay their debts.[20]

Robertson's favorite quote on economics is Proverbs 22:7: ". . . the borrower is servant to the lender." When debt grows exponentially through interest added every year to the unpaid balance, eventually government becomes dependent on bankers and the economy suffers. During the Carter years the total national debt amounted to about 33 percent of the gross national product (the total value of goods and services produced in a year). But by 1986, the debt was almost 66 percent of the gross national product. Business cannot borrow when government has drained the supply of available investment capital. Robertson says at the bottom of this insupportable debt problem is what he calls the miracle of compound interest.

> The compounding principle is simply astounding, and it grows so enormously when the exponential curve begins that the numbers are overwhelming. I think that most intelligent business people today have understood the tremendous power of compound interest. If businesses can grow at 25 percent a year, they double in less than three years and it just continues. It is a very wonderful thing, but the same laws of economics that work very beneficially also are inexorably cruel if they work against us, because the same principle of compounding which can bring about enormous wealth and prosperity can also bring about insupportable debt and bondage.[21]

To help people understand compound interest, Robertson teaches the rule of seventy-two. Dividing the interest percent into the number seventy-two gives the number of years that it will take to double the amount owed. By this measure, he calculates a debt with a 20 percent compound interest rate will double in about three years.[22] He points out that this explains why the total national debt has recently grown so fast from $1 trillion in 1981 to $2 trillion in 1986, to $3 trillion before 1990.

Taking figures from Peter Grace, the head of the Grace Commission that studied government efficiency, he predicts that the interest on a debt of over $12 trillion by the year 2000 will be above $1 trillion a year which is more than the total federal budget today. To lend credibility to this terrible prediction, he reminds listeners that the present annual interest charge on the debt of over $170 billion is larger than the total annual budget of President Lyndon Johnson during the Vietnam War.[23] Robertson concludes that once one gets on the wrong side of an accelerating debt curve, there is not enough money to make payments.

> The interest on that debt will exceed the current federal budget, which is $1 trillion. We can't support that kind of money. We can't support it in the states; the federal government can't support it; the American people can't support it, and the world can't support it. So, something undoubtedly is going to happen, because when this compounding reaches a particular point there is nothing else for an economy to do except to stall.[24]

According to Robertson, debt compounded leads eventually to bankruptcy and depression; compounded savings lead to wealth. For example, a twenty-five-year-old worker saving twenty dollars a week at 12 percent interest will receive a million dollars in interest by age sixty-five on a total of less than fifty thousand dollars actually saved. Using the encouraging example of Japan, he reports that the Japanese save about 17 percent of their national income every year, compared with America's 3 percent. The result is that they have abundant capital to invest, most of the largest banks in the world, and corporations that literally operate debt free. He reports that Toyota, for example, has no corporate debt; this enables them to produce cars more cheaply because they have no interest payments to make on loans. If America could increase savings rates, there would shortly be enough money to reduce and pay off the debt, and even pay for significant new advances in technology.[25]

Robertson has personally avoided consumer debt. This has allowed him, he says, to give generously, to buy more for his family, and to invest. He objects to even minor government measures that increase the debt; for example, he would have preferred that a Saturday or Sunday be set aside to commemorate Martin Luther King because of the huge costs involved in losing a work day by federal employees. This one holiday he estimates will cost the nation $5 billion in ten years.

The national economy does show signs of health, he says. Under President Reagan, inflation dropped to almost zero, and more than 8 million new jobs and hundreds of thousands of new businesses were created. However, Robertson is convinced the larger problem of debt must be dealt with to preserve these gains. Worldwide debt amounts to over $17 trillion, and both the American government and banks carry responsibility for this problem.[26]

He refers to the negative example of Argentina. Argentina once had the ninth highest standard of living in the world. They borrowed themselves into poverty, he says, and no longer rank even in the top fifty. Americans have already lost their top ranking to Japan and to other nations. Robertson wonders how far America will decline before it learns not to go the way of Argentina.[27]

The Next Depression

In speeches before business groups in 1987, Robertson warned that a general financial collapse was coming. He said the economy was "skating on extraordinarily thin ice," and he wondered when something might break.[28] Linking his understanding of compound interest and the exponential curve to a theory of economic cycles, he predicted a likely, though not inevitable, worldwide depression by 1989, and said, "I don't envy the person who is going to be president in 1989, be it me or somebody else, because there's going to be some very serious problems in our society."[29]

The cycle that Robertson sees operating in economics takes about fifty years to run its course. Beginning in the post–World War II period, he says, America experienced rebuilding, increased demand, and an active economy. The stock market took off, credit increased, and the inflation battle began. Eventually, a combination of debt and excess manufacturing capacity will bring the economy down, he predicts, pointing out that before a recession or a depression, there is a good deal of false prosperity with inflated real estate values and inflated stock prices.

Debt creates wealth—creditors end up with large amounts of capital. When inflation is controlled and interest rates drop, this money tends to flow into the stock market and not into savings. This powerful flow of funds, however, is based more on debt than on sales, profits, and the efficient production of goods and services. Furthermore, foreign nations are investing in the United States stock market more than they are buying American products. Eventually this will hurt the world's economy because the value of the corporate stocks will be worth far more than the goods and services the companies produce. Robertson says that the strength of the stock market hides the overall weakness in the economy caused by American debt. With such debt, people have less to spend, and eventually demand for goods and services will decline. Investments even in the stock market will slow, and as the economy takes a downturn, the deficit will accelerate further as less taxes are collected, and confidence in business, banking, and government drops.[30]

It is one thing for the world's economy to move in cycles and another to have a depression. What makes the present so precarious in Robertson's mind is that the policies of governments and banks are about to make the normal downturn of an economic cycle into a disaster. He says that we face an "extraordinarily serious financial collapse" largely because the banks and governments engage in almost unlimited debt financing.

Robertson estimates that bank loans to nations in South America, Africa, and the poorer nations of Asia amount to between $800 billion and $1 trillion. These governments simply never will be able to repay them, nor can they afford the yearly interest payments. The fault in his opinion lies with the banks, not so much with debtor nations.

Bankers assumed, Robertson argues, that governments could at least make payments on the interest that they owed. Describing what was a cynical policy at root, he says,

> Whether the sovereign nation was Zaire or Brazil or the Sudan or Venezuela or the United States, and whether the loans were made in pesos or piasters or pounds or kreuzers or dollars, the thought was—loan as much money to these people as you have to because they can always turn the screws of the taxing power up on their people and therefore your loans will be paid back.[31]

Much of this loan money went for corruption, graft, and foolish prestige investments. The response of investment bankers was to demand further tough measures by the debtor governments that in turn made their poor people pay the price for loans that never should have been made in the first place, according to Robertson.[32]

The response of the banks, he says, is to delay the day of accounting. Refinancing debts, moratoriums on payments, even partial cancellations are all cosmetic and temporary expedients. What must be faced is the relentless pressure of compounded debt that eventually outstrips the total amount of real money that actually exists.

> The problem begins to manifest itself very quickly when you can see that compounding of interest escalates debt to a totally unrealistic level. The second thing that happens is that exponential compounding results ultimately in the total slavery of the debtor or it results in a level of debt that completely jeopardizes the financial stability of the lender. The third thing is that there never is enough money in the money supply to pay back compounded debt. The last thing that we find is that the creditor, the bank, would come against you and say, "If you don't pay, we're going to sell your business or your

merchandise or your inventory," but that act would automatically force down the prices of the commodities that you were dealing with.[33]

When banks begin to seize the collateral used to secure their loans, then the value of these goods or properties begins to decline. A vicious cycle can ensue that leaves debtor nations unable to repay debts, and what little wealth they do have in their agriculture or industry is worth less than before. Meanwhile, he says that banks list the debts owed to them as assets, and that, too, is fraudulent, because the banks know that these debts will not be collected.[34]

Robertson writes that the world's banking system rests partly on real assets and partly on trust that there are enough resources to handle loans. When the banks rely more on trust than on real wealth, they will be vulnerable to panic. At any one time, he says, the amount of money in the world is at best half the size of the public and private debt. As debt goes up rapidly before the year 2000, it will simply overwhelm the money supply and productive ability of nations. Then if people begin to pull their investments out of banks, banking and the economy will be in jeopardy. Robertson believes that a stock market collapse or banking failures or a disruptive war in the Persian Gulf could precipitate a general depression.[35]

Behind the complex interplay of banking, business, and government policy is the single problem of growing debt and compound interest. Some economists also speak of a fifty-year economic cycle; Robertson says that this cycle is tied to the exponential curve of compound interest. "The Bible," he says, "long ago recognized the incredible nature of compound interest."[36] The idea of the Year of Jubilee in ancient Israel, though it may never have been implemented, provided that every fifty years all debts would be cancelled. Robertson argues there must be some systematic provision for the cancellation of debt on a worldwide basis on something like the Jubilee model, so that the obligations of governments and private debtors can be kept within reasonable boundaries.[37]

> At some point in time the game is over. No amount of monetarist tinkering will make much difference. Then debt is eliminated by bankruptcy, debt repudiation, hyperinflation, dictatorial slavery, or a brand-new money system. The world is near that breaking point now. We will continue to have increasingly turbulent economic times until the final resolution of the problem takes place when debt is eliminated.[38]

Robertson defines the role of government in such a breakdown as easing the burden on debtors and on creditors, and restoring confidence as quickly as possible in the economy and its future. He recommends that banks be given a ten- to fifteen-year period to write off their losses against their earnings. The government, he says, should "guarantee their solvency during this period," and with restrictions allow them to operate with less capital.[39]

Farmers in deep debt from loans they made to buy land at inflated prices must be protected too, according to Robertson. He favors a government program that allows banks to reduce the amount owed to them by farmers. A farmer who paid $4,000 an acre must be allowed to reduce the original loan to the fair market value of the land, such as $1,800 an acre. If the bank foreclosed when the farmer could not afford the interest on $4,000 an acre, and then turned around and sold the land for $1,800, the farmer loses, the bank assumes the cost of the foreclosure and resale, and no one really wins.

Rather than just subsidize crops to give farmers profits that they will use to pay for loans that were too high in the first place, Robertson favors a general reduction of farm loan values, and remortgaging at lower interest rates. Paying less for their land will release farmers from the intolerable burden of compounding land debts. The alternative is massive bankruptcy and a wave of foreclosures that threatens the health of the entire farming structure.[40]

Farm programs that encourage the removal of marginal acreage from production will continue to be useful, he believes. Farmers need a good price for their product, but this will not help much until the unreasonable debt burden is removed.[41]

In a depression, America must at all costs avoid the mistakes made in the early 1930s. High tariffs restrict trade and prevent recovery, and high interest rates would add to the burden of business. Credit must be eased and the temptation to close out imports resisted. Robertson is especially concerned that the Federal Reserve Board that sets interest rates be held accountable for its actions in hard times. If it raises interest rates when they should be lowered, he fears that this will delay economic recovery.[42]

> We don't want to overcontrol the economy like we did during the Hoover Administration, and let the Federal Reserve tighten the money supply fearing inflation, and take us into some ghastly recession. If we'll allow this thing to move through the economy so this surplus production and capacity is taken out, and if we will just keep our heads up, I think we'll come out of it very well. And while we're doing it, we have to cut the federal budget deficit. If we don't do that, if we continue to pile up billions and billions of dollars of debt, the resulting crash one day will be so horrible, none of us even want to discuss it.[43]

If he could, Robertson would abolish the Federal Reserve banking system. The system's banks are owned by stockholders and managed by people largely independent of public authority; they also issue currency, and are doing what he thinks government alone should do. In his opinion, America's banking system has a serious conflict of interest between private ownership and a public role. The banks set interest rates and then loan money to the United States Treasury at rates they have determined. He calls this a theft of public funds; the government should issue money; privately owned banks should not have the authority to set interest rates for the nation. The quasi-public banking of the Federal Reserve system is an unnatural mixture. "Unquestionably," he asserts, "this monstrous evil must be abolished, and the power to issue interest-free money restored to the United States Congress where the Constitution put it."[44]

Federal Reserve Board members presume that they know more than they in fact do, Robertson contends. The economy of the United States is so vast, complex, and fluid that the board's efforts to control money flow is almost always poorly done; he thinks they generally overreact to changing circumstances, fighting yesterday's battles and making recessions worse. He blames them for making the stock market crash in 1929 truly disastrous by tightening the money supply at just the wrong time. They might do worse when another depression hits.

For years, Robertson has been giving advice to individuals on how to protect their savings in a depression. His counsel is to invest in government securities or gold, favoring these measures over savings accounts, certificates, bank deposits, or real estate. He encourages above all the development of skills that are useful no matter what happens to the general economy.[45]

Robertson is persuaded that people who follow wise financial counsel and avoid personal debt can prosper even in a depression. He reminded CBN supporters that ancient Israel received blessings during the time of the plagues in Egypt, and so there is no reason to be passive or fatalistic as a depression approaches. Those who prepare can weather a storm, or several storms, and even receive an increase.[46]

What about unemployment and the creation of jobs to help people cope in a depression? Robertson's solutions are to put the nation's financial house in order. Runaway debt is the problem, he says, both private and public, and that issue must be resolved for other remedies to help. More jobs will be needed to reduce severe unemployment, but they do not revive the economy. Despite the terrible suffering that a depression brings, he says:

> I am optimistic about the future. I think we have a tremendous hope of the future, and if people like you who understand—believe in government policies which can see us through what could be a very difficult situation—somebody who knows the answers would be better off than somebody who doesn't and who does the wrong thing. The Democrats talk about massive government programs to

provide jobs, and massive tax increases, massive tariffs. . . . We will
be right back where we were in the 1930s.[47]

Once America puts the debt problems behind, Robertson is very
optimistic about the economic future. Resources, skill, and initiative are sufficient for a sustained period of economic growth.
Assisted by new technologies paid for by healthy savings, he
foresees American business booming and the best days for the
world's economy ahead.

When the process was over, debt would be gone and along with it
inflation and bogus paper money. The rich would still be rich and
the poor would be poor, but all people would be released from the
throttle-hold of money lenders, and the people would once again be
in charge of their governments. . . . Ultimately, there must be some
cancellation of debt.[48]

Strengthening the Economy

Without blaming Ronald Reagan for the American debt, Robertson promises to do more than Reagan to cut government spending.
Congress was partly to blame for the budget problems, but when
pressed on this issue and asked how he could do better than
Reagan, he responded that White House pressure on Congress
should be greater and the cabinet could cooperate more to reduce
costs.[49]

In the last generation, starting with Lyndon Johnson's administration (1963 to 1968), there was a change in the thinking of
government that prepared the way for huge deficits. Entitlement
programs—the allotment of benefits to those who qualified—that
had no budget ceiling destroyed fiscal restraint. There was also a
subtle redefining of the role of government, giving people supple-
mentary assistance in addition to their own wages, so that government, instead of making possible the "pursuit of happiness," was
instead supposed to be "the ultimate guarantor of happiness
itself." This thinking is wrong, he feels, and with the greatest need

of the hour to reduce spending, Robertson calls for a careful review of entitlements.[50] He wrote in 1980 that too few leaders really cared to cut costs:

> Over 53 percent of all Americans are getting something financially from Washington and little public sentiment exists for sacrifice. Consequently, despite the election year smooth talk, there is little heart in the administration or Congress to do battle with the entrenched bureaucracy and the vested interests that are draining our economy.[51]

Seven years later, Robertson is especially concerned that large corporations are abandoning their independence for some form of assistance from government. He complains that Washington "just crawls with lobbyists who are looking for favors."[52] Even fiscally conservative Republican congressmen go against their own principles if cutting the budget means losing jobs in their districts. But despite this lack of support and much resistance, he is confident that he can succeed where others, including Reagan, have failed.

> I told Senator Phil Gramm that I had to cut 20 percent of my [CBN] budget, and I did it in an afternoon. And he said, "Well, Pat, the difference between you and us is that you wanted to and we don't." So there has to be a desire somewhere to do this.[53]

When asked where he would cut the federal budget, he lists the Departments of Education and Energy, the Small Business Administration and the Legal Services Corporation, the federal rail system—Amtrak and Conrail, and certain defense programs including one unnamed weapon costing $10 billion a year. Robertson is critical of the B-1-B bomber; he wants to improve the purchasing practices of the Defense Department to save more billions. Furthermore, Robertson thinks we must sooner or later tackle the huge medical costs in the Medicare and Medicaid programs.

Questioned in the fall of 1986 on how much should be cut immediately, Robertson responded that $100 billion, about 10 percent of the budget, was a good figure.[54]

To better equip the president and the Congress to deal with the budget, he suggests a new law or a constitutional amendment requiring a balanced budget. He also favors a biannual budget that would cover two years instead of the usual one, suggesting this might reduce conflicts in government. He supports granting the president the line item veto power that would enable him to sign an appropriations bill while rejecting any part of it he found unacceptable. These measures would greatly increase presidential authority.[55]

In general, Robertson strongly favors reducing the percentage of American revenue going to government. Presently, 25 percent of the gross national product goes to Washington; it ought to be reduced and the money saved left in the hands of citizens. He objects to the suggestion that the government ought to raise taxes to reduce the deficit, saying that the nation must leave most of its resources in the private sector where they can be used to create new wealth and opportunity. He believes the tax system should be carefully engineered to support savings, investments, and charitable contributions.[56]

The huge trade imbalance is also a serious issue. If America has debits of $1 trillion that it owes to foreign trading partners, its credibility and currency will suffer. The value of the dollar dropped substantially, down 40 percent by 1986 compared with Japanese and German currency, and this Robertson said was primarily because of the federal debt. What must be done is to reduce debt, and then expand foreign markets for American products. A cheapened United States currency is not the way to expand exports. Not until "Made in the United States" is equal to the best in the world will the trade battle be truly won, according to Robertson.[57]

He would also recommend a change in American business practices to meet more demanding markets. For too long Americans have focused on quarterly (four times a year) earnings. Government must encourage business to plan long range and make investments with no profit for five or ten years if necessary. Gone are the days of quick and easy profits. By providing more tax incentives for capital investments, business could begin to think in terms of winning the competitive trade war.[58]

America cannot lose basic industries like steel and expect to prosper. A service or information economy will always be dependent and weak compared to a full economy that makes physical products too. America cannot afford, Robertson says, to "write off the automobile, the steel, the plastics, the chemicals, the major industries in America."[59]

Energy, too, is critical for economic development. Robertson supports safer nuclear reactors until some better, cheaper form of energy is found. He does not favor an import tax on foreign oil and argues that even domestic oil producers will favor free market conditions if they are allowed to make a profit when prices rise. Government restraints like the windfall profits tax, or existing limits on the oil depletion allowance, should be removed to encourage domestic oil production.[60]

Looking ahead to the next generation, Robertson sees a serious threat to Social Security in what he calls the "depopulation of the West." In 1950, 30 percent of the world's population lived in Western democracies. Today only 15 percent live in Western democracies and this figure is dropping rapidly. Fertility rates per couple in Japan are 1.7, Great Britain, 1.8, West Germany, 1.3, and the United States, 1.8. A fertility rate of 2.1 will sustain a population under most circumstances. Robertson says that these figures have enormous economic consequences for the retirement systems of the nation.[61]

When the Social Security system began, "There were seventy workers for every retiree." This figure dropped to four workers per retiree. Robertson hopes to solve the retirement problem by adding voluntary or compulsory private programs to supplement Social Security. This money, unlike most Social Security taxes that are directly paid out in benefits, would be managed by private companies and would also increase investments in the economy. He also favors additional tax breaks to encourage larger families.[62]

Robertson's prediction of a depression conceivably before 1989 is a matter of dispute. Some think that banks can handle their bad debts by setting aside assets to cover them and that, after a dip in stock prices, the market will hold steady. In this view, good economic management by banks and by the Federal Reserve Board will suffice. Robertson disagrees, not because of the severity of the 1987 stock market crash and not because he thinks there is a fifty-year cycle that guarantees a depression, but because compound interest makes large debts eventually unsupportable. There is a predictable recession or depression once government and banks let debt get out of hand. Robertson believes that public and private debt together will soon bring an economic collapse.[63]

Getting out of debt, cutting costs, changing our thinking about entitlements, keeping taxes down to keep a larger percentage of the economy in the private sector, increasing savings and pensions, improving products, holding on to basic industries, increasing energy production by deregulation, and bringing tax relief to families are all in line with the original Reagan program. However, Robertson rejects supply-side economics that simply reduces taxes so that consumers can buy more products, favoring instead a balanced approach to the economy that reduces taxes and government spending—especially government spending.

Across-the-board cuts in government expenditures, in particular entitlement programs like unemployment, welfare, and Social Security, are not easy to make, and without the cooperation of Congress, nothing can be done. However, if a depression were to occur, then Congress and the nation would have to face the debt issue. Events may force government to act, and Robertson is ready to be president for that time.

Fiscal and monetary matters concern him greatly. In a period of American politics when television preachers are being exposed for loving money too much, Robertson unabashedly makes the economy the centerpiece of his politics. Only national defense and foreign relations are more important to him, and he thinks defense depends fundamentally on a healthy economy. Furthermore, he argues that a debt-burdened economy has devastating effects on family life for generations.[64]

·4·
Responding to America's Social Crises

- ♦ *Can illiteracy be licked?*
- ♦ *What is undermining national morals?*
- ♦ *What would Robertson do about pornography, abortion, and AIDS?*

By the mid-seventies, Robertson's CBN television operations were booming. But there were doubts in his mind. Building a system was one kind of accomplishment, but what was it for? He wondered who would benefit from it. How was it to make a difference to America, and to the Kingdom of God? He saw the danger in creating a system without a clear mission; he did not want just another religious talk show.

> . . . All too many Christians had forsaken their role as "salt and light," bringing a godly influence to the major areas of American life. Instead, they had withdrawn from society into private religiosity, and abandoned these areas to the leadership of the ungodly, with the horrifying results we see all around us.[1]

Robertson pondered the direction of his ministry in 1978 as he prepared for yet another "700 Club" telecast. Turning to the Bible he found a passage in Isaiah that gave him both direction and strong motivation. The Hebrew prophet asked Israel to consider what would please God. Religious services and sacrifice were not enough, said the prophet. God desired that people share food with the hungry, shelter with the wanderer, and clothes with the impoverished. Isaiah asked Israel to stop gossiping and to spend themselves helping the poor break free from poverty's oppressive chains.[2]

Robertson's motivation to set up a relief operation came partly from the biblical command and partly from the promise made by Isaiah that he would be rewarded after helping the poor: "Then your light will break forth like the dawn . . . then your light will rise in the darkness . . . you will be like a well-watered garden, like the spring whose waters never fail." Compassion contained the secret of success. As long as CBN stayed close to the poor, centering part of its program on them, its own operations would be secured. The recognition and praise of people for these good works would naturally follow. He wrote confidently, "God will bless the giver. He'll bless the receiver. He'll bless us for pulling the two together. Everyone will be blessed." Soon he established Operation Blessing, the food, clothing, and shelter program of CBN, that grew to help more than 5 million people a year during 1986–1987.[3]

Through his CBN telephone-counseling systems set up in cities around the nation, Robertson keeps in touch with America's social problems on the grass-roots level. More than 25 million calls have come to CBN's counselors. Many of the people who call are desperate and have nowhere else to turn.

As his awareness of their problems grew, Robertson looked deeper into the nation's social crises; no services seemed adequate. Many of the difficulties could be traced back to education, to family life, and to the need for spiritual renewal.

Literacy was the other area that most concerned him. Reading and writing skills are essential for family, work, and creativity. Without literacy, the key to communication, people are cut off from life. Food, clothing, and shelter are necessary for physical survival, but literacy lays the foundation for participation in society.

Illiteracy is mounting, especially for the children of poor single women supported by government. Later on, these children have difficulty getting jobs and end up dependent. In some places, Robertson reported, almost half the high school students never graduate and many cannot read.[4]

Drugs, crime, and a gripping sense of helplessness turn vulnerable children into dangerous and destructive adults. Robertson reports that over 60 percent of the Texas prison population cannot read or write. Building more prisons simply delays the day of accountability when the nation faces up to its responsibility for poverty and crime. Blaming families for illiteracy that leads to crime is not the answer either, he believes. Failed government programs and schools bear much of the responsibility.

Frustrated at public education in America for failing to equip the poor with basic reading skills, Robertson created a volunteer literacy program. He claimed that 2 million functionally illiterate people left American schools each year, and something had to be done.[5]

Literacy and Education

Operation Heads Up, Robertson's national literacy project, taught 105,000 students to read in 1987. His goal was to reach 500,000 young students by 1988, using a phonics method, "Sing, Spell, Read and Write," that has a vocabulary base of 22,000 words, more than ten times the number of words taught by most public schools. If he had $1 billion, a fraction of the current $18 billion spent annually by the Federal Department of Education, he claims that he could teach all 27 million functional illiterates in America how to read.[6]

When told that children from poor families cannot learn to read, Robertson responds, "You know that really is not true." Not only has his program worked in the poorest of ethnic neighborhoods, he says it also is effective with children who barely know English. He recounts a story of a teacher in Chicago, Marva Collins, whose students were able to read classics by the seventh grade. By striving for excellence and by requiring that students speak English correctly, she got results. The proof that the poor can be taught, he argues, is in the product that comes out of good schools.[7] He claims that his literacy project has shown how easy it is to teach reading:

I can guarantee that a child can learn to read, whether that child is Hispanic, black, American Indian, or Cambodian. . . . I can teach that child to read and write with fluency in English in thirty-six lessons. Guaranteed, 99 percent. We had one child in Pittsburgh who was reading at a second-grade level. After twenty days, that child began reading at the seventh-grade level. I have seen little black children in Chicago, little fellas four years old, stand up and read a book. Tremendous. They were so excited, they didn't know what to do. I've seen them take newspapers and read words that would be jaw-breakers for most adults, read with fluency because we taught them the syllables and phonics the way that God made people to talk. That's the way our brains work. That's how we talk and with this program, it costs us, using volunteers, eight dollars a child. That's all it costs, eight dollars a child. It works. I mean, it isn't a question about some theory. We've seen it, and it works. We've demonstrated it in Selma, California, with the children of migrant Hispanic farm laborers. They didn't have any education. They all spoke Spanish, and the school system had those children reading with considerable fluency at the end of the year. Yet with that demonstration project, the powers that be in the educational system in California say, "No way. That would make us change our system, and we're not going to do it."[8]

Illiteracy is a problem for the rich and the poor, and even the poor can be helped to overcome it. What also alarms Robertson is that high technology jobs that require good communication skills cannot be done by those who are illiterate. A technological society demands brighter and more competent students.

Surveys show that students who are above average today cannot read or comprehend facts as well as students could ten years ago. In fact, university students interviewed for CBN could not remember the names of recent presidents. They did not know which nations fought in World War II, and could not remember who was president during the Civil War. Such ignorance makes intelligent conversation impossible and weakens culture. Furthermore, American students will not be able to compete as equals with gifted and disciplined Asians and Europeans who will move into leadership in their nations. Robertson was shocked to discover that the stereotype of a dumb California "valley girl" was becoming common in America.[9]

He attributes the breakdown of literacy to the progressive philosophy and educational techniques of John Dewey (1859–1952). The evidence is in from schools that have used this method for fifty years, and Robertson thinks Dewey's approach can be judged a failure.[10]

In a recent book, *Cultural Literacy: What Every American Needs to Know*, E. D. Hirsch of the University of Virginia confirms Robertson's diagnosis of the problem. Hirsch documents the illiteracy problem and also reports that America proportionately produces less than half as many excellent readers as it did ten years ago. He largely blames John Dewey for this result. American educators once stressed reading skills by teaching students factual material that was important for them to know as adult citizens. Dewey stressed skills with less concern for ideas, facts, or content.[11]

Hirsch explains that literacy is not simply learning to give the right sound to the appropriate word; it is more important to know something of what that word means. When students do not know that the Civil War occurred some time between 1850 and 1900, then they may be able to read the words *Civil War* but they will not truly understand those words in conversation, in a book, or on television. Literacy combines the ability to speak a written word with some minimal knowledge about what that word means.[12]

Young children can be taught to say the right sounds, but after about the fourth grade if they are not also learning American history, geography, literature, and culture, they will mentally lose out. Hirsch advises that reading becomes a meaningless chore if it is based on sounding out words that have no sense to the child. Reading becomes enjoyable when it builds a picture of the world where the parts fit together and opens up the child's mind to the adventures of learning. In short, Hirsch concludes that children cannot learn to read without memorizing thousands of facts about the world and human experience.

The benefits of being able to read are great. Communication depends on it in a modern complex world, and business requires rapid and accurate communication. But even more significantly, Hirsch says that a democratic nation's very identity rests on literacy.

In the past, American children knew the same stories about the Pilgrims, Thanksgiving, Valley Forge, the cherry tree, Abe's log cabin, slavery, and California gold. They also studied the Declaration of Independence, the Constitution, and the Gettysburg Address. These same facts and ideas were familiar to all Americans; they bound diverse people together. They were American, declares Hirsch, because they were literate.

America's future depends on literacy. Without it, Hirsch claims, the poor will remain poor, the economy will be bogged down, patriotism will disappear, cultural ideals transmitted from generation to generation will be lost, and democratic political participation will decline. Thomas Jefferson argued that in a democracy newspapers and literacy were more important than government, and Hirsch agrees wholeheartedly.[13] Looking back at education in America before Dewey, he writes,

> In a study of American school materials of the nineteenth century, Ruth Miller found an almost complete unanimity of values and emphases in our schoolbooks from 1790–1900. They consistently contrasted virtuous and natural Americans with corrupt and decadent Europeans; they unanimously stressed love of country, love of God, obedience to parents, thrift, honesty, and hard work; and they continually insisted upon the perfection of the United States, the guardian of liberty and the destined redeemer of a sinful Europe.[14]

Robertson would not want to teach children that the "United States is a redeemer of a sinful Europe," yet in the current curriculum, he says there is little sense of a national identity, morals, or even the bare bones of names, dates, places, and events. Neither Hirsch nor Robertson blame parents, television, or rock music for the problem. Both argue that decades ago education in America made a wrong turn. There are "high stakes" for the nation in the decisions now required of educators. Hirsch concludes that education involves

> . . . breaking the cycle of illiteracy for deprived children; raising the living standard of families who have been illiterate; achieving greater social justice; enabling all citizens to participate in the political process . . . in short, achieving fundamental goals of the Founders at the birth of the republic.[15]

Because literacy is connected to understanding all of life, there is no teaching of reading without teaching morality. Robertson is angry about false moral teachings in the schools, where sexual immorality is condoned. This is the problem of "situational ethics," where any values chosen are approved; the other is silence on the moral standards that reflect the convictions of the community. More significant than banning voluntary prayer in schools, in his view, is the removal of moral instruction. Cultural pluralism has respected ethnic differences, but it has made it impossible to teach morals in public schools, and the results speak for themselves. Robertson believes stealing, lying, cheating, and killing are the same things in every language and must be condemned in American schools.[16]

At one time, education in America recognized God as the source of community morals. Hirsch advised that this nonsectarian religious approach to ethics worked well into the 1900s. It was tolerant and humane while it gave people a strong sense of right and wrong and taught neighborliness. He argues, in agreement with Robertson, that democracy requires some religious values held in common for it to work. Furthermore, he says the American founders knew and agreed to this.

> The American founders were well aware of the paradox that precisely because established sectarian religion must be forbidden, a non-sectarian civil "religion" must be put in its stead to secure a good and harmonious democracy. Since the people are to govern themselves, they must govern on high, broadly religious principle for the larger public good as well as for their own private good.[17]

Schools once taught that America was "One nation under God." This was based on some agreement on the beliefs taught in the churches and homes of most Americans. George Washington believed that public morality depended on some teaching of religious principles.[18]

Robertson's four goals for education include a religious aspect:

1. Get back to basics—teach reading and writing.
2. Teach the facts of math, history, science, and geography.
3. Give clear instruction in morals that all civilized people respect.
4. Respect the religious convictions of the nation and allow children at least to pray voluntarily in school.

Each part of this four-point program contributes significantly to rescuing education. Discussing how to implement his reforms, Robertson is convinced that they are better left to the fifteen thousand local education districts than to the National Education Association and the Department of Education. Education unions are an obstacle to his reforms, he feels, and because the Department of Education is too much the tool of unions and not an aid to better education, he would completely abolish it.[19]

More fundamentally, he opposes the near monopoly of education held by public schools. He challenges Congress, the Supreme Court, and the states to approve a voucher system that would allow parents to select any school for their children and to pay for it with a government-financed voucher. This would benefit under-privileged children. The children from poor neighborhoods deserve the best education, public or private, that can be made available to them. Vouchers in his opinion would also upgrade quality, for if parents chose schools, then educators would have to compete for children. Robertson says in effect, "May the best school win."[20]

To restrict the poor to the worst schools divides Americans into two classes, one primarily illiterate and the other capable of technical jobs. He thinks the nation must end the kind of discrimination that forces the poor to attend public schools that in their current condition have little to offer them. Robertson thinks that voucher-based education must forbid discrimination based on race or ethnic origin but be open to religious schools along with other private schools.[21]

While government has the power to increase the number of educational alternatives, families—not government—ought to be in control of their children's education, he believes. A realistic and affordable choice of schools available to parents would also encourage increased commitment of parents to quality schools. He offers this solution as a radical but workable plan.

Community Health and Morals

Discussing censorship before the New York Academy of Television Arts and Sciences, Robertson advocated the banning of filthy songs and lewd talk shows, pressing the television industry to acknowledge its heavy responsibility for community morals. However, he did not call for more government censorship, but rather self-regulation by the television professionals to live up to their public trust to support family values.[22]

He also favors tough local enforcement of the law against all forms of pornography. He believes that if the attorney general of each state enforced the laws as they stand, this alone would "go a long way toward taking care of pornography." Believing in state and local responsibility for health and morals, he opposes "passing federal laws to solve all the ills of society." State programs ought to care for victims of crime, institute more stringent divorce laws, provide for child support, and take legal action against abortion. These can be encouraged by the federal government with information and recommendations for the states, but he opposes most efforts to have uniform national health and moral standards. These would give the federal government too much power, he feels.[23]

Abortion especially concerns Robertson. He thinks this difficult problem should be left to citizens and their elected representatives at the state level where it can be more quickly and effectively dealt with. The president, he says, does not have the major responsibility to halt abortions. The states should act immediately to save life, and the Supreme Court must remove its obstruction to these efforts.[24] When asked what should be done, he responded,

> Well, the first thing that has to be done on abortion, we have to realize that abortion is an individual decision. The government doesn't have abortions, women have abortions. We need a massive educational program to show people that this wonderful life within them is created in the image of God, and to take that life is murder.
>
> The court, however, overruled the laws of fifty states and said that a woman has a constitutional right to abortion. Well, that's nonsense. There's no constitutional right to take the life of another human being. We don't have such rights. So *Roe v. Wade* has got to be overturned. This would put the matter of abortion back in the hands of the people, in their legislatures.
>
> Once that is done, we could then talk about a human life resolution in Congress or a law that says life begins at conception; and if indeed the holocaust of abortion continues, we could indeed go in for a federal amendment to the Constitution, a human life amendment. But that is impossible politically right now. It will take us to the year 1995 or 2000 to get it passed, and I want to stop the slaughter of innocent children right now.[25]

Robertson supports traditional laws against adultery and sodomy. Laws supporting marriage and forbidding such sexual sins are guides to "liberty and happiness."[26] He compares sexual promiscuity to driving through a red light.

> If there is a red light at an intersection, and you drive through the red light, and you're hit by a car going through the green light, and you are injured in the car, did the city smite you? Did the city strike you and cause your accident? Well, you say, that's ridiculous. Of course not: I caused it myself. But there was a law there, wasn't there? And you broke the law. You drove through the red light, which was a warning sign; and when you crossed through it, you got it. Well, people in this country are violating certain moral laws and standards, and as a result, they're getting diseases.[27]

When asked if AIDS is the direct punishment of God for sexual sins, Robertson has two answers. First, he thinks Americans must understand that when someone contracts AIDS by having sexual relations outside of marriage, they have put themselves and others at risk and reap the results of promiscuity. Marriage protects people from infectious diseases; promiscuity is dangerous. Second, he argues that although God does not directly cause AIDS, He designed the natural world with laws that cannot be violated without consequences. The Bible says sin leads to death. Biological processes encourage people to follow right principles for living. This disease, as terrible as it is, "is a consequence of promiscuity," even when others are innocent victims, and is directly related to morals.

> I think it's high time we start making moral judgments in our society. The problem of AIDS in the homosexual community is well known to most Americans. . . . It is a tragedy . . . but homosexuality was written about in the Bible. This thing was prohibited. We are able to make moral judgments. This thing is morally wrong, and God warned us of the retribution that comes.[28]

Robertson is concerned that the American people lack the moral and political will to deal with AIDS. This plague could become the worst in history, with promiscuous victims endangering the innocent. He believes securing the purity of the blood supply in the nation's hospitals is a first priority. Research for cures must accelerate, he feels, but government must encourage citizens to "sexual continence and sexual fidelity within marriage" as its first line of defense. Unless the nation follows biblical standards on sexual matters, he thinks AIDS will overwhelm all efforts to prevent or cure it.[29]

Robertson wants the people to get tough on anything that undermines community health and morals, and he wants the government to adopt a moral agenda centered on family development. America needs to act quickly against pornography, abortion, and AIDS. Schools must teach morals to equip people for life. All this can be done without unduly expanding the federal government's role in communities, if most of the responsibility for health and morals is left to state and local government, to private groups, and to citizens.

What is particularly religious about Robertson's approach to social issues are his priorities and his urgency. He wants a healthy climate in which to raise children. Government today is swamped with chores too great for its resources—law enforcement officers are already busy keeping the streets safe in large cities. Nevertheless, America also needs to deal with pornography, abortion, and AIDS. Often politicians have other priorities. Robertson's views are more long term. He is concerned about the results of social breakdown in the next generation, not just the safety of streets tonight.

·5·
Giving
Families Support

♦ *What can be done for single-parent homes?*
♦ *Can the poor be helped more effectively?*
♦ *What incentives can strengthen families?*

Pat Robertson knows how easy it is for a father to get so busy in business or education that he neglects his own family. In his autobiography, *Shout It From the Housetops*, he recalls how, early in their marriage, his wife, Dede, complained to him, "You spend all your time running around the city, and your children never even know they have a father. Just because you never knew your father very well as a child is no excuse for your not spending time with your children."[1]

A few days later when his young son, Tim, came down with a high fever, Robertson cried out to God for his son's recovery. While praying, he felt guilty for his own lack of fathering. At the same time he was overwhelmed with what he understood to be God's perfect father love both for him and his son. No longer pleading for help, he confidently entrusted his son to God's care. Almost instantly the fever broke, and Robertson began to cry, amazed at what he took to be God's love for Tim and His acceptance of him as a poor neglectful father.

It was a lesson Pat Robertson never forgot.

But Robertson is also aware that many children do not even have a father at home. Fifteen million American children now live in single-parent homes because of divorce. Often these children blame themselves for their parents' divorce. As they grow older, they are more susceptible to drugs, to peer pressure, and to divorce when they become adults. Cycles of divorce and related poverty result.

Traditionally government encouraged husbands and wives to stay married. State laws made marriage vows hard to terminate unless there were sufficient grounds or both parties consented to a divorce. Under "no-fault" divorce laws, government now does little to keep marriages together. Robertson advised that government had good reasons for requiring grounds for divorce: The family unit is the building block of a stable society. He feels strongly that nothing destroys individuals and family relationships like divorce. When marriages crumble, everyone in America pays a high price.[2]

There are over 1 million unmarried-teen pregnancies a year, claims Robertson. These babies are either aborted, or the mothers often end up on welfare. The direct cost to government is $19 billion a year, and as this problem grows worse, it produces others.

Robertson says that his proposals differ from conservative and liberal solutions. Conservatives want to spend less money for poor families and liberals want to spend more, but neither look much at the impact of government on families. Conservatives in particular deserve criticism, he thinks, because they care nothing for the plight of families and simply work to keep the welfare state from costing too much for the taxpayer. Conservatives do not fight for white or black families, while liberals who do care make things worse.

Government programs even encourage divorce by subsidizing the desertion of women and their children by negligent fathers. Speaking to a conservative group, Robertson said,

Two Ohio University economists, Lowell Gallaway and Richard Vedder, have demonstrated that more than 50 percent of the increase in the United States divorce rate since 1965 can be explained by the growth in welfare spending . . . while the eligibility rules of AFDC (Aid to Families with Dependent Children) created the economic incentives for single-parent homes, another government program, the Legal Services Corporation, stood by to help with divorce. The greatest number of cases handled by attorneys of this agency, funded entirely by the federal government, ostensibly to provide legal aid to poor persons, is divorces and separations. In 1984, they handled over 220,000 divorces—over 20 percent of all divorces in the United States that year.[3]

Relating divorce to poverty, Robertson reported that intact families produce most of the nation's wealth. Family-owned businesses generate 60 percent of the gross national product and broken homes produce most of the poverty. Less than 16 percent of America's intact black families are poor, compared with well over half of the black homes without fathers. Once on welfare, mothers are penalized by reduced benefits if they work, and they become ineligible if they get married. Although it acts in the name of compassion, Robertson thinks almost everything government does in the Aid to Families with Dependent Children program encourages poverty. He believes it is time to carefully consider major reforms in this program.[4]

Care for the Poor

When poor families are given freedom to earn money and the opportunity gradually to provide for themselves, they will generally take good care of their family members, Robertson believes. Government should be minimally involved as the provider of last resort. But in situations where families lack resources, he does believe that government and private groups should help.[5]

Charities are generally much more efficient than government social programs. For example, Robertson estimates that over the past several years, CBN distributed $130 million worth of furniture, clothing, blankets, food, and other necessities to over 5 million Americans through cooperating churches and charitable groups. Working with volunteer forces, the immediate cost of distributing these items was less than half of 1 percent of their value. He compares this with government welfare programs where sometimes 50 percent to 70 percent of a program is eaten up with the overhead of salaries, offices, and record keeping involved in delivering services.[6]

Today there are fourth-generation welfare families. He insists, "Now, we can't just push that off in a corner and say, 'Well, 25 percent of the folks are going to be in trouble, and the other 75 percent of us are going to live in Westchester and live it up.' "[7] America now faces

> . . . a cycle of continuing poverty, and nothing is being done to get them out of it. But, along with government, there need to be these mediating agencies. The churches and the synagogues and the individual social agencies can move in with a spiritual help that the government can never give. There needs to be a partnership, if you will, between the private sector and the government sector. We can't throw it all on government, because government can't handle it. It doesn't do a good job of it. The churches don't have enough money to do it all. But working together, it can be very successful, if we'd acknowledge some of the problems.[8]

His solution involves the cooperation of government funding, private organizations, paid staff, and thousands of volunteers. Churches and private agencies can give counsel and spiritual help too. For the elderly, he proposes a national private retirement system to supplement Social Security, because eventually, care for the elderly at a comfortable level will require a much larger effort. Any tax on this pension should be minimal for those over sixty-five.[9]

Robertson claims over $400 billion a year is spent on all government benefits to those who are dependent and on Social Security.

Yet people remain poor. Crime is one major reason, he believes, for this poverty. Once it was assumed that poverty caused crime; in many cities it is now clear, he explains, that crime produces poverty, because owners in heavy crime areas refuse to invest in their property, stores leave, and businesses shut down long before nightfall to avoid robbery and vandalism. This reduces the number of jobs. Insurance and security systems are costly in high crime areas, discouraging business development. In this way, crime devours whole communities.[10] He cites these statistics:

> Americans earning less than three thousand dollars a year are twice as likely to be robbed as those earning twenty-five thousand dollars. For poor women, the statistics are even more threatening: An unemployed woman—or a woman earning under three thousand dollars annually—is three times more likely to be a rape victim than a woman earning seventy-five hundred dollars or more. Welfare families—those who have least in the way of material possessions— are robbed as often as families making twenty-five thousand dollars or more per year. For the poor, the consequences are devastating. In 1980, the economic burden of crime on a family making less than six thousand was five times greater per incident than that for families making twenty-five thousand dollars.[11]

To help the young break out of crime and unemployment, he recommends that there be a minimum youth wage that is lower than the federal minimum wage to create more entry level jobs. Robertson would also allow families to establish businesses in their homes. He wants to remove the many legal restrictions supported by labor unions which make it difficult to work.[12]

Government welfare agencies have a monopoly on the delivery of social services, but he proposes opening up the system to allow the poor to receive help through private agencies that could be partly funded by government. He also thinks that poor families with both parents living together should be rewarded, not punished, for keeping their homes intact. Taxing public assistance once a reasonable income level is reached would be preferable to deducting all earnings from the welfare benefits that they receive. Government needs to reward work and marriage as it assists the poor.[13]

The Needs of Families

While Robertson warns against government control of family life, he does have a vision for government helping to strengthen families. For too long government programs have neglected or damaged families, he feels. Fathers deserting families have unleashed terrible problems for women and children and the rest of society. Fathers can be encouraged to return home, and mothers can be given incentives to care for their children.

Robertson thinks Americans need to resist efforts by government to interfere with parental authority. Whenever government begins to replace parents, he warned, this leads in the end to totalitarian rule. In Illinois, for example, there was debate in the state legislature on compulsory education for three-year-olds. One advocate said, "Well, why shouldn't we get children when they're three years old? The state can do a whole lot better job with them than the parents can." Robertson reports that an attorney general in Texas said, "The state owns your children." He wants Americans to know that government can be a threat to family life.[14]

Today almost 60 percent of the women in America work full time outside their homes. The trend is increasing this number. Younger women especially are making good wages. Robertson reports that average salaries for young women are about 85 percent that of men; he does think that a woman should receive the same pay as a man for the same work. However, with their duties at home and the costs of child care, professional clothing, restaurants, and taxes, typically women have little money left to show for their labor. Many women would prefer to be full-time mothers and wives, but financial pressures keep them at work.[15]

There are other factors affecting family finances. Taxes have gone up twice as fast as the average family income. Inflation cuts into the budget, making it much more difficult to buy houses and automobiles, and consumer expectations and debts pressure women to work. Government subsidizes this by allowing a tax credit for mothers who have baby-sitters. But government could help mothers much more in another way. Robertson recommends that there be an extra tax deduction for women who want to stay at home and raise their children.[16] Women should have a choice about what kind of work they will do and whether or not to be mothers at home, and he believes government can help make this a possibility. When asked if mothers on welfare should work before their children start school, Robertson responded that he would want to study the problem, but he would prefer that all children under six years old have full-time mothers.[17]

He recalls the contribution of his own mother, Gladys Robertson, to his early development and later ministry.

> I know my own mother. I can't tell you what an influence she had on me when I was growing up—the concepts, the ideals, the tenderness, the warmth, the compassion for other people—came from my mother. She prayed for me for hours, and went with me through many struggles of life. What it is that I am, standing here to do, in large part, is attributable to my mother. Now, she wasn't in business, she wasn't a professional lady. She was a mother.[18]

Robertson wants government to encourage mothers to stay at home when their children are young. If the tax deduction for children was increased to five thousand dollars per child, as many as a quarter of the women who now work would stay home, he claims. Government today penalizes young families rather than encouraging them.

With opportunities for careers, more women are choosing to have fewer children. Each child is expensive to clothe and to care for, and living only for present pleasures undermines a commitment to have children. The reduction in family size is dramatic and long term. Someday a very few younger adults will have to support a great many older people on Social Security, and government is partly responsible for this, according to Robertson. At present rates the population will decline, and he points out that this will be tough on the economy as well.

Robertson tells people that one exception to the general trend toward small families with less than two children are the traditionally religious homes. Religious parents tend to have hope for the future and are thus prepared to make long-term, sacrificial investments for their children. They are fulfilled in having children. Robertson remembers his early days as a father:

> Dede and I . . . didn't have those disposable, throw-away diapers. We had those buckets and we washed those things out. I've had my experience with dirty babies' bottoms and walking them when they cried at night and all the rest of it. . . . It's a sacrifice.[19]

Mothers and fathers give generously to their children so that the next generation will have a good start in life. Government, says Robertson, must assist these families. He believes that Americans should plan for the future of their children.

Robertson believes that men and women are significantly different, and gender-based roles enhance harmony at home and in society. By recognizing differences between men and women, government can avoid setting the sexes against each other. Special protection should be given to women where appropriate, he says, such as in the military draft.

Robertson is opposed to the Equal Rights Amendment. He is convinced that ERA would protect individuals at the expense of the family, and it could take benefits such as alimony away from women. Women deserve the full respect of the law, Robertson claims, without losing equal protection. Furthermore, he believes ERA is socially destructive: "If ratified, it could be interpreted to give constitutional protection to homosexuals, lesbians, sadomasochists and to anyone else who engaged in any other sexual practice, whether or not that practice was prohibited by the Bible, religious dogma, or existing federal or state law." He argues that the mere fact that the homosexual community and antireligious groups strongly support ERA is evidence that it is not the innocent proposal that it appears.[20]

The poor need America's attention desperately. Robertson is confident of the simple answer to the problem:

All people have got to do is three things and they can almost guarantee they won't be in poverty. Number one, they have to finish high school. That's not too hard. Number two, they have to get a job, even at an entry-level wage, and stay at it. And number three, they've got to get married and stay married. That's all they've got to do to guarantee that they will not come to the poverty level because the overall statistics t to those three things as the key. That isn't very difficult in any society as free and good as ours.[21]

Without literacy, work, and marriage, no assistance to the poor, public or private, will make much difference, he feels. The Bible promised a reward for those who cared for the destitute, and the evidence available should warn America that the costs of poverty and illiteracy are not bearable in the long run. America has a bright future, he believes, if it cares properly for the poor and the young.

According to Robertson, government must recapture the confidence that it can contribute to the social welfare of its people. Average Americans can be helped, the poor can be assisted, the illiterate can be taught, and government action can make the difference. Failed policies are not the only policies. He asks government to focus on two specific areas, literacy and the family. He favors a cooperative and complementary approach that releases private initiative, supporting it somewhat with government funds. His distaste for centralized control in Washington leads him to favor local and state action with Washington assisting but not managing programs. Healthy families create wealth, good schools produce literacy, and wise government will promote them both.

·6·
Endangered
<u>Liberty</u>

- ♦ *Does religion support freedom?*
- ♦ *How has liberty been eroded?*
- ♦ *Has confusion captured American schools?*

On a day maybe similar to this, Captain John Smith took his boat up the Chesapeake Bay, went into the waters of what is now Pennsylvania, got off his ship, went into the fields and up into the hills, and looked at the beautiful blue skies, breathing the air of a free land. When he got back in his ship, he penned these words, "I would rather be a settler in America than Good Queen Bess over all of England." He said, "This is the place where a man can spread his wings and fly like an eagle. These are the days to live!"[1]

When he speaks on liberty, Robertson frequently tells this story from earliest colonial Virginia. Almost four hundred years later, another Elizabeth, Queen Elizabeth II, occupies the throne in England, but Robertson feels that America is still a place where "a man can spread his wings and fly like an eagle." While respecting his British roots, he reminds Americans that theirs is a unique heritage, a revolutionary heritage, that began when fresh ideas were given room to grow in a new land.

Recently in Great Britain, politics again turned to the theme of liberty. Margaret Thatcher, Prime Minister of Great Britain, had not, she said, run out of ideas. Campaigning for reelection in June

1987, this Conservative Party champion produced a seventy-seven-page Manifesto to trumpet her successes and to announce further "radical conservative reform." Her goal was "building One Nation of free, prosperous, and responsible families and people."[2]

Under Thatcher's leadership, since 1979, British Conservatives have sought to reduce government control over the industry and life of their people. More Britons now own their own homes and shares in the private corporations in which they work, and new industry thrives, particularly in the south of England. Committed to "steadily reducing the share of the nation's income taken by the State," Thatcher wants her people "to have more freedom of choice about what they do for themselves, their families and for others less fortunate."[3] The Manifesto states:

> In this way One Nation is finally reached—not by a single people being conscripted into an organized socialist programme but by millions of people building their own lives in their own way.[4]

The most visible part of this program is owning your own home instead of renting from the government; the other parts of the program—debt-free government, no inflation, more private industry, schools teaching basic skills and moral values, strong defense, and free trade—are basic conservative measures.

Certainly building one nation of free and prosperous families fits with Pat Robertson's new vision for America. What is missing from Thatcher's platform, for Robertson, is the phrase "under God." There is no mention of God or religion in the Manifesto. Liberty and justice in Britain, according to Thatcher, come from the "British instinct for choice and independence," and the good instincts of conservatives will be sufficient, she thinks, to insure the preservation of what is noble and useful of this ancient tradition.[5]

An appeal to an instinct for liberty makes some sense in Great Britain. For generations the phrase "the rights of Englishmen" meant a great deal to Americans, who revolted when they felt those rights threatened by the British Parliament; however, the historic basis for liberty in America, in principle and in fact, is quite different. This is stated clearly in the Declaration of Independence, the nation's founding legal document, where reference is made to "the Laws of Nature and of Nature's God" and to the belief that

> We hold these truths to be self-evident, that all men are created equal, that they are endowed by their Creator with certain unalienable Rights. . . .

Liberty in America was based on both reason and God, and both were thought to be beyond dispute. These truths were considered self-evident, which meant that they could be discovered or understood by anyone, anywhere, with or without the help of the Christian faith or the British tradition, to be considered valid and correct. The nation agreed on this essential point that all people had rights and were worthy of respect because they were made in God's image. This conviction, which the Bible taught and reason supported, was the foundation of American government. Reason and God together secured liberty.[6]

The belief that all persons, whatever their religion or cultural background, were worthy of respect was in fact a religious teaching. Yet Americans today are slow to trust anyone who claims there is a spiritual basis for American government and law. History gives credit to the Anglicans, the Pilgrims, the Puritans, the Quakers, the Catholics, and others for helping to establish the first colonies. Scholars respect Baptists for their contribution to religious liberty. But when a religious broadcaster like Pat Robertson claims far more for religion, based on the Declaration of Independence and his reading of American history, people doubt those claims for three reasons: first, because of his personal religious bias; second, because religion seems a poor foundation for secular government; and third, because few are confident that religion or government can be understood clearly. So in the face of considerable opposition, Robertson presses his case for liberty.

Robertson published his views on the founding of America in a recent book, *America's Dates With Destiny*. This book begins by reporting that religion has largely been removed from American school textbooks. Textbooks virtually ignore the contribution of the Bible to the foundations of the nation. He places the responsibility for this on educational leaders and scholars. Robertson says that this distortion of history has affected his life goals. When he finished college and law school he was a person without any concern for the nation. His view of life had become warped. His purpose in life after graduating was to make money: "I had been bitten by the entrepreneurial bug, and making big deals in business and a lot of money were my principal goals."[7]

Personal ambition replaced public service, which had been modeled for Robertson by his senator father. He blames his education, because in it the "spiritual dimension of man was ridiculed, caricatured, or ignored entirely." Law was only a game by which the strong controlled the weak, or so he thought, and he became somewhat cynical and disillusioned. He failed the bar examination after law school, not seriously preparing for it and having no higher purpose to motivate him to study. Robertson already had an excellent business position with W. R. Grace and Company, and this seemed sufficient to secure his future.[8]

His own experience of being lost without a direction or purpose beyond himself helps to explain why Robertson is so exercised by these issues. According to Robertson, a combination of factors is needed to provide the necessary nurture for his own life and the life of the nation: personal faith in God and a deep appreciation and positive belief in the principles of the Bible as they relate to common life and government. To meet the needs of America requires that the nation get back in touch with what has been removed from most accounts of American history.

What Robertson has been saying is uniquely expressed in the best-selling book by Allan Bloom entitled *The Closing of the American Mind*. Professor Bloom, a teacher for thirty years and a scholar at the University of Chicago, is concerned that if America forgets that it was "conceived in liberty and dedicated to the proposition that all men are created equal," it will be vulnerable to dictatorship.[9] In his book, Bloom warns the nation and its leaders:

This is the American moment in world history, the one for which we shall forever be judged. Just as in politics the responsibility for the fate of freedom in the world has devolved upon our regime, so the fate of philosophy in the world has devolved upon our universities, and the two are related as they have never been before. The gravity of our given task is great, and it is very much in doubt how the future will judge our stewardship.[10]

Bloom, a political philosopher who studies the classics of Western thought, does not write from a Christian or even from a religious perspective. Although Bloom and Robertson have little in common in their personal and professional experience, they share a similar understanding of America and a concern for the classrooms of the nation. Both agree that citizens are being taught to doubt and even to reject the nation's most basic institutions and beliefs. Robertson looks at this from a religious perspective; Bloom discusses the same subject as a political philosopher. Both see the education of children as highly significant for America's future.

Robertson on Liberty

In *America's Dates With Destiny*, Robertson claims one cannot understand America without including the role of religion. The Declaration of Independence stated that the colonists had a right to be independent because of their relationship to the "Laws of Nature and of Nature's God." The idea that independence is just plain politics with no connection to religion is completely foreign to the Declaration. Religion, he argues, must be understood if one is going to deal with the founding of this nation and its later history.

The idea that all people had inalienable rights given to them by their Creator was something average Americans understood in the eighteenth and nineteenth century because they were familiar with the Bible. They understood that Americans were protected by God's law from tyrants and from the arbitrary acts of those in authority.[11] Robertson recently explained:

In 1776, when our forefathers decided that the burdens of the English Parliament and King George III were intolerable, they declared they were writing a revolution. A man named Thomas Jefferson penned the immortal words, "We hold these truths to be self-evident." Why were they self-evident? Truth isn't always self-evident to anybody. They were evident to those colonists, to those early founders of this nation, because they had heard them from the pulpits of America for one hundred and fifty years at least—that all men are endowed by their Creator with certain unalienable rights of life, liberty, and the pursuit of happiness. In the founding documents that began this nation, we affirm belief in a Creator that gave us our rights. And that was the unique genius of the American experiment that we gave God credit, and that we took our freedoms from Almighty God. No government gave us freedom, and no government has the power to take it away from us. Our freedom comes from God and is inalienable. It cannot be separated from us because it is part of our possession as human beings created in the image of Almighty God.[12]

The Declaration's statements were made in a clearly religious context. In particular, "all men are created equal" is a statement based on Genesis, says Robertson, where it states that all are made in the image of God and obtain their nature from Him. The phrase "life, liberty, and the pursuit of happiness" is also religiously grounded. The founders believed that God is the source of life for every human being and that all true liberty comes ultimately from God, who created mankind to enjoy His creation. These basic rights are not granted by the state, and government is not their source, Robertson points out. They came with creation and are inalienable because they are in our very nature, our created identity, and cannot be taken away.[13] The purpose of government, writes Robertson, is to protect these rights and to enable people to live in health and prosperity.

Religion helps to define what government can and should do. It sets limits on the powers of leaders and directs the energies of government. Law and the actions of government, from Robertson's standpoint, must be in line with godly principles.

Man's law is important, but it must reflect God's law to be truly valid. The colonists tried diligently to obey their king. When the king refused to grant them justice, however, they appealed to a higher authority. What a gift our forefathers have given us. By their example we learn that it is our right and duty as citizens to judge the laws and lawmakers of this nation by the laws of God in the created order and in God's Word, and then to act.[14]

There is no question that the *Roe v. Wade* abortion ruling by the Supreme Court, more than any other recent event, focused the attention of religious Americans on the law and on the role of the Supreme Court in the nation's life. This one decision has driven Christians back to their biblical and historical foundations to defend what they believe is right.

For people to challenge laws and oppose rulings of the Supreme Court at a time when crime and lawlessness are increasing the disorder in America puts the general political order and the institutions of the country under even more pressure. If Christians stand up in this way, what will others do?

Robertson's desire to apply biblical standards to issues like abortion will expose him to the charge of being a religious troublemaker—an anarchist. How will he maintain respect for the institutions and leaders of this nation if he calls their actions illegal? This is not an easy question, but it is one that he is willing to wrestle with and discuss in public.

This is not the first time the nation has faced such issues. Before America was one hundred years old it had almost lost its unity and its vision, Robertson reminds us. At the heart of national life in 1860 was a terrible contradiction long noticed but unresolved: Slavery held some Americans as property. Yet no rationalization of slavery could overcome the issue raised by the words of the Declaration of Independence: "All men are created equal." In his Gettysburg Address, President Abraham Lincoln kept alive the Declaration's understanding of liberty. Robertson writes that the primary issue of the Civil War to Lincoln was "what liberty means and who should have it."[15]

In his political debates with Senator Stephen A. Douglas (1857–58), Lincoln argued against the expansion of slavery into the federal territories. He believed that the federal government should not allow slaves in these territories even if a majority of the white settlers wanted them. Douglas replied that the majority vote of local settlers should decide the issue. Lincoln disagreed, because democracy had its limits: A majority vote would not make slavery right, nor should the federal government allow slaves in the territories.

> So I say in relation to the principle that *all men are created equal*, let it be as nearly reached as we can. If we cannot give freedom to every creature, let us do nothing that will impose slavery upon any other creature.[16]

Lincoln provides for Robertson the clear and authoritative interpretation of the Declaration of Independence. Once Americans committed themselves to believing in God-given rights due equally to all people, they had released a power into the nation's life with which to resist oppression. Robertson quotes Lincoln's explanation of this ongoing influence of the Declaration:

> I think the authors of that notable instrument intended to include all men, but they did not intend to declare all men equal in all respects. They did not mean to say all were equal in color, size, intellect, moral developments, or social capacity. They defined with tolerable distinctness in what respects they did consider all men created equal—equal with "certain inalienable rights, among which are life, liberty, and the pursuit of happiness." This they said, and this they meant. They did not mean to assert the obvious untruth that all were then actually enjoying that equality, nor yet that they were about to confer it immediately upon them. In fact, they had no power to confer such a boon. They meant simply to declare the right, so that enforcement of it might follow as fast as circumstances should permit. They meant to set up a standard maxim for free society which should be familiar to all and revered by all; constantly looked

to . . . constantly approximated, and thereby constantly spreading and deepening its influence and augmenting the happiness and value of life to all people of all colors everywhere.[17]

Robertson stands against the cynicism about human rights that some have in America because of the abuses of those rights in practice. The nation needs to recapture the realistic vision of Lincoln, he says. He finds in Lincoln a model for his own participation in politics. Lincoln stood in the gap against a false democracy that would let slavery expand and lead to mob rule. Through the Republican Party, he mobilized people to defend the founding principles of liberty and equality. Lincoln stood for those principles clearly even when he could not implement them to free all the slaves.

American principles are universal, says Robertson. They are meant by God to be "enjoyed by people everywhere in this land and around the world."[18] He is committed to this extension of liberty where people desire it, as his foreign policy reflects.

The two founding documents of America, the Declaration of Independence and the Constitution, are both legal documents. The Constitution is the supreme law of the land. Any reading of one, says Robertson, is "incomplete without the other." The Declaration refers to God, and the Constitution is rooted in a religious tradition but makes no mention of a deity. Seeing this difference in the documents, he notes, "Some read the Constitution quickly, and because it contains no direct reference to God, conclude that it has no Christian roots, no biblical precedents." Nothing could be further from the truth, he says, because the Constitution is a means of implementing the principles of liberty and equality stated and assumed by the Declaration. Originally it also involved making practical political choices that included protecting temporarily the institution of slavery. Robertson argues that since the Constitution combined American ideals with compromises, such as its tolerance of slavery, it was hence very much "man-made." He argues, "The

Constitution is not an appropriate or necessary place to speak of God."[19]

Governments commonly rule by force or by tradition. A government by the consent of the governed and under law was unique in 1787, and is still rare. In fact, most peoples do not seem yet to be able to institute this kind of government.[20] Robertson believes that what made the American government work were both the principles taken from the Bible and the restraint made possible by the religious convictions of the American people. In America, a clear understanding of law and political rights preserved the peace, but Robertson says liberty began within the hearts and minds of people.

> Our free society depends on one essential element, the self-restraint of its citizens. And the self-restraint of the citizens in turn depends on one primary belief, that God exists and that one day He will judge us and reward or punish us according to His divine standard. Believing in the just and powerful God of the Old Testament makes a tremendous difference in a society. Believing in the ancient promise of eternal rewards or eternal punishments helps foster self-control.[21]

Bloom on Liberty

The thesis of Bloom's *The Closing of the American Mind* is that American schools are hostile to the liberty taught by the Declaration and the Constitution. Because Indians have been abused, blacks enslaved, Roman Catholics and Jews excluded, and women refused suffrage, "liberty" is said to be hypocrisy. Teachers often claim that American ideals are a cover-up for a government controlled by dominant white Protestant men.[22]

Schools once taught patriotism and respect for national ideals and American heroes, Bloom argues. Now they attack the Declaration and Constitution as slave documents written by slave owners like Thomas Jefferson and George Washington. Abraham Lincoln is condemned as well for allowing slavery to continue—the

Great Emancipator has become in our classrooms a pragmatic, unprincipled politician, he says. Schools now teach that there are no real heroes to remember or learn from, and no sure ideals to pass on to our children.[23]

Bloom contends this was once not so. Until recently, Americans were confident of their ability to comprehend fully the meaning of liberty and the basis for it. The essentials of good government were known and taught to everybody.

> The American Revolution instituted this system of government for Americans, who in general were satisfied with the result and had a pretty clear view of what they had done. The questions of political principle and of right had been solved once and for all.[24]

Europeans, on the other hand, began their thinking with doubt. Bloom describes how the French, for example, are torn between faith and reason, between religion and atheism. Europe has had a mental, spiritual, and political civil war at its heart for generations, he says. Instead of having confidence in a few principles and building on them like the Americans, Europeans are unsure of themselves. Bloom states that they believe truth can only be dimly perceived and is easily misunderstood, and perhaps contradictory anyway. He implies that for Europeans, the result is conflict in politics, uncertainty in education, and, in both, something of a sophisticated confusion.[25]

American faith in basic truths rested on the Bible and on a real trust in the human mind.

> Most students could be counted on to know the Bible, that ubiquitous source of the older traditions. In America it was not filtered through great national interpreters, but approached directly in the manner of early Protestantism, every man his own interpreter.[26]

People who knew the Bible ended up learning from:

> . . . great scholars and thinkers who dealt with the same material, not from outside or from an alien perspective, but believing as they

did, while simply going deeper and providing guidance. There was a respect for real learning, because it had a felt connection with their lives.[27]

There was then in America harmony between religion and scholarship and between education and politics. Bloom relates that Americans were at peace with their traditions because they believed them to be true.

> America tells one story: the unbroken, ineluctable progress of freedom and equality. From its first settlers and its political foundings on, there has been no dispute that freedom and equality are the essence of justice for us. No one serious or notable has stood outside this consensus.[28]

This common way of thinking was liberating, he says. It made it possible for anyone without any prior training to quickly become an American. Bloom writes,

> Americans were, in effect, told that they could be whatever they wanted to be or happened to be as long as they recognized that the same applied to all other men and they were willing to support and defend the government that guaranteed that dispensation. It is possible to become an American in a day.[29]

Newcomers could join this experiment in self-government by agreeing to respect the rights of others protected by law. This liberty relied on the confident and free approval of citizens. Civic education, says Bloom, was essential for its success. This training was not the rigid, ideological indoctrination so characteristic of most nations. American education stressed ideals and praised the prudent leaders who strove to live by them. Speaking of the American student, Bloom says:

> Above all he was to know the rights doctrine; the Constitution, which embodied it; and American history, which presented and celebrated the founding of a nation "conceived in liberty and

dedicated to the proposition that all men are created equal." A powerful attachment to the letter and the spirit of the Declaration of Independence gently conveyed, appealing to each man's reason, was the goal of the education of democratic man.[30]

American civic education taught principles, documents, institutions, and heroes that people were to study to be good citizens, Bloom reports. Students learned Revolutionary War slogans, such as "Give me liberty or give me death," and whole classes memorized portions of the Declaration, the Constitution, and the Gettysburg Address. They analyzed the separation of powers and federalism; they heard stories from the lives of Washington and Lincoln. These were the essentials of informed citizenship. They bound Americans together, making democracy possible. Although the nation's divisions were many and its conflicts at times exploded, common principles helped to bind it together.

Bloom concludes that up until recent times the nation's schools, supported by a largely Protestant Christian faith, sustained an American way of life. Eventually Americans made room, although with some pain, for Jews, Roman Catholics, agnostics, and Orientals. All assumed that ethnic and religious groups would be very different in their doctrines and practices. Groups were even expected to be hostile to one another's most cherished beliefs, but all were to be protected by the same law and were recognized to have the same rights.[31]

Robertson and the Loss of Liberty

For Pat Robertson, the truths that sustain liberty, representing the shared American perspective, are theological in nature. People have rights because they are brothers who have a common Father who watches over the welfare of each of His children. Human beings made in God's image owe one another respect; they have rights given to them by God. God has been central to the American political vision and has sustained it providentially, in Robertson's view.

Abraham Lincoln's victory in the Civil War preserved the Union, abolished slavery, and his Gettysburg Address kept the meaning of liberty clear for all to see. Yet one generation after Lincoln's accomplishments, American liberty faced a threat in the nation's schools that is yet to be overcome, and according to Robertson, that threat grows daily.

In *America's Dates With Destiny*, Robertson suggests reasons for the loss of the meaning of liberty in American classrooms. The fundamental problems are intellectual and, ultimately, spiritual. He makes no claims to be a professional scholar, yet when he looks for an explanation for why liberties are in jeopardy he knows that ideas count, because liberty begins as an idea.[32]

Robertson traces current problems back to intellectual developments after 1865. Charles Darwin, Karl Marx, Friedrich Nietzsche, Sigmund Freud, and the American John Dewey all had large parts to play in a mental revolution of enormous consequences. He notes:

> Contemporary thinkers with roots in the eighteenth-century Enlightenment began to advance new ideas about humanity and its place in the universe. With all their wisdom, the use and misuse of these new ideas tended to undermine the spiritual foundations laid so carefully by our forefathers.[33]

Science and theology parted company, he says, and the result was the removal of the "Laws of Nature and of Nature's God" from America's vocabulary and awareness. The scientific method, as interpreted by great scholars or by their followers, became separated from values and replaced the Bible and God in human affairs, giving people a different philosophy of life and a false sense of optimism about the future.[34]

In America, John Dewey taught that an experimental method was appropriate in the classroom, and according to Robertson this replaced traditional moral and political instruction. The result of Dewey's position was to teach children that ethical rules and laws could be devised and were not related to fixed principles. The clear implication and result, says Robertson, is that the Bible and the

Declaration of Independence were both attacked and removed from the classroom.[35]

In simple terms, Americans changed from a God-centered mental universe, where human reason is respected and where the Bible is taught, to a man-centered perspective that gathers information but loses sight of basic principles of life. This contemporary view is based on modern science, Robertson asserts, leading to loss of respect for religion, law, and humanity. He draws this conclusion recounting a series of destructive events that have hit America in recent years—World War I, the removal of religion from public life, the Depression, World War II, communism, political assassinations, budget deficits, legalized abortion, and defeat in Vietnam. An intellectual and spiritual bankruptcy helped to cause these problems and made it difficult to solve them. Robertson writes in summary,

> At the beginning of the century, America had turned from her spiritual and political foundations. As a result, the nation had suffered great loss. Her spirit had been broken. Her will to win had been crippled dangerously.[36]

For Robertson, the basic problem is spiritual. To deny God removes Him from personal and political life and leads eventually to the loss of respect for "life, liberty, and the pursuit of happiness." Allan Bloom has a somewhat different but confirming explanation for the same result.

Bloom and the Loss of Liberty

Bloom understands liberty in the American sense to be a relatively recent idea developed by philosophical thinking, not religion.

> The notion that man possesses inalienable natural rights, that they belong to him as an individual prior, both in time and in sanctity, to any civil society, and that civil societies exist for and acquire their

legitimacy from ensuring those rights, is an invention of modern philosophy.[37]

Bloom agrees, however, that liberty, whatever its source, took root deeply in America.

> But almost every thoughtful observer knows that it is in the United States that the idea of rights has penetrated most deeply into the bloodstream of its citizens and accounts for their unusual lack of servility.[38]

What we must understand now, says Bloom, is that the best schools no longer teach the basic truths that produced this freedom of the American spirit. He writes that America is substituting tolerance for liberty. Any idea, no matter how false or destructive, is considered acceptable if it works for someone, but it is not to be imposed on others. Tolerance has become the one absolute rule of America's cultural elite, and this is increasingly true of its schools.[39]

What governs increasingly in America, according to Bloom, is doubt—doubt that may not even want to examine evidence or arguments. This recent rejection of reason has dreadful consequences waiting. He writes, "There is no doubt that value-relativism, if it is true and it is believed in, takes one into very dark regions of the soul and very dangerous political experiments."[40] When people are less controlled by their thoughts, their passions and impulses will begin to rule. Eventually, if this is unchecked, anything goes.

> The soul becomes a stage for a repertory company that changes plays regularly—sometimes a tragedy, sometimes a comedy; one day love, another day politics, and finally religion; now cosmopolitanism, and again rooted loyalty; the city or the country; individualism or community; sentimentality or brutality. And there is neither principle nor will to impose a rank order on all of these.[41]

Bloom has taught in the best secular universities. He is an astute observer of student thinking. He says students deserve to be understood, because they are children and neighbors, and some-day they will be in government.

> There is one thing a professor can be absolutely certain of: almost every student entering the university believes, or says he believes, that truth is relative.[42]

Bloom's explanation for this state of mind, or condition of the soul as he would prefer to call it, is interesting. Professors don't have answers for students, and even more troubling, students don't ask questions about life, death, God, or immortality. Broken homes have produced insecurity that makes it difficult for students to ask questions or to examine their foundations for fear they have none. Rock music replaces books that cannot compete with its erotic beat, its universal language. Casual premarital sex reduces curiosity, as the mystery of the other sex is violated—there is less to look forward to.[43]

Most fundamentally, says Bloom, relativism and tolerance have replaced the "inalienable natural rights that used to be traditional American grounds for a free society."[44] The reason for this is simple: Students blame the truth, or people who say that they know the truth, for conflicts in the world. Truth divides and tolerance unites, and they believe that the world needs unity at all costs. Bloom states that students assume:

> The study of history and of culture teaches that all the world was mad in the past; men always thought they were right, and that led to wars, persecutions, slavery, xenophobia, racism, and chauvinism. The point is not to correct the mistakes and really be right; rather it is not to think you are right at all.[45]

This would not be of great concern if this skepticism were only a passing phase. Bloom thinks that valuing tolerance more than truth is being hardened into dogma with the assistance of professors and scholars.[46]

Bloom is concerned that everyday language is being destroyed in this battle. When Americans can no longer use words to call tyranny what it is, then they will neither recognize tyranny nor be able to resist it.

> When President Ronald Reagan called the Soviet Union "the evil empire," right-thinking persons joined in an angry chorus of protest against such provocative rhetoric. At other times Mr. Reagan has said that the United States and the Soviet Union "have different *values*" (italics added), an assertion that those same persons greet at worst with silence and frequently with approval.[47]

Bloom gives explanations for this problem that are only indirectly religious. He partly blames German scholarship and the profound influence of Friedrich Nietzsche, Sigmund Freud, and Max Weber on American thinking: "The self-understanding of hippies, yippies, yuppies, panthers, prelates and presidents has unconsciously been formed by German thought of a half-century earlier."[48]

Bloom's intent is not to attack German scholarship. His concern is with the effects of the popularization of that scholarship and its dominance over Americans. It is one thing to read these scholars and quite another to let them become the gatekeepers of thought.[49]

The true genius of American scholarship, according to Bloom, has been its freedom to study the great masterpieces of Western literature afresh. Americans have gone to the Bible, to the Greek classics, and to the European masterpieces directly to learn for themselves rather than through interpreters. The tragedy of this day, he declares, is that universities have given up this independence.[50]

Bloom concludes that liberty in America requires that teachers again boldly affirm and defend with reason certain fixed truths—the founding principles that are true for all people at all times. Above all, they must not substitute mere relative tolerance for the law of liberty, or Americans will end up tolerating tyranny.

The axioms that Americans agree on actually set them free to explore the universe of ideas, Bloom says, confident of their ability to comprehend both deep mysteries and the meaning of a single word. For Americans, respect for reason, in his view, is a distinctive national trait that must never be surrendered. Liberty requires respect for truth to survive.

Robertson enjoys saying the Statue of Liberty belongs to the whole world. Immigrants from every part of the earth pass by its torch when they come into New York Harbor. It symbolizes a welcome and equal rights for each person as he or she makes a new home in America.

> More than 60 million immigrants have come to America fleeing oppression and revolution. They came seeking religious and political freedom. They came to plant farms and build houses, to raise families, and to seek a new life in a new world. They came seeking life, liberty and the pursuit of happiness, and most of them have found it here.[51]

One of the rights that Americans have is the freedom to leave and choose another country. "From the beginning, our forefathers believed that the freedom to leave one country and take up residence in another was a God-given right."[52] No one is bound by law to be an American; citizenship is voluntary and can be relinquished.

Robertson contrasts the Statue of Liberty with the ancient statues of Greek and Roman civilization built in honor of conquest. America was to be a beacon of opportunity, not an empire. He eulogizes the immigrants who took enormous risks to come to this country. Here, he says, there is an equality that leads to opportunity for distinction, and that has made this country great.

Robertson says that America belongs to the world and was created by the peoples of the world. It is respected not as a perfect nation, but because of its progress in the direction of liberty and the protection of the dignity of individuals and groups. America must remain a refuge for the oppressed, Robertson feels.

> . . . When the first settlers and their children began to complain about the numbers of new arrivals who also came seeking liberty, President Jefferson asked, "Shall we refuse to the unhappy fugitives from distress that hospitality which the savages of the wilderness extended to our fathers arriving in this land? Shall oppressed humanity find no asylum on this globe?"[53]

Respect for the rights of people in theory should lead to their proper treatment in practice. America boasted to the world on its great seal, which is printed on its money and used on its documents, that it had established a *Novus Ordo Seclorum*, a "New Order for the Ages." Robertson sees a fulfillment of this vision in the mix of peoples gathered voluntarily and peacefully under one flag.

Religion and reason once stood together in America to support liberty. Now they largely stand apart. Robertson hears the Declaration when it speaks of the "Creator" as the source of liberty. He rejects the idea of "self-evident" truth. Truth is extremely difficult to find, in his view, and was self-evident in America only because they already believed in it: From April 12, 1607, "until the day of the signing of the Declaration of Independence, the pastors throughout the colonies had proclaimed one central truth—God is sovereign. You are creatures made in the image of God. You have rights because God gave them to you." Bloom, on the other hand, affirms the "self-evident" nature of liberty, and is confident that reason does not need religion or a belief in God to discover it.[54] For him, the greatest book on education is Plato's *Republic*, not the Bible.

Margaret Thatcher's belief in the instinct of a people for liberty has no appeal for Robertson or Bloom. Neither trusts instinct as the source of liberty. They also agree on another issue: A very special kind of education is required to enable people to be citizens in a successful democracy. For Robertson this must include room for the Creator in the classrooms of America, "under God." Bloom would place religious instruction in the home. He wants schools to teach children that, "We hold these truths to be self-evident."

For Bloom, educational reform includes reading and teaching great ideas and talking with friends. For Robertson, it involves instruction on the original meaning of the Declaration of Independence accompanied by a spiritual and social revival, more like a river in flood stage than Bloom's thoughtful dialogues. With their significant disagreements and different starting points, both of these men have this concern—to see a renewed America where the same liberty is understood and loved.

·7·
Law:
The Backbone
of Liberty

- ♦ *What about separation of church and state?*
- ♦ *Is secularism America's established religion?*
- ♦ *Would Robertson obey the Supreme Court?*

Without rules that limit government, tyranny results; without laws that restrict individuals, anarchy follows. Trained in law, Pat Robertson believes that liberty in America presumes the restraint of both government and individuals for the common good.

In the late seventies, conservatives grew alarmed at growing social anarchy and government encroachments. Led by the Reverend Jerry Falwell, the Moral Majority was founded and the new Christian right jumped into politics with strong reactions and not much knowledge or experience. In the fall of 1981, Yale University President A. Bartlett Giamatti warned incoming freshmen to beware of the Moral Majority. In his estimation, rising popular religion equipped with television power was a terrible threat to liberty and to education.[1]

From Giamatti's perspective, the religious right was trying to impose its idea of biblical rules on people for whom those rules meant nothing. He assumed that there was no single morality that could be agreed upon, no laws for everyone on which to base human community. All that was needed was a general law to preserve respect for different persons and groups who may choose to live as they wish. Giamatti defined public good as primarily "the practical protection of the several individual freedoms," and he was closed to any position that would seek to legislate uniform behavior.[2]

Why was Giamatti so offended at the Moral Majority and the evangelicals? When he said, "What disgusts me so much about the 'morality' seeping out of the ground around our feet is that it would deny the legitimacy of differentness,"[3] he did not speak with detachment or moderation. Perhaps he spoke as an alarmed citizen, but his contempt showed.

Part of the answer is that there is a great deal of conflict over what the law should prohibit or allow in areas of personal morality. The university community favors the liberalization of restrictions, and conservative religious groups want to uphold traditional laws. Giamatti's opinions are actually part of this conflict.

When he denounced the Moral Majority for being intolerant, what Giamatti really meant, of course, is that they were wrong on the issues. The charge of intolerance is one way to attack religious people. From the university perspective, however, popular religion is trying to outlaw everything that it calls sinful, and that, of course, is unjust. This argument was used against the abolitionists who opposed slavery in the early nineteenth century and later against the prohibition movement. However, its validity stands or falls on the merits of a specific issue alone: whether or not something should be illegal.

The fact is that many religious people consider adultery and homosexuality unlawful and sinful socially destructive acts. This is perhaps the single most dangerous aspect of Moral Majority activity from the standpoint of the university.

Playboy magazine, in its interview of candidate Jimmy Carter in 1976, pursued him on this point. Carter assured the interviewer that he would not batter down any bedroom doors to investigate, but he did view sexual morality laws as useful; they at least placed a social taboo on what had always been considered wrong and socially damaging practices. But the tolerant today want to strip the law of such "unenforceable" restraints.

Pat Robertson would uphold traditional laws on adultery and sodomy. A Supreme Court decision in *Bowers v. Hardwick* (1986), upholding a sodomy statute in Georgia, is the kind of ruling that Robertson wants to see more often from the Court. In this decision, the Court upheld the rule against sodomy, refusing to strike it down as an invasion of privacy. Community morals are a legal matter and nothing in the Constitution, these justices said, forbade this kind of legislation.[4]

Robertson understands homosexuality to be a sin against nature that cannot be tolerated by a nation and quotes from the Bible that the "very earth itself will vomit you out." For him, laws protecting marriage and forbidding such sexual sins are guides to "liberty and happiness."[5]

Biblical religion may sustain civic virtue, but it also brings with it a price that many people do not wish to pay. The whole package of biblical morality makes demands that offend much contemporary thinking. Roman Catholic educator John Henry Newman explained this issue well:

Knowledge, viewed as knowledge, exerts a subtle influence in throwing us back on ourselves, and making us our own center, and our minds the measure of all things. This, then, is the tendency of that liberal education, of which a university is the school, viz., to view revealed religion from an aspect of its own—to fuse and recast it, to tune it, as it were, to a different key, and to reset its harmonies, to circumscribe it by a circle which unwarrantably amputates here, and unduly develops there, and all under the notion, conscious or unconscious, that the human intellect, self-educated and self-supported, is more true and perfect in its ideas and judgments than that of Prophets and Apostles, to whom the sights and sounds of Heaven were immediately conveyed. A sense of propriety, order, consistency, and completeness gives birth to a rebellious stirring against miracle and mystery, against the severe and terrible.[6]

Laws prohibiting adultery and homosexuality are part of the original "severe and terrible" biblical law, and for many religious people they are absolutes that should remain in America's civic laws.

Falwell and Robertson are convinced their views are well within the American constitutional order. They defend laws that others may not accept, but which they consider necessary for the survival of any people.[7]

Traditional cultures from China to the Americas historically have thought that they must find and follow the correct path, the way, if they were to prosper under heaven. They shared a common ground of virtue for all people, including universal taboos against incest, adultery, and murder. The awesome diversity in the myriads of cultures and peoples did not contradict this common "law of the earth." Today increasingly only diversity is respected because it is thought that no agreement is possible on the laws necessary for different communities.[8]

The Separation of Church and State

Speaking at the Eisenhower Symposium at Johns Hopkins University in the fall of 1986, Robertson defended separation of church and state, quoting from the original Virginia disestablishment legislation:

> Be it . . . enacted by the General Assembly that no man shall be compelled to frequent or support any religious worship, place, or ministry whatsoever, nor shall be enforced, restrained, molested, or burdened in his body or goods, nor shall otherwise suffer on account of his religious opinions or belief; but that all men shall be free to profess, and by argument to maintain, their opinion in matters of religion, and that the same shall in no wise diminish, enlarge, or affect their civil capacities.[9]

Baptists in particular supported Jefferson and Madison in this landmark Virginia law, helping to lay the foundation of separation of church and state later put into the Constitution by the First

Amendment: "Congress shall make no law respecting an establishment of religion or prohibiting the free exercise thereof.' The
only mention of religion in the text of the Constitution itself was
that "No religious test shall ever be required as a qualification to
any office or public trust under the United States." These two
provisions together helped to keep peace between government
and religion in America; they create a space for both to flourish.
Congress could never impose a national church, no denomination
could lay claim to special treatment, and a personal belief in
religion was never to be a legal requirement for public office.[10]

The separation of church and state allows a religious candidate
to claim no conflict of interest when running for public office. If
government subsidized and established a church in America, as in
Great Britain or Germany, or as in Virginia up until 1786, then
religion would be an impossible liability for Pat Robertson. Because
of separation, he fights for free exercise of religion without having
to defend government preferential treatment for a state church.

But the separation of church and state was never meant to isolate
religion from political life, according to Robertson. Having defined
some boundaries of authority, the doors of influence were left wide
open, giving to each the right to learn from and to help the other.
America, says Robertson, had the full benefits of wisdom, morality,
and law taught by the Bible. He traces these influences on the
development of this distinctive way of life:

> Supreme Court Justice William O. Douglas said, "We are a religious
> people, whose institutions presuppose the existence of a supreme
> Being." If you will look at our foundational laws, you can track the
> Ten Commandments and how they became the laws of the states,
> and of course, the United States of America. We celebrate weekends.
> Why? Well, the Fourth Commandment says, "Remember the
> Sabbath." And so we have weekend rest in this nation. We're told to
> look after and honor our mothers and fathers. We now have Social
> Security. We have Medicare, and we have other health insurance.
> We have a prohibition against murder; "Thou shalt not murder."
> We have the same law against theft. The Ninth Commandment
> speaks out against perjury; we also have laws against perjury in

court cases. Now, there is Old Testament provision for industrial safety; we have enacted laws concerning the safety in the work place. More than anything, though, is the concept, and it's a biblical concept, of equal justice for all. "Thou shalt not give favorable treatment to the poor, nor shalt thou give favorable treatment to the rich." Justice should apply to all. And that's been foundational in our society. . . . At least with the blindfold on and the scales, the concept is that justice is blind, and that is equal justice, regardless of who the plaintiff is and who the defendant is. That does not happen in a case always, obviously. But it's a goal that we seek to fulfill.[11]

When told that religious beliefs are only a private matter and should not be brought into the public arena, Robertson disagreed and quoted from Virginia's declaration of religious freedom: "All men shall be free to profess, and by argument to maintain, their opinion in matters of religion, and that same shall in no wise diminish, enlarge, or affect their civil capacities."[12]

Americans have turned everything upside down, he says, if the separation of church and state turns into a license to exclude Christians from public life and to discriminate against them. This would violate the practice of equal justice for all, setting up a new state anti-religion, secular humanism. To exclude all religions from seeking to influence public life is far more oppressive than any established church in the colonies. He foresees America coming around full circle to an established religion more insidious and destructive than any his Baptist ancestors fought, because it is hidden within government. Robertson's concern has been to protect the true exercise of religious liberty once gained and now being lost.[13]

The National Legal Foundation

Learning from how the American Civil Liberties Union (ACLU) defended minorities, Robertson recently set up the National Legal Foundation, a tax-exempt, nonprofit organization to fight for religious liberty. Headed by an experienced trial lawyer, Robert

Skolrood, the NLF receives some funding from CBN, but is designed to operate independently of the television ministry or Robertson's involvements in politics. As founder, Robertson often speaks on behalf of the NLF, but is not an officer or director. The NLF's purpose is to protect any person or group whose religious liberty is threatened. Skolrood says the NLF defends Mormons, Jews, and even cult members if they are suffering religious discrimination.

> There are times when I've had to be supportive of the Church of Scientology, although I absolutely disagree with them. But the thing that's very dangerous is that the people that are sharp will pick out a group like Church of Scientology or Moonies and figure, well, Christians and others aren't going to come to their help. So a principle is established, and then the next move is to move in and hit the Christians with it, and we can't allow that to happen. As long as the principle is right, I've got to join with them.[14]

Beyond legal protection of individuals and groups, the NLF wants to see the principles of religious liberty clearly stated and defended by courts and by legislatures. There is little point in winning one local case if most state courts continue to deny religious people their rights. The NLF seeks cases that will serve as precedent-setting cases for the whole nation. Clear rulings on principles that protect everyone will have an influence far beyond winning a particular case. Courts can still defend the Constitution. Three NLF cases illustrate this strategy developed earlier by the American Civil Liberties Union and the National Association for the Advancement of Colored People in their struggles to protect the civil liberties of individuals and minorities.

In Omaha, Nebraska, the NLF assisted a Bible club that met in a public school at the same time as other voluntary clubs. In 1984, an Equal Access Law was passed by Congress that protected religious groups from discrimination. No school that receives federal financial aid may treat religious beliefs differently from other forms of legitimate speech. In short, the law says that if any voluntary club, like a chess club, can meet on campus, a Bible club can too. Working with a local attorney in Omaha, the NLF defended a club in a case before the Federal District Court. Skolrood commented:

> In Omaha we maintained that there was a violation of Constitutional rights, specifically the First Amendment, of the students who desire to have a Bible club meet on the school premises during noninstructional time the same as other clubs. The First Amendment was violated in regard to their free speech, freedom of assembly or association, and the free exercise clause of the First Amendment. In addition, we cited the Nebraska Constitution as having been violated. In 1984, the Equal Access was passed, which provided that any secondary school which receives federal financial assistance could not discriminate on the basis of the philosophy, politics, or religion of the club.[15]

The second example was settled out of court. "Jesus Loves New York," a group of small ethnic churches near Central Park, held rallies in the park. The New York Park District refused this group equal treatment, denying them the right to hold their rally when and where other groups met. The NLF filed a suit against the Park District, the City of New York, Mayor Koch, and the New York Police Department for the violation of free speech, assembly rights, and the free exercise of religion. Under the pressure of a lawsuit this small group of churches finally received permission for their September 17, 1987, rally.[16]

A third case, the Alabama humanism textbook case, attracted national attention in early 1986 when the Federal District Court ruled in favor of the plaintiff and the NLF position. This case dealt with textbook bias against biblical religion, and government-supported secular humanism. Skolrood said, "We maintained there was a censorship of the history, social studies, and home economic textbooks so as to effectively remove all references to the contribution of the Judeo-Christian faith to America, its culture, its history, and development." For example, one book printed part of the Mayflower Compact, deleting all references to God and religion.[17]

Beyond this use of silence to avoid any mention of religion's role in America, there was present in these Alabama textbooks evidence of a secular belief system. According to Skolrood, this violated the First Amendment clause against establishment of religion and the Supreme Court's recent rulings that public schools were to be neutral in all matters of religion. If you can't teach theistic religion in the schools, Skolrood argued you had to be fair and not teach an anti-religion either.[18]

At one time, atheist parents objected when their children went to public school and were taught about God; now believers object when their children go to school and are taught that God does not exist or that religion does not matter. For instance, Skolrood reports that the Protestant Reformation may get a few sentences in a book while some obscure tribe gets nineteen pages. This is not simply an accidental omission, says Skolrood, because there is enough evidence to point to a deliberate attempt to distort or to revise the place of religion in history. Furthermore, the treatment of parental roles, religious authority, and differences between the sexes in these textbooks are all contrary to traditional religion and are essentially part of a belief system hostile to religion.

The Eleventh Federal Circuit Court of Appeals reversed the earlier favorable District Court decision in August 1987, declaring that neutrality on religion did not require that textbooks "speak about religion." The books never actually denied that religion could be one source of truth. There was, in the court's judgment, not enough evidence that "omission of certain facts regarding religion from the textbooks of itself constituted an advancement of secular humanism or an active hostility towards a theistic religion." Skolrood saw the decision as a constitutional disaster, removing the protections of the First Amendment and endorsing secularism.[19]

Robertson wants to see the appropriate mention of God put back into textbooks, not as a national religion forced on people, but in full recognition of religion's ongoing place in American life. As long as most Americans believe in God, references to religion in textbooks or voluntary prayer and Bible reading in public schools should not be removed, in his view. He points out other examples of public prayer:

> The Senate has a chaplain, a paid chaplain, and the Senate opens with prayer. The House of Representatives has a paid chaplain; they open with prayer. The Supreme Court opens with prayer. "God bless this honorable court." When the president takes the oath of office, he puts his hand on a Bible and swears before God, "So help me God." Now, why are little school children second-class citizens? Why can't they have the same privileges and rights as a senator, a congressman, or a justice have? If it's constitutionally permissible for the House of Representatives to pray, it's certainly constitutionally permissible for a little child to pray as well.[20]

Asked if the state should write the prayers for schoolchildren, Robertson disagreed, responding that the Supreme Court would not even allow a moment of silence for people to pray as they wished. He called this nonsense and said that increasingly this kind of ruling was an "intellectual scandal." The government in his view was not to interfere with normal and voluntary public expressions of faith or to establish a secular religion.[21]

At a Jewish Federation meeting, Robertson was asked to distinguish his position from that of someone like the Ayatollah Khomeini—was he planning a Christian fundamentalist takeover of American politics? Comparing this to Islamic fundamentalism in Iran, they asked Robertson to defend his outspoken views.

Robertson's response was, in short, "I'm for freedom. As much as is possible." He did not believe his position on religious freedom had anything in common with that of the Ayatollah who favored total church domination of government, religious fanaticism, holy war against Israel, and terrorism. He also rejected the concept of a "Christian America," calling Americans instead a people who believe that God the Creator is the source of their inalienable rights, who believe in religious freedom, and are "largely Christian." If any reference to God is removed, making it impossible to speak of Him in public life, and if basic morality is no longer taught in the schools, then ne predicts that the whole structure of liberty that historically has made room for Baptists, atheists, and Jews, will fall.[22]

The Supreme Court

In the spring of 1986, five years after Giamatti's notable warning against religious fundamentalism, Robertson accepted an invitation from the deans of law and theology at Yale University, to return to his alma mater and speak at a joint meeting of the two schools. A few weeks later he gave essentially the same address to the University of Virginia School of Law.[23]

Robertson began his discussion of the law with an admission of weakness: "I've got to confess that while I was a law student, during that whole three years at Yale, I never read the Constitution once." Although he had read many Supreme Court cases dealing with parts of the Constitution, no one required that the document itself be read and studied as a whole, nor had he bothered to do so. He implied that sophisticated education has lost sight of the Constitution itself, and its founding purposes.[24]

Up until 1932, he said, there was an historic framework for government provided by the Constitution, including the separation of powers between the legislative, the executive, and the judiciary with the legislature the stronger of the three branches. The Bill of Rights limited the national legislature by prohibiting certain actions by Congress and by leaving most powers in the hands of the states and the people.

Beginning with the Great Depression and the presidency of Franklin Roosevelt, Congress dismantled this framework by giving the president too many emergency powers, according to Robertson, and later, in the fifties, the Supreme Court under Chief Justice Earl Warren further upset the balance. Eventually, the Court usurped powers never intended for it by the Constitution, he thinks, and even the powerful presidency constructed by Roosevelt and his successors was vulnerable to judicial attack. By the time of President Jimmy Carter, after Watergate, Robertson considered the American political system all but unmanageable. His concern was to explain what happened, especially in the Supreme Court, and to suggest how America could return to a balanced constitutional system.[25]

The Court is beyond accountability and "out of control," he said, noting that judges are no longer simply interpreting the law and applying it to specific cases and controversies, but are turning into administrators, running prisons and school systems, getting involved in the details of government and the daily lives of people. They have more power than they can handle without becoming corrupt.

Robertson mentioned a famous case, *Marbury v. Madison* (1803), where the Supreme Court Chief Justice John Marshall declared that Congress, in a law that it had passed, had empowered the Court to decide a matter beyond their jurisdiction as stated in the Constitution. As chief justice, Marshall refused to exercise a power that he considered unconstitutional. This case was the first Supreme Court case to establish the "right of judicial review," which meant that if the Court determined that the law violated the Constitution, the Court would not enforce it. Thomas Jefferson later objected saying that if the Supreme Court had the last word on what was or was not constitutional, this would be "a very dangerous doctrine indeed, and one that would place us under the despotism of an oligarchy."[26]

Robertson mentioned Abraham Lincoln's view that neither the people, the Congress, nor the president should assume that the Court was correct. Lincoln objected to the infamous Dred Scott decision (1857) which would have prohibited Congress from outlawing slavery in the federal territories. He said the Court had no authority to establish by itself the correct view of the Constitution on this matter, for the American people or for the rest of the American government. Lincoln believed the Court could only rule in cases under its jurisdiction and demand that those who were parties to those cases submit to its interpretation of the law.[27]

While Robertson doubted that the Supreme Court had the authority to declare a law of Congress unconstitutional, he was sure that it had no authority whatsoever to compel the president, the Congress, or the people to agree with its decision; that would destroy the democratic process. He left open the door for the president or the Congress to ignore the Court if they were not involved directly in the specific case decided. In this view, only parties in a case must submit to the Court because the Constitution limited the Court's authority to judicial rulings in specific cases.[28] Robertson once facetiously suggested,

Let us amend the Constitution to say as follows: "The Supreme Court shall be the paramount branch of government, and a simple majority of the judges ruling in any case between two litigants shall hereafter be considered the supreme law of the land and shall take precedence over all other laws and bind all the citizens." Now I don't think that amendment would get through our government, but that is what, in essence, we have accepted.[29]

The supreme law of the land, according to Article VI of the Constitution, includes three things: the Constitution itself, laws passed by Congress in accord with that Constitution, and treaties made and ratified by the United States government. Court decisions are not the law, but rather a judicial opinion about the law, and the difference between law and a Court decision needs to be maintained if the Supreme Court is to be kept in check, according to Robertson. He objected to the *New York Times* using the term "Constitutional right to abortion." No such law had ever been written, he said, and what the Court had done in *Roe v. Wade* (1973) when it refused to allow the enforcement of state laws prohibiting abortions, was unjust, contrary to the law, and a totally irresponsible misreading of the Constitution.[30]

The fault lay not with the people or the Constitution, but with the Supreme Court, Robertson claimed. Its too broad or too restrictive interpretations of the Fourteenth Amendment are the problem. This amendment protected all citizens from any state government that would deprive a person of life, liberty, or property without due process of law or the equal protection of the law. Designed initially to protect former slaves from discrimination,

Robertson thinks this law has come to mean almost anything the Court wants. It has become an open license to uphold or refuse to uphold state laws, without any respect for the original meaning of the amendment or the intentions of state legislatures attempting to regulate public life within their boundaries. For example, the Fourteenth Amendment as interpreted by the Court does not protect unborn babies, but it does stop people from praying in public school. Jefferson's worst fears of despotism have proven true, and Robertson asserts that Americans now live at the mercy of an oligarchy of five Supreme Court justices.[31]

In addition to opposing the Court's abortion rulings, Robertson saw an ongoing miscarriage of justice in restrictions placed by it on the free exercise of religion. He was especially offended because he saw this as a violation of the classical separation of church and state put in place by his ancestors in Virginia.

> The First Amendment dealt with the establishment of a national religion by Congress. And the people in Virginia, and my ancestors were among them, fought the Church of England, which was an established church. Some of my ancestors went to jail because they would not pay taxes to support Anglican clergymen who only could give civil weddings and civil privileges to those in the Anglican community. But an establishment of religion . . . didn't have anything to do with letting a little child pray in school. It didn't have anything to do with putting up a manger scene in Pawtucket, Rhode Island. It didn't have anything to do with a little Vietnamese girl saying the Rosary beads on a bus in El Paso, Texas. It didn't have anything to do with a black teacher in Charlotte, North Carolina, reading a Bible during her lunch break in the school cafeteria as she was prohibited from doing by her principal in the school there. It never meant any of those things. Because, when you look at the history of this nation, you find that James Madison, who drew up the First Amendment, had as his first official act entering into the new Congress of the new Constitution to select a chaplain to lead the Senate and the House in prayer.[32]

By restricting the voluntary exercise of religion, a secular rather than a pluralistic society is established. Robertson argues that the people never voted to remove all reference to God from public places. Instead, when Congress or the people acted, they gave religion recognition—"In God we trust" on our coins; "One nation under God" in the pledge of allegiance; starting Congress and sessions of the Supreme Court with prayer for God's help. Yet in public schools, even the Ten Commandments cannot be posted on the walls, according to the Supreme Court.[33]

Robertson called this a "constitutional crisis." The authority of Congress and the state governments was cut off so completely that it undermined democratic government. The will of the majority was now at the mercy of groups that could influence the courts. In *America's Dates With Destiny*, he wrote that through the efforts of the ACLU and others, the rights of the majority in America have been lost.

> In 1986 the ACLU chapter in Los Angeles was able by court action to prevent all prayers or public mention of God in the high school baccalaureate services in that great city. It has become apparent that the ACLU has determined to strip all signs of faith from the culture of this nation by attacking or threatening to attack in the courts such American traditions as Christmas manger scenes, Easter sunrise services, public invocations and benedictions, and even the spiritual songs and stories of our children.[34]

These issues were never meant to be decided on by the Supreme Court or the federal government in the first place—matters of religion were to be left to the states and the people by constitutional design, says Robertson. Now any public expression of religion is said to be a threat to some individual's right not to hear others express faith in God. The right not to be religious or the legitimate freedom of conscience has taken precedence over the constitutional right of free exercise of religion.

Boldly expressing his dissent from current judicial practice before his audiences at Yale and Virginia, Robertson issued a challenge to the American public to rethink the basics of the constitutional order. But would he as president refuse to obey the

Supreme Court on an issue like abortion? On this Robertson hedged. He was reluctant to submit to the Court, questioning its authority to tell a president or Congress what to do, but he was not fully prepared to disobey either.[35]

This issue erupted into full public controversy after an encounter between Robertson and the editorial board of the *Washington Post*. In June of 1986, David Broder of the *Post* reported that Robertson refused to be bound by any Supreme Court decision that was contrary to the Constitution (if he were not actually a party to the case). The *Post* in a later editorial said that Robertson's belief that "a Supreme Court ruling is not the law of the United States" was destructive of political order. The *Post* argued:

> There is room here for a politician to say, as Mr. Robertson and so many others do about the abortion case of *Roe v. Wade*, that a Supreme Court decision is wrong, and should be overturned by new justices or a constitutional amendment; there is room for a private citizen to engage in civil disobedience in order to get the law changed. But public officials and politicians who may seek the highest office do have a duty to obey Supreme Court rulings, even those they disagree with.[36]

In a political system already riddled with conflict over issues of authority, it is not surprising that Robertson's position was attacked. What was not so visible in public was that Robertson's own position had changed just prior to his meeting with the *Post* editors. He was confident that the Court could not force anyone to agree with it; Congress was not required to pass or to change any law to support a decision of the Court; he also said the president did not have to obey the Court if he were not party to a case. But did the Court have judicial review authority? Robertson had questioned the authority of the Court to refuse to endorse a law they considered unconstitutional.

To question judicial review as such was to undermine a long accepted principle of American government. This issue was not finally resolved in his own thinking until late June 1986 just before his meeting with the *Washington Post*. Up until that time he saw the issue in political terms: The Court undermined the other branches of government and was a tool of minorities. But judicial review also raises a different kind of issue, namely, the rule of law above politics.

Each branch of government was bound by oath to consider what the Constitution meant and to uphold it in its daily tasks. For the Court this required measuring all actions of government against the Constitution in the cases before it. Otherwise, the Court, as John Marshall argued, would be forced to rule on cases without considering the Constitution. The rule of law was what established judicial review, not some political ambition of the Court to usurp power from the other branches of government.

Robertson communicated with the faculty from the School of Public Policy at CBN University prior to his meeting with the *Post*. The history of judicial review that actually preceded the famous *Marbury v. Madison* (1803) decision helped to persuade him that Chief Justice John Marshall had not in fact invented this power, as he had assumed. In his mind, this established the Supreme Court's authority to refuse to uphold laws. However, the Supreme Court still had a serious problem with its own identity and responsibilities, he thought, and this could not be glossed over.[37]

In his interview with the *Post*, and in the published defense of his position written by Dr. Herbert Titus, Harvard-trained Constitutional Law professor and now dean of the College of Law and Government at CBN University, Robertson cited Lincoln's position, accepting judicial review with limits.

We oppose the Dred Scott decision in a certain way, upon which I ought perhaps to address you a few words. We do not propose that when Dred Scott has been decided to be a slave by the court, we, as a mob, will decide him to be free. We do not propose that, when any other one, or one thousand, shall be decided by that court to be slaves, we will in any violent way disturb the rights of property thus settled; but we nevertheless do oppose that decision as a political rule which shall be binding on the voter, to vote for nobody who thinks it wrong, which shall be binding on the members of Congress or the President to favor no measure that does not actually concur with the principles of that decision. We do not propose to be bound by it as a political rule in that way, because we think it lays the foundation not merely of enlarging and spreading out what we consider an evil, but it lays the foundation for spreading that evil into the states themselves. We propose so resisting it as to have it reversed if we can, and a new judicial rule established upon this subject.[38]

The president, the Congress, and the people should work within their legitimate spheres of authority to limit and to reverse the damage done by incorrect Supreme Court rulings, according to Robertson; what applied to slavery in the territories in 1857 applied to contemporary issues like abortion. He believed that Supreme Court decisions that are rejected for good reasons need never be considered authoritative or final in the larger political sense.[39]

Like Lincoln, Robertson rejects rule by the judiciary. Not until a Court's interpretation has been widely accepted for a long period of time, been confirmed by other Court decisions, and is supported by history and further reflection by the rest of government and the general public can it be considered authoritative, and even then it is not the same as law. Court decisions in America, Robertson believes, are never law itself, but only evidence of law or interpretations of the Constitution, laws, or treaties already passed and ratified.[40]

The dispute with the *Post* was not resolved. The newspaper editors said a prior commitment to obey Court decisions was required if he were to run for president. Robertson would promise obedience in advance only if he were a party to the case. Otherwise, he had the basic duty as did all citizens and officials of government to obey the Constitution as he understood it.

Commentators responded in differing ways to Robertson's dispute with the *Washington Post*. Joseph Sobran, a conservative editor of the *National Review*, called his arguments brilliant and unconventional. However, Sobran argued that most people no longer can think clearly enough about law to follow the arguments in such a dispute. But he agreed with Robertson's position that the president must follow the Constitution and not the Court's interpretations of it. Otherwise, the Court would be given clear supremacy over the other branches of government. "The point is that there is no last word," said Sobran. The Congress, the people, or a later court can prevail eventually over any Court's opinion.[41]

Other commentators were not friendly to Robertson's position. We need a referee in our system, argued one, and without it, "anarchy would prevail." Even though the Court may have been wrong in *Roe v. Wade*, its decision is the law and the president has to execute it. After all, this writer asserted, disputes over Court rulings are matters of opinion. Someday the Court may reverse on the issue of abortion, for example, and Robertson would then ask everyone to comply with the Court's ruling. "He would say that the Supreme Court must be obeyed. And he would be right."[42]

Robertson's position would be that one should obey the written law, and whether or not the Court ruled rightly was beside the point. Herbert Titus's newspaper article defending Robertson stated that the Supreme Court could not decide all vital questions "affecting the whole people."

> In a newspaper report on June 27, Pat Robertson, a potential candidate for the Presidency, rejected *Roe v. Wade* as the law of the land. He, like Lincoln before him, contended he was not bound by the Court's ruling because he had not been a party to the case. He explained his opposition, as did Lincoln, that a Supreme Court ruling is not law and that neither Congress nor the President has a duty to obey judicial rulings contrary to the Constitution.[43]

One newspaper in a major city claimed that Robertson's position clearly disqualified him for the presidency. The paper assumed from the *Post* story that Robertson rejected judicial review. However, the real issue was missed by that commentator. Robertson accepted judicial review, but wanted more respect for the authority of the presidency, the states, the Congress, and the people, that preserved their independent authority and their right to resist a wrong Court decision by appropriate and lawful means—by constitutional amendment, by passing new laws, by Supreme Court appointments, and by additional Court cases. If the Court can only command the obedience of the particular parties in a case, as Robertson argued, then one cannot obey or disobey the Court until one is a part of a case under the judicial authority of the Court.[44]

The difference between a law and a Court ruling is difficult to distinguish. According to Robertson, "Thirty percent of the people in America think the Supreme Court writes laws like a legislature." He blamed the press for some of the confusion but he also blamed the complexity of the topic. Courts interpret the law in particular cases and their views are evidence for what the law means, but he believed they are not the law itself.[45]

Robertson argued that if the Constitution is out of date or in some respects unjust and needing to be changed, it should be changed by the amendment process provided in the document, not by Court decision. He believes that judicial interpretation that expands meanings beyond the accepted definitions of words, or the author's clear intent, will eventually undermine trust in the Constitution. If words can mean anything, then they mean nothing.[46]

In his address to the Yale Law School, Robertson denounced what he called a "distorted" approach to the judicial role where in particular cases decisions were made with little regard for the letter or spirit of the law. Quoting from past presidents and others, he attacked recent Supreme Court rulings, especially on religious rights and the rights of the unborn. He warned that these decisions have ". . . started a political backlash in this country that is going to have serious consequences." Robertson himself is determined to warn the American people, and especially Christians, to deal with runaway courts.[47]

Robertson reminds the nation that the founders placed only limited trust and authority in each branch of government, "and they didn't trust sinners—forgiven sinners or just plain ordinary sinners." He finds the Court usurping power and without a clear sense of the constitutional limits to its own authority.[48]

Law in America cannot be restricted to constitutional law. Most statutes and the rules of criminal and civil law go back to the common law established over the centuries in England and in America. Preserving this priceless heritage of common law at the state level that was deeply influenced by biblical faith is part of Robertson's personal and political agenda. Restrictions on pornography, limits on divorce and sexual behavior, and provisions for capital punishment are parts of the law that are now debated and revised without much thought for how this will affect community life. Judges and legislators care more for individual rights than for families and the public good.[49]

Robertson's answer to this problem is to appoint the right justices to the Supreme Court. Justices have enormous influence for good or for ill. He wants to stop subjective interpretations of the Constitution that amount to a rewriting of its meaning. Laws in the states must be protected from this kind of attack. Reagan's appointment of Chief Justice Rhenquist and Justice Scalia, and his nomination of Judge Robert Bork were in line with Robertson's views.

> The thing that I'm concerned about is respect for the historic interpretation of the Constitution, what is known as "the intention of the framers" as opposed to a sociological interpretation which means that it is a constantly changing document that can be amended at will by five Supreme Court Justices. And I would like the Rhenquists, and the Scalias, and the people like that who hold to a more traditional restrained view of judicial power. . . . I wouldn't ask a candidate, "Are you for abortion, are you for this. . . ." That's not the issue. If a person cares about the tradition of the Constitution, I think that's what we're more concerned about.[50]

Much of the ferment leading to radical legal reforms begins in law schools. Robertson wants to see legal education changed in America. As his contribution to this effort, he established a law school at CBN primarily for Christians, in an effort to help restore the Bible's influence on legal education.[51]

Speaking at Yale from his historic Protestant assumptions, Robertson refused to allow religion to be quarantined as Giamatti had in effect argued. Religion was meant to influence the rest of life. From this biblical perspective, tyranny and anarchy were two distinct threats and were to be guarded against with equal vigilance. Law was to be the great protector, restraining government from tyranny and citizens from anarchy. Political liberty and religious freedom were the result.

· 8 ·

Foreign Policy: What Robertson Would Do Differently

- ♦ *Would Robertson pull out of the United Nations?*
- ♦ *How would he deal with communism?*
- ♦ *How would he work for world peace?*

When he comments on foreign affairs, Robertson often points to the British example in the nineteenth century. He says that while the Royal Navy kept the peace, the British pound backed by gold sustained the world's economy, and in addition, Victorian morality, London's alliances, and a unified parliamentary system together contributed to British success.[1]

In other words, Robertson says that to build an effective foreign policy, a nation must be strong. But the prerequisites for a strong American foreign policy are not in place at present, and national reputation and influence internationally have been declining. America has difficulty sending forces to the Persian Gulf. Because America is saddled with huge debts and disagreements between the Congress and the president, its commitments are not trusted by allies.[2]

Turning from these specifics that limit America's ability to act in the world, Robertson points out two obligations to guide foreign policy. First, there is the duty of the government to protect the "life, liberty, and pursuit of happiness" of American citizens from threats inside or outside the nation. This he calls a moral duty and a constitutional requirement.

Second, he believes America must strive to help liberty advance for "men and women who desire to be free." He is especially concerned that the United States in its weakness not turn its back on other nations or their peoples. This creates a dilemma for him, because he knows that American resources are not yet sufficient to face this challenge.[3]

Foreign relations is not a topic of popular discussion in America. In his *Foreign Affairs* article, "Realism and Vision in American Foreign Policy," political historian James H. Billington wrote, "The American citizens may come to see foreign policy as a soap opera which some invisible hand occasionally turns on to distract it from its real problems."[4] To the extent that foreign relations have been reduced to entertainment for the public, Billington compares America with ancient Rome—ripe for distintegration and even conquest.

America's "historical commitment to both enlightenment and religion" made us great, Billington argues. Enlightenment provided thoughtful detachment, the clear thinking that is needed to master circumstances and maintain self-control. Reason alone, however, was not enough to motivate citizens. This motivation came from biblical religion, he claims.[5]

Before there was a Constitution, there was a "covenant" binding American people into a community. Billington reminds us that this covenant, rooted for most in Christian beliefs, gave Americans a sense of duty toward their neighbors and a concern for justice and for freedom at home and abroad. Religious convictions helped to unite a people so large and diverse that without them there would have been no radical experiment in self-government. He argues, "Religious values are in fact by far the controlling ones in the United States; it is hard to envisage effective leadership in a democratically accountable society that does not build on, rather than snipe at, these values."[6]

To turn against God, "the ultimate source of justice and judgment" in the American tradition, will leave this nation with no standard to guide its politics. Universities may alienate secular leadership from America's religious population, but the answer, writes Billington, is not for the population to become secular; instead leadership must once again affirm that God is the source of public values. More leaders need to affirm their responsibility to God, he says.

> Unless that answer can be given more firmly by more people in the educated American opinion-making elite, there will continue to be a polarization that will make it impossible to define any common values. America will remain divided between those who are spiritually committed but not intellectually trained and those who are highly educated but deficient in moral and spiritual conviction.[7]

This nation has a democratic heritage, the greatest system of higher education in history, and religious traditions that are universal in their message and appeal. Billington says, however, that America lacks a clear sense of who it is as a largely religious people and where it is in the world as a nation among nations. After saying that the United States must strongly resist Soviet ambitions, Billington turns to the third world and reports that most nations have chosen to work toward democracy and to look for non-Communist answers to their problems. Liberty is far more attractive than impoverished equality, and capitalism is more promising than stagnant socialism imposed by communism. Education is rising in importance in the world, bursting with new life, and religion is far from dead, with spiritual concerns increasing dramatically. What is needed, Billington says, is a combination of reform, education, and revival. A politics of liberty, an education of enlightenment, and a revival of the sacred—these are the three most powerful positive forces he sees operating in the world. In this dynamic context, any new American leadership will be tested.[8]

A Community of Nations

Robertson's effort to give direction to American foreign policy is a contemporary example of what Billington calls "religion with enlightenment." Both believe America needs to secure its spiritual identity and its economy if it is to make its mark in the next century.

Standing before the Council on Foreign Relations in New York in the spring of 1987, Robertson presented his vision for the world in a speech entitled "Toward a Community of Democratic Nations." Calling the United Nations an example of failed idealism, Robertson issued a summons for the creation of a "Community of Democratic Nations." He named the United Nations the grandchild of people who had moved away from their spiritual roots, who were unprepared for global wars, totalitarian oppression, and genocide. Nothing in history prepared the largely Christian peoples of Europe, Russia, and the United States for the traumas of death camps and World Wars I and II, he said. False optimism from the nineteenth century and not just nationalism was the cause of many modern problems, and it died hard.[9]

Both Woodrow Wilson and Franklin Roosevelt spent their last energies trying to create a League of Nations and a United Nations to reach lasting peace, but they both ignored the hard tasks of making peace, he said. Wilson cared too little for the Versailles Peace Treaty that ended World War I, and Roosevelt abandoned eastern Europe to Joseph Stalin. Both errors contributed to war, he believes. Out of the Versailles Treaty's harsh treatment of Germany rose Hitler to take revenge on the democratic powers, and Roosevelt's supposed generosity simply encouraged Stalin's aggression and the cold war. Blinded by idealism, in Robertson's view, America's leaders failed to negotiate with the care needed to protect the West.[10]

Idealistic fervor replaced a genuine confidence in God and a realistic dedication to liberty. Since then, when wars or genocide have occurred, instead of restraining evil, the United Nations turned the very language of liberty and peace into propaganda weapons, justifying any horror.

> The most grotesque example of the emerging morality of the United Nations took place on October 1, 1975, when Ugandan dictator Idi Amin, then Chairman of the Organization for African Unity, addressed the General Assembly. . . . According to one historian, when he spoke, he denounced the Zionist-U.S. conspiracy and called not merely for the expulsion of Israel from the United Nations but for its "extinction." The Assembly gave him a standing ovation when he arrived, applauded him throughout, and again rose to its feet when he left. The following day the U.N. Secretary-General and the president of the General Assembly gave a public dinner in Amin's honor. Amin had murdered at least 200,000 of his fellow citizens including Anglican Archbishop Luwum.[11]

For Robertson, justice has no home in the United Nations because its foundations are an illusion, a utopian vision with no hold either on reality or "the bedrock of honored principles." Talk of brotherhood without a true understanding of liberty took the French into the bloodbath of the French revolution, and the same false dreams produced holocausts in the twentieth century. Attacking the United Nations' "New International Economic Order" and the "Charter on the Economic Rights and Duties of States," he claimed:

> The new thrust is for a world devoid of ideological differences; with a built-in poor versus rich bias; with a new information order severely restricting press freedom; and a new international legal order mandating by fiat world peace as an inalienable right of humanity—in other words, peace at any price—a proposal that could ultimately result in a loss of all other human rights under a one world dictatorship.[12]

Overlooking human rights violations everywhere between 1980 and 1984 except in El Salvador, Guatemala, and Chile, the United Nations finally dealt with Afghanistan in 1986. This was the first time in recent years that it cared to address human rights violations by a Communist nation. Robertson reported that the nonaligned, supposedly neutral nations have voted with the Soviet Union 85 percent of the time in the General Assembly of the United Nations, and yet the United States continues to pay about 25 percent of the United Nations' assessed budget. In his view, however, America is merely reaping what it has sowed. An organization that welcomed the Soviet Union from the start could never remotely be considered a defender of human rights. It has become what it could only be, a defender of human rights violations.[13]

One alternative rejected by Robertson is a retreat into a fortress America; giving up utopian thinking leaves the door open for more false dreams, Communist or otherwise, to replace it. Instead, we need a set of limited ideals, he said, and a community of nations dedicated to them, to compete successfully with the delusory hopes of the United Nations and the false promises of communism. Neither the United Nations nor communism can be removed quickly. But they can be labeled for what they are, and America and the world can go on to better things. He hopes that his proposals will stir leaders to act.

In his presentation to the Council on Foreign Relations, Robertson proposed a new organization that would "run parallel to the United Nations and ultimately supplant it." There would be no division between first, second, and third world, or East and West; the same concrete and practical principles would apply to all. He names these principles:

A community of sovereign nations based on democratic institutions, representative government, respect for the rule of law, respect for individual freedom, private property, the basic rights of freedom of speech, freedom of assembly, freedom of religion, and freedom of press. Those nations which neither use terrorism against other nations nor torture and terror against their own citizens. I call for a new "Community of Democratic Nations" which would be open to all nations whose governments have achieved legitimacy because they embrace democratic processes. When a nation was able to move from totalitarianism or dictatorship to true democracy for a specified period of time, it would become eligible for membership in the Community of Democratic Nations.[14]

This group could serve as a defense system for its members, he said, perhaps replacing the North Atlantic Treaty Organization (NATO), for example. As for rich and poor, the community would have great resources available without the "obstructionism" of the Soviet Union to hinder their use. Robertson proposed that the United States immediately set aside perhaps 25 percent of the money that it sends to the United Nations, about $250 million, and use this to help start the "Community of Democratic Nations."[15]

He suggested that the United Nations could continue to function as a forum for discussion by opposing nations. Its agencies could render technical assistance having to do with postal service, weights and measures, and technology. But the strength of international assistance efforts would increasingly be channeled through the new "Community of Democratic Nations." Robertson says,

> The problem with the United Nations . . . it was based on muddle-headed idealism. Dean Acheson said it was presented with the evangelical fervor of a revival meeting. Franklin Roosevelt had stars in his eyes when it was done. There was never any attempt to be hard-nosed and realistic. The most realistic type of international diplomacy that we've had was that advocated by Count Metternich after the Napoleonic War, when he set up the European balance of power. He based it on strength as opposed to some utopian view that all nations would live together in peace, even though some are Communist and some are capitalist. It was just a totally mistaken view of mankind and of the world we live in, that we advocated when we entered the United Nations.[16]

Combining ideals like liberty with realistic goals and methods was the genius of the American constitutional founding, and Robertson believes that is what it will take to get beyond the current ideological struggles. Nations that agree on liberty need to lead the way to help those less fortunate. He is convinced, he told the Council on Foreign Relations, that the time is ripe for this initiative to set the stage for a more just and peaceful twenty-first century.

Expanding Democracy

To encourage respect for human rights in other nations, Robertson suggests that America link what it has to offer in aid and trade to improvements in other governments. Moral persuasion, economic assistance, and diplomatic pressure are legitimate tools of influence. There are, of course, limits to American responsibility, and conflicts that arise because of American security interests and human rights violations by allies. In general, he favors a consistent use of American influence abroad instead of choosing targets like South Africa and imposing especially tough sanctions.[17]

> I believe in the concept of constructive engagement where our corporations, our businesses were beginning to open the doors. And that could be pushed along much faster. For the good of the blacks in South Africa, for the good of the strategic mineral interest in the United States, it seems to me that we would be far better to engage and pressure those people, rather than to put them in a bunker mentality where for five or ten years there'll be nothing but bloodshed and war and ultimately . . . a Communist takeover, which then would link Mozambique, South Africa, Angola, and Zimbabwe into one major Marxist stronghold over the mineral wealth of Africa. That's the game we're playing.[18]

Robertson does not see South Africa as simply a racist problem. Its location and wealth give it strategic significance; he thinks its black people deserve protection during this tough period—"It doesn't matter whether a black person is put out of work in Chicago or Pittsburgh or whether he is put out of work in Soweto, he still suffers." Robertson is totally opposed to apartheid, calling it a ruthless system, but he does not want to see American policy lead to the deaths of millions of people or to a Soviet takeover that would be a worse fate for all involved.[19]

In this instance, Robertson's two principles of American foreign policy—national security and concern for the liberty of others—are in direct tension. When two such important issues come together as they do in South Africa, Robertson supports a middle course that refuses to surrender either goal. Prudence dictates some compromise in such a situation and he would avoid extreme solutions, preferring less pressure to a complete embargo on trade with South Africa.

Terrorism needs to be resisted more directly, Robertson says. He supported negotiating with Iran for the release of hostages in Lebanon, even though Iran sponsors terrorism, but he would not give Iran "a cap pistol, much less missiles," to get them to release terrorist victims. He praised President Reagan's objectives but thinks his methods compromised his antiterrorist position. Concerned that retaliatory raids against Libya will not suffice, Robertson suggests further political and military preparations.

> My solution for terrorism is, number one, the establishment of a Community of Democratic Nations which would be parallel to the United Nations and would bring into that organization those nations which did not practice terrorism against other people, and who did not practice torture and terror against their own citizens, that have afforded them the basic rights. I think that organization should move in concert against terrorism. It is very difficult for the United States to go it alone, and I'm shocked that England, France, and Germany and Italy will not move against terror. The next thing I'd like to see is a beefing up of the Delta Strike Force. Terrorism is an act of war, and I believe we have to treat it as such, with certain preemptive military action that would interdict terrorists before they strike, and that would also bring punitive action against them when they take hostages.[20]

Robertson is impressed by how the United Nations is a haven for terrorism. When asked if he thought Colonel Khadafi ought to be killed for his sponsorship of terrorism, he responded,

"You don't strike the king unless you kill him." That is a political term that has been around for years. What it means is, unless you render a leader impotent, it's best to leave him alone . . . it's best not to attack a president unless you think you can beat him in the next election. . . . We should render Khadafi impotent. We didn't want to leave him in charge of oil revenues, and of the army and all the facilities he had before just to make him mad at us. It looks, though, like the president aimed at his house in the bombing raid, and I think he had on his mind actually killing him. It looked like that was the attempt of that raid. And that frightened Khadafi enough so he's been pretty much out of the picture of terrorism since then.[21]

Asked if he could justify this as an act that a Christian could do, he said, "Absolutely." Acting in an official capacity, the president of the United States wields a sword given to him by God for just that purpose, he declared, to bring judgment on killers of innocent people, including foreign government leaders like Khadafi. In this view, international terrorism is both criminal and an unjust form of war, and ought to be resisted.[22]

Robertson realizes that helping the poorer nations to build healthy economies will not be easy. For many nations, "bribery, graft, and corruption are a way of life." Nations are poor for a variety of reasons including the faults of governments. "I do not think that we can continue to pour money into a system that is full of leaks." For example, in Africa, governments mismanaged agriculture and destroyed what strength there was in their economies—"and the people suffer." Regretfully, he says, "In the world of sin and evil, and inhumanity of man to man, we are always going to have some kind of poverty."[23]

He argues that in South and Central America, religion shares some of the blame for poverty, because it supported the ruling dictators, representing a few rich families that controlled the government, helping to create the problem. Healthy religion brings material and spiritual prosperity to people, and recently Christians in some of these countries have recovered respect for prosperity.[24]

Robertson especially wants to free other nations from debt to international banks. He would encourage foreign governments to reassess their priorities and to turn away from prestige projects like high-rise buildings and city highways that increase their debt burdens. The key to wealth for most of these nations, he says, starts with food and agricultural production. When the needs of farmers are met, the rest of their economies will begin to grow.[25]

As these poorer nations begin to establish democratic capitalism, Robertson is confident that they will prosper. As they do so, he wants American, European, and Japanese aid and trade available to them. This effort by democratic nations to assist growing, healthy, soon-to-be-democratic nations unburdened by debt, is one of Robertson's first concerns.

Resisting Communism

Pat Robertson believes that communism will disappear from this earth one day. He believes that day is closer than we think. Communism is no longer attractive to thinking people. Nations are rejecting it and people under its control are now more ready to get rid of it. These are encouraging signs for those who love liberty and want to resist tyranny.

However, America should not be fooled, Robertson says, by the new leadership of the Soviet Union. The government of Mikhail Gorbachev was put in place by Yuri Andropov, the head of the Soviet KGB (the secret police), and the heart of this system remains the same despite its pretense.[26] Robertson warns,

> If anybody in America thinks that the KGB is for an open society, they may also believe in the Great Pumpkin. I don't think that what we're seeing over there is anything but a tactical ploy on his part. It sounds good; but the KGB is for the ultimate elimination of freedom, and it certainly has worked to that end . . . They appear, however, very sophisticated. They wear the best clothes and they smoke Western cigarettes, and they probably like jazz music, but they also torture people and put people into mental institutions because they

desire to be free. They also tried to kill the Pope. They're not nice people at all. And they are the backers of Gorbachev.[27]

Robertson's fierce love of liberty is deeply offended by tyranny of any kind. History is not on the side of the Marxists, as they claim, and though they have been in power for seventy years, their days are numbered. He believes God's judgment is coming against it.

When people read the Bible, when they know the truth of God's Word, they will not be slaves. It just won't be that way. They'll revolt ultimately against tyranny. This is what is going to happen sooner or later in that Soviet Bloc. . . . Communism is a monstrous evil, Satanically inspired, which brings out the absolute brutality and cruelty in people in a way that is indescribable and inconceivable in a society that is permeated with Christianity.[28]

He vividly expressed his opposition to communism on television in this prayer:

Father, this is not Your will. Your Kingdom has not come in the Soviet Union and in those East-bloc countries, where people are being persecuted and tormented and suppressed in their freedom. And in Africa, because of Communist revolution and warfare, millions of people are suffering. . . . Lord, this evil has been allowed to go unchecked in our world, and we pray, Lord, by Your power, in Your anointing, break the hold of communism on this world. Bring it down, Lord, from the Kremlin to every satellite nation in the East-bloc—wherever they are, Lord. Bring down those evil people, we pray in the name of Jesus. . . . Lord, whether it's dictators of the right or dictators of the left, may there arise, Lord, those who care for people and who love them as leaders . . . May the people of God come into prominence that they might lead and show mercy and compassion on their own people.[29]

For over forty years this nation lived by the Truman doctrine of containment which Robertson thinks served it well for a time. This doctrine stated that America would resist the armed takeover of any nation by Soviet-backed internal or external forces. It also presumed that where communism already ruled, Washington would not intervene. Robertson compares this approach to putting a tiger in a cage. "We contain until the Soviets take a country by subversion, and then we back up and contain there; then they subvert another and we back up and contain there." Meanwhile, he says, the tiger grows, by taking in new nations one by one and must either be killed or starved to death before it jumps out and eats up the rest of the world.[30]

Containment by itself is now a dangerous doctrine in his view, and since communism is itself vulnerable in a new way, Robertson calls for American policy to stand in principle for "the ultimate elimination of communism from every nation on the face of the earth, including the Soviet Union." This calls for a complex and somewhat flexible new strategy. He asks,

> Should we support the Freedom Fighters in Nicaragua, Angola, and Afghanistan? Absolutely. We should build up our support for these people. I think we should roll back the Soviet empire at its fringes. And once it begins to unravel in Afghanistan, Angola, Mozambique, Nicaragua and these other places, ultimately the whole thing will begin to unravel because the word will get back to Moscow, "We're losing. We're losing." We want them to have the mentality that they are losing. And we want to have the mentality that we are winning. And the best way to do it is to win a few.[31]

The Soviets have a global objective and they are out to seize strategic minerals and bases in Africa, oil in the Middle East, and eventually take over the world. Instead of losing out to such aggression, Robertson believes that with an active policy America can see the shrinking of Soviet rule. It might take fifty years, but it can be done, and it is time to begin, he says.[32]

Robertson outlines five strategies for a rollback policy:

1. Do not provide bank loans, credits, or modern technology and equipment to Soviet governments. He says, "It is common sense that tells us that we cannot, on the one hand, spend $300 billion to arm ourselves against the Soviets, while at the same time permitting our bankers to grant long-range, low-cost loans to shore up their tyranny and their economic machine . . . We should insist that our nation stand for freedom, in every aspect, and that our international business stand for it too."[33]

2. Put pressure directly on the Soviet Union to stop the human rights abuses of Jews, Christians, Muslims, and dissidents by further economic sanctions. Connect non-strategic trade like agriculture to improved Soviet behavior. "They have thousands of people in concentration camps and the other people have been denied basic human civil rights, and I think we should not give them trade and credit and benefits unless they lift the oppression of the people and the oppression of the satellite countries."[34]

3. Link trade with China and other Communist nations that are independent of the Soviet Union to further improvements in their treatment of foreign visitors and internal religious and political dissenters. To restrain any aggressive move against Taiwan, for example, "Strong linkages of our Chinese trade with our fundamental goals will ensure that we do not become an 'American card' for China."[35]

4. Use every opportunity to persuade Communist nations that American ideals are right for all people. This nation needs to fight the war of ideas, for liberty and justice, with a will to win, because, "Deep inside there is a yearning for freedom. I think that is true for every human being everywhere, and the United States, in my opinion, should stand for freedom."[36]

5. Give more support to armies that are fighting the Soviet governments in Ethiopia, Mozambique, and Angola, so that winning these conflicts is possible. Help nations to

establish democratic governments even in exile. He argues, "There are two things that have got to be done. Number one, those three Communist countries have got to go—their governments have got to be taken out so the people can be free and we can establish normal market conditions. And the second thing: We have to reforest the land to get it back like it used to be a hundred years ago."[37]

Democratic resistance, internal Soviet conflicts, and spiritual renewal will all help in dealing with Moscow, according to Robertson. Soviet decline, encouraged by American resistance, will speed up, he predicts, as internal conflicts break loose within the Soviet Union. He believes that the Bible itself predicts that the worst Soviet military defeat will occur not at the hands of NATO or American forces but as the Soviet system self-destructs in domestic struggle.[38]

He is encouraged by reports of spiritual revival within Russia. Thousands of Russians are now meeting secretly in homes and in parks to celebrate their faith in God, he says. It appears that the atheist propaganda of two generations failed to remove the spiritual need for the eternal within the Russian people. He tells Americans, "We should love the people of the Soviet Union, but pray against a despotic dictatorship that has tortured and maimed and hurt the lives of millions of their own citizens."[39]

The so-called cold war will continue to require great patience, as it has already. He says that Soviet strategists are like chess players. They display great tactical flexibility and tenacity. Robertson expects Moscow to keep its agreements when it is to its advantage to do so, but says the West should expect more deceit and harassment. Negotiations with the Soviets ought never to presume good intentions until Russia rids itself of its Marxist system, he says. Washington can expect them to use every trick of diplomacy and espionage to get the upper hand in their relations with America.[40]

Global nuclear confrontation seems a remote possibility to him. Instead he expects more aggressive action where the West is weak, such as the Persian Gulf.[41] The best way to prove Soviet willingness to compromise, says Robertson, is to press for substantial conces- sions. If they are serious in arms negotiations, get them to demobilize fifty divisions in their huge conventional army. If they claim to respect human rights, ask them to release 30,000 Jews a year and to stop using mental institutions to house political prisoners.[42]

Deterrence and Arms Control

Reporters and observers have asked Robertson, "Given your professed views that a cataclysmic day or second coming is an imminent reality, can we trust your finger on the nuclear button?" He responded by saying he believes the Bible does not predict a nuclear incineration of the globe, but he did think nuclear weapons may be used locally, as in the Persian Gulf.[43] He claimed "no religious significance to the most awful weapon that has ever been devised by mankind." On the "700 Club" after the national TV special "The Day After" described a nuclear attack on the United States, he announced:

I have a definite message of hope. God is not going to let that happen. The Bible indicates things are going to keep on going until Jesus Christ comes back again. God is not going to turn this world over to a couple of madmen to push buttons and blow us up . . . Armageddon isn't a nuclear war. Armageddon is Jesus Christ destroying the forces of Anti-Christ and taking the world in His own hands.[44]

If Robertson believes the Bible does not predict world destruction by nuclear war and thinks the nations eventually will handle this terrible problem successfully, would he fail to take the nuclear issue seriously enough? He is caught on the horns of an apparent dilemma: If not trigger-happy, would he be slow to negotiate arms reductions? Would he think hardheaded negotiations with the

Soviet Union unnecessary? From his comments it would appear that he would negotiate cautiously and with low expectations. Mere arms reductions will not, he thinks, create the necessary conditions for peace.

> Obviously, we should work to reduce the threat of nuclear warfare. But in my own belief the Soviets are liars. They are evil men, who do not have the same benevolence that we do in this part of the world. They're not motivated by the milk of human kindness . . . the thing that's kept us from nuclear warfare since World War II, when they were used twice, is the fact that we have comparable forces, where the Soviets don't dare do anything without fear of United States retaliation. It's a balance of terror, granted, but at least it's kept it balanced. We've got to be strong. And we cannot unilaterally disarm and freeze our capability without making them do the same things. It's a dangerous game, but we're in it. And we have to ask God to bless us in it.[45]

Robertson does not have reservations about nuclear deterrence as the best way to stop the powerful Soviets from starting a war with the United States. Nor would the awful possibility of nuclear war stop him from threatening to use nuclear weapons should the Soviets move. He answers the "nuclear button" question:

> The chief executive of the United States has a responsibility to let his enemies know that every weapon in the arsenal is available for use, and that he won't shrink from that terrible decision. And I would not shrink from it either. I would hate it, but it would be one of those things that any chief executive would have to do in order to defend the long-range interests of this country. Otherwise, if we just sent a signal of weakness that these weapons were meaningless, at that point the Soviets would move at will throughout the world with their conventional forces. The answer is yes, I would do it, but I would be very reluctant, as any thinking person should be . . . I would be terribly reluctant to begin something like that. But we have to be willing to retaliate and to use what's available to us.[46]

There is every evidence that Robertson's religious views influence and support his approach to defense, encouraging him not to give up in despair or to move too quickly on these complex questions. He does not fear immediate nuclear war and sees the short-term value of deterrence.

Robertson prefers President Reagan's Strategic Defense Initiative, better known as "Star Wars," to having no defense against a strategic nuclear attack. He thinks a missile defense system that would simply destroy incoming missiles would contribute to deterrence, provide a backup if deterrence ever failed, and put pressure on Moscow to negotiate arms reduction. He would develop and deploy it as quickly as possible. To him it is a defensive, not an offensive weapon and makes sense given the great number of Soviet missiles targeted on the United States. Robertson would not recommend giving up SDI for arms reductions of any size.[47]

However, he has no illusions that SDI will protect America completely. Even if the system worked perfectly, it would not stop low-flying bombers, cruise missiles, attack from the sea, or bombs planted secretly on land. Nuclear terrorism or conventional war could still happen at any time. A "Star Wars" defense would be a limited measure to reduce destruction from strategic missiles.[48]

Western Europe is confronted with a huge buildup of Soviet forces. Considering the weakness of European defense, Robertson wants to expect more help from Europeans. Their recovery from World War II is complete and their resources for defense ample. He says, "In my opinion, they should be asked to share a much larger burden in defense than they are now." The reduction of missile strength on both sides in Europe will place greater need to build up conventional forces, and this will increase defense costs, he says.[49]

Arms reductions of intermediate-range missiles in Europe should include a careful look at conventional force levels and verification of all missile removals, but Robertson does not expect arms reductions to solve the underlying political fact that Western

Europe faces a powerful enemy across its borders. He warns against any move by the United States motivated by a utopian desire to make a lasting peace; such a mark in history, he says, is beyond American capabilities.[50]

Central America and the Persian Gulf

As part of his overall strategy for stopping Soviet aggression and beginning to roll back its influence, he wants to strike back where he feels the opportunity for victory would be realistic and the consequences of defeat for America and the West would be devastating. Two areas of the world concern Robertson greatly. First, working from Cuba, the Soviets are establishing their first base in North America in Nicaragua. American aid to the Contras is totally inadequate in his view, and if not linked to a systematic policy, it will confuse the American public and be a mere annoyance to the Communist Sandinista government. Robertson wants to win the war for Central America and throw the Marxist-Leninists out of power.[51]

Most immediately, if the Communists succeed in Nicaragua, they will proceed to dominate the region from Soviet bases. Costa Rica, El Salvador, Honduras, Guatemala, and then Mexico itself will face direct Communist subversion. Before this happens, he wants the United States to apply even more pressure on Nicaragua.[52]

Robertson recommends that the Nicaraguans set up a government-in-exile outside of Nicaragua. They should have a written constitution, a leadership structure, and be committed to elections once there is peace and the people of Nicaragua are able to vote. This government should be recognized by Washington, and diplomatic relations severed with the present government in Managua. He is confident that as many as 85 percent of the Nicaraguans would support this kind of real alternative to oppression or endless civil war. Contra aid by itself neither helps to win the war nor solves the political problem of Nicaragua, he says. Robertson would favor giving substantial money and equipment to guarantee the democratic government enough strength to win their civil war.[53]

Second, Robertson is concerned for the Persian Gulf because of its strategic importance for oil and the close proximity of the Soviet Union to this area. In 1977, Robertson predicted that Israel's Arab neighbors, Syria, Egypt, Lebanon, and Jordan would eventually make peace with Israel, while nations farther away like Iran would become belligerently opposed to the Jewish state. Arguing from prophetic biblical passages, he said, "Again, we must understand that from a biblical standpoint, there will be peace between Israel and her Arab neighbors." When Egypt and Israel subsequently made peace, he was not surprised.[54]

Well before the downfall of the Shah of Iran, Robertson predicted trouble for the Shah's government. For more than a decade, he pointed to the Persian Gulf and Iran in particular as a future source of difficulty. He foresaw conflict and strange reversals in the Arab world. In 1978, he said, "It is not inconceivable that one day United States armaments sold to Saudi Arabia and Egypt will be used to defend Israel, while sophisticated weapons sold to Iran will be used both against Israel and the United States."[55]

Following the seizure of American hostages in Iran late in 1979, Robertson looked ahead to the security of oil interests in the Gulf. He warned, "It will only be a question of time before we are facing Russian forces or Russian surrogates in a life and death struggle for Middle East oil." The trigger for this struggle may be the death of the Ayatollah Khomeini, he feels. Robertson says that Communists have infiltrated key positions in Iran and are securing their control of Afghanistan.[56]

The oil coming out of that waterway is critical to Europe. If Europe loses Middle East oil, their economic machinery will go down, maybe as quickly as ninety to one hundred and twenty days. There isn't enough in the North Sea to supply their needs, and we certainly don't have enough to supply their needs. So, this is strategic to them and ultimately strategic to us. We must maintain a presence in the Middle East in that Persian Gulf region. We have no other choice, it has to be done. Our economic and security interests are inextricably linked, at this point in time, to petroleum. There's just no way out of it.[57]

The ultimate destiny of Iran is clearly the focus of Robertson's Middle Eastern politics today. Appalled by the lack of discussion or public concern on these fateful issues, he asks, "Would we, indeed, send a force into the Middle East to keep Middle East oil from going under Soviet domination?" The problem is not Islamic fundamentalism itself, he says, but the instability that it creates and the circumstances that can lead to war.[58]

As Iranian attacks on oil tankers intensified in the summer of 1987, Robertson supported keeping the shipping lanes open and favored putting American flags on Kuwaiti ships. Fearing a Soviet initiative in the Persian Gulf, he advised that America must without hesitation send powerful forces into the Gulf.[59]

> We must guarantee peaceful shipping in that region The thing that is the concomitant of that is that our vessels should be armed and ready, and the message needs to be sent to all those in that region that we put on our flag in the early days of this republic—"Don't tread on me." And if they come near us, we should be prepared to shoot and down any planes or missiles that show a hostile intent. And I think with that, we'll send the message to the Iranians, and we'll send a proper message to the Soviets.[60]

Iran's influence extends to Israeli relations with Arab neighbors. Shiite extremists trained and aided by Iran do all that they can to undercut Arab ties with Israel. Robertson wants the United States to continue to support Israel and friendlier Arab nations like Jordan so that Iranian efforts to isolate Israel will fail.[61]

Relations With Israel

Robertson relates that on Christmas Day 1974, he was in Jerusalem, considering the isolation of Israel during the Arab oil embargo, "And I made a solemn commitment to the Lord that night that whatever happened, and however unpopular it might be, I would stand as a friend of Israel and a friend of Jewish people around the world."[62]

Asked if his public support for Israel is "based on your vision of a return of the Messiah or on its importance to the United States," Robertson responds that if American support for Israel was based simply on national self-interest, it would not last. He sees a conflict between the need for Arab oil and support for Israel. "Israel is an outpost of the Western civilization and culture and the democratic tradition and ideas in the Middle East." But for him it is more than a friendly democratic nation or a military ally. Israel is uniquely tied to the Western world by history and by religion.[63]

Robertson's biblical views lead him to focus on the importance of Israel in current events. He sees the Soviet Union dangerously hostile to Israel. Eventually he thinks that Moscow will actually attack Israel as part of a move to dominate the Middle East. He is confident the Soviets will lose when they attempt to do so. When Israel recently invaded Lebanon, he saw this as another step toward that day of confrontation.[64]

People fault Robertson for using the Bible to interpret current events. Asked if it would be his foreign policy guide, he responded that he was well-informed on Middle Eastern affairs, and like some Jewish leaders in Israel, he would not hesitate to consult the Scripture for guidance.[65]

On specific issues, he favors moving the United States embassy from Tel Aviv to Jerusalem. He thinks that once other nations fully recognize the authority of Israel over all of Jerusalem, it will help to remove this inflammable issue from discussion. Robertson took this position as early as 1980 and repeated it in 1987 on a trip to Israel.[66]

The West Bank issue involving Palestinian Arabs and their future is more complex. He does not favor American pressure on Israel concerning it. Control of this narrow neck of land is vital for Israel's security. He faults the Israeli government for not fully incorporating this territory when it was initially seized in 1967. By administering it as occupied territory, he says, problems multiplied. Meanwhile, counseling patience, he is confident that Israel can work out this problem with its neighbors.[67]

Robertson's concern for foreign affairs reflects his effort to construct a thoughtful and realistic international perspective, avoiding extremes, utopian and isolationist. His communication network has extensive overseas operations in the Middle East and elsewhere, and he has commented on foreign affairs in these broadcasts. He has traveled to forty-two nations and spoken with international leaders often over the years. He is confident of his understanding of foreign policy issues, addressing them in a manner that most Americans can understand.

Daniel Boorstin, the retiring Librarian of Congress, recommended a list of books to presidential candidates. One of these books, George Kennan's *American Diplomacy*, helped to lay the foundations of American thought on how best to resist Soviet aggression. Kennan first published his ideas in *Foreign Affairs* in 1947, forty years before Billington's recent article. In "The Sources of Soviet Conduct," Kennan advised a "patient but firm and vigilant containment of Russian expansive tendencies." He called for "the adroit and vigilant application of counter-force at a series of constantly shifting geographical and political points, corresponding to the shifts and maneuvers of Soviet policy." These now-famous lines described containment at the start of the cold war between the Soviet Union and the United States following World War II.[68]

Kennan warned against excessive moralism in American foreign policy, that inflamed conflicts and could lead America on crazy and impossible crusades. He said that Woodrow Wilson's war to "make the world safe for democracy" was an example of this thought operating in American foreign policy. After World War II, Kennan thought a modest and rational policy was what was needed, facing the Soviet menace with its grandiose ambitions.[69]

I see the most serious fault of our past policy formulation to lie in something that I might call the legalistic-moralistic approach to international problems. This approach runs like a red skein through our foreign policy of the last 50 years.[70]

Kennan and Robertson share a contempt for utopian idealism. Both believe utopianism took root in American foreign policy after World War I. Prudence is the rule of foreign policy for Kennan. Faith in liberty, in the future, and in God are Robertson's platform. Kennan thinks compromises are necessary for policy to work; Robertson focuses on modest and realistic ways to advance his principles. The reasoned and the religious approaches of Kennan and Robertson, although certainly different, are not totally at odds.[71]

Robertson thinks that failed dreams like the United Nations make way for a Soviet-run world. Neither the progressive idealism that produced the United Nations nor passive retreat before the threat of communism provide answers. Furthermore, he says, the United States is at a point in its national history when it ought to be asking different questions. For forty years it sought to quarantine or restrict communism, to "put the tiger in a cage." Now it needs to ask how to help get rid of the tiger altogether, he says, to build a better world.

Soviet ambitions bring subversion to Central America and threaten oil seizure in the Middle East, but neither problem is quickly solvable. As Washington wrestles with these priorities under the restraints imposed by circumstances, the nation needs to deal with its own evident weakness and confusion.

Soviet imperialism is only part of the problem, according to Robertson. Lack of confidence in the principle of liberty hinders the nation when it is most needed to give direction and strength to its policy. He questions whether the United States can defend its own freedom without a commitment to liberty for the whole world. Efforts to export democracy frequently fail. But America can help others to discover the true meaning of liberty and the respect no government can rightly deny to its own people. Liberty is a gift from God, he believes, and ultimately it is meant for the whole human race and not just for Americans and a few other fortunate peoples. As Washington struggles to protect national interests, Robertson warns that there is no responsible withdrawal from a liberating role in world politics.

·9·

Robertson's Principles
for Success

♦ **Are there biblical principles that will work
in Washington?**
♦ **How can America discover a way out of its
difficulties?**
♦ **Could Robertson's ideas bring unity to the
nation?**

Robertson's religious and political ideas are based on the Bible.
He believes biblical principles always work in every area of life
because they are the laws of creation underlying all of reality.

Surprisingly, a number of political scientists and researchers are
beginning to look to the Bible to see if it can offer any guidance in
the current political confusion. One of these is Professor Aaron
Wildavsky, past president of the American Political Science
Association (1985–1986). He writes of his own intellectual journey
that took him to a small orthodox synagogue in Berkeley,
California:

> . . . I listened to that week's portion of the Pentateuch (the five
> books of Moses), which concerned the Golden Calf. When Moses
> comes down the mountain and sees the Hebrew people cavorting
> before the calf, he slams down the tablets containing the law, calls
> for supporters, asks every man to kill his guilty brother, has the calf

ground up and mixed with water, and makes the people eat it. Wow! There it was, just what I had been looking for—or, perchance, what had been looking for me—fanaticism with a moral purpose.[1]

Profoundly disappointed in American leadership, Wildavsky was looking for what he called a "good fanatic" or a fanaticism that he could justify. Over the next years, he found healthy and unhealthy leadership defined by principles described in the Bible. He then wrote *The Nursing Father: Moses as a Political Leader.*

James Reichley of the Brookings Institution, a major research center in Washington, argues strongly that theistic religion is necessary for America to survive politically. He is convinced that a democracy only works if citizens care about their neighbors, and they will only do this if they love and obey God first. He argues this position in his book *Religion in American Public Life.* Wildavsky and Reichley demonstrate that today scholars are considering religion indispensable to the understanding of politics.[2]

At the same time that some scholars and journalists are learning from religion, many religious people are becoming more alert to politics. Government itself clearly contributed to this change. As Professor Kenneth Wald observed, "The actions of secular authority not only offended traditional moral values—which was reason enough to act—but also seemed to threaten the ability of evangelicals to protect themselves and their families from corrupting influences."[3] Endangered by government actions, Christian groups mobilized, while some said that what passed as religious politics was simply interest group politics by another name.

The religious in America increasingly care about politics, but do they do so in a thoughtful fashion? One study of Christian magazines found that articles dealing with political issues had almost no biblical or theological teaching on the subjects addressed. Do religious people cover their conservative *or* liberal politics with biblical language? Is religion a real influence on politics? Some say that this is a takeover of religion by political activists of left and right. They wonder if Robertson is anything more than a conservative in religious clothes.[4]

In the seventies, Robertson began to be concerned about the severing of virtue from strength that he saw in the religious community and in America. If the net effect of religion was to make people weak and unproductive, then it truly was a form of slavery as Marxists and others have argued, and not the Good News of the Kingdom promised by Jesus Christ. However, his concern extended to politics that seemed to lack direction and moral foundations. His own questioning of fundamental assumptions led him to ask, "How do you run a just government? How do you run a world?" He searched in the words of Jesus and discovered that He had dealt with these basic questions.

> That's why Jesus talked so much about the Kingdom. He let His apostles teach about the church. He, the King, talked about His own Kingdom and the way it works. He wants us to master those principles so we will be able to serve with Him properly.[5]

Robertson's confidence in the message of salvation by faith in Jesus Christ remained unshaken, but what he needed were teachings that would help him to deal with political life on God's terms. He asked, "What does the Lord of the Universe desire for the nations of this world?" He went back to the beginning in the Bible, to creation as it is taught in Genesis.

> I was praying and fasting some years ago, seeking to understand God's purpose more fully. I heard His voice, level and conversational, "What do I desire for man?" A bit surprised, I replied, "I don't know Lord. You know." "Look at Genesis, and you'll see," He said.[6]

Robertson then looked throughout the Bible for principles on which to base his thinking on how to live in the world—he developed his own practical "worldview" as a Christian.

Pat Robertson

The Secret Kingdom

While Robertson's openness to prayer and miracles lends credibility to his claim to be genuinely religious, the convincing proof of his claim to have a distinctive candidacy will be in his thinking and his policy proposals. The core of his thought is contained in his book *The Secret Kingdom*.

Robertson's political thinking begins with his discovery of the New Testament teaching on the Kingdom of God. This Kingdom is an invisible realm of the Spirit that has great influence on the world of men partly because its principles structure all of creation. Entering this Kingdom personally as a subject requires spiritual conversion, but he believes that the relational truths of the Kingdom work if followed by anyone, individuals or nations.[7]

Some are confused by Robertson's views, assuming that he is simply talking to Christians, telling them what to do in politics. Robertson speaks of one interchange with such a person:

> A reporter from NBC was asking me all those questions. And she said, "Well, you know, this book you wrote, it won't apply to me because I'm not a Christian." And I said, "Do you think the law of gravity only applies to Christians and Jews? You know, it applies to everybody."[8]

One would expect at least religious people to understand the rules of creation, but Robertson sees the church without much influence, ignorant of how these teachings apply to politics and economics. Without true beliefs about basic questions of life, Robertson sees today's leaders taking the nation into worse problems, while the church knows the Bible but is largely silent and divided, confused and ineffective.

> Unhappily, Evangelical Christians have for too long reduced the born-again experience to the issue of being "saved." Salvation is an important issue, obviously, and must never be deemphasized. But

rebirth must be seen as a beginning, not an arrival. It provides access to the invisible world, the Kingdom of God, of which we are to learn and experience and then share with others . . . We have fallen short. Occasionally we have perceived God's hand at work in the world. But we have not striven to understand how the Kingdom functions, nor have we fully participated in its manifestation on earth.[9]

One of Robertson's favorite phrases in political speeches is *noblesse oblige*, which means "nobility obligates." As an educated son of a senator and the founder of a television network, he felt a heavy responsibility to God and the world. As a Christian citizen wanting to help America, he worked to apply his understanding of the Kingdom to the real problems he encountered.[10]

Robertson did not identify the Kingdom, this spiritual realm where God's will prevails, with American democratic capitalism. Pure democratic capitalism, if it is based solely on greed, leads eventually, he thinks, to gross materialism, to the collapse of political order, and to the rule of the rich and powerful or to anarchy and dictatorship. He says that the American capitalistic system will fail if left to itself. Only the strong and virtuous activity of the Kingdom within it can keep it alive and healthy.[11]

To Robertson, the Kingdom is a powerful reality—solid, structured, with practical implications, and not an unapproachable ideal. Secular thinking, by contrast, while focusing on problems with great accuracy, provides few creative answers. Knowledge and methods alone, without wisdom based on true principles, ends in despair and confusion. What the world needs, says Robertson, is not more scientific diagnosis so much as confidence in unchanging truth as a basis for answers.[12]

In simple terms, Robertson is saying that religion without a clear grasp of biblical truths fails to bring help to the world. Unless America can once again understand and follow true principles of action, it is doomed to gamesmanship. His candidacy, then, is an effort to recover the principles of the Kingdom for public affairs. The Lord's Prayer that Jesus taught encouraged people toward politics, to bring life and truth from the Kingdom to the earth,

Robertson says. This is a necessary part of Christian faith and is what democratic politics needs to survive.

Confidence in the invisible markedly increases Robertson's discontent with conventional religion and politics. When his prayers are answered, sometimes dramatically, he wonders why more of the power and reality of God is not brought into everyday life. If people begin to accept the goodness of God as a resource available to them through faith, Robertson is convinced that they will not be able to remain aloof from the challenges of their day.[13]

Robertson believes the realm of Spirit is close at hand and "undergirds, surrounds, and interpenetrates the visible world in which we live." Complete access to the "unrestricted, unlimited, infinite" resources of this other world comes by faith in Jesus Christ; however, anyone who lives humbly and does right will receive its help. Robertson feels that God wants to assist nations with their needs and problems. Jesus lived fully in both worlds, the visible and the invisible, he says, exercising authority over even the wind and the waves. Christians as well must learn to live fully in both worlds—the world of the Spirit where there is power and truth unlimited and in the finite and broken world. Involvement in politics is an opportunity for Robertson to bring spiritual life to the secular arena. *Secular* here for him means outside the direct control of the church but under the authority of God.[14]

The Kingdom power is brought in first of all by people learning to be more virtuous. Robertson calls the Sermon on the Mount the constitution of the Kingdom, and living the Golden Rule its practical expression. However, personal virtue is not enough; he believes religious citizens have failed to connect it appropriately with other Kingdom principles. He complains that we have produced good people but we have not generated leaders.[15]

The second essential step is to follow certain laws that develop leadership. "The people of God are to live out the Beatitudes and the virtues of humility, wisdom, faith, hope, and love while at the same time becoming leaders." This is a paradox, because virtue seems to soften a person. How does a leader turn the other cheek and maintain respect for authority? Robertson finds solutions to this dilemma in the laws of God in both the Old and the New Testaments that add strength to virtue. They are universal laws, he believes, governing the way life works, and are open to all people. The results of following them are practical and predictable, but first, they are the right way to live.[16]

The Laws

Robertson's study of the Bible led him to define eight laws that build strength. In *The Secret Kingdom*, he explained how they work and some of their implications for government.

1. The **Law of Reciprocity** says that one's actions have a power to influence others; they can help to change people. This is the Golden Rule amplified: "Give and you shall receive," or whatever you give, good or bad, is what you will receive in return. This means that the quality of life in the end has more to do with one's own actions than with circumstances.[17] Giving results in receiving. In Luke 6:36–38, Jesus taught:

> Be merciful, just as your Father is merciful. Do not judge, and you will not be judged. Do not condemn, and you will not be condemned. Forgive, and you will be forgiven. Give, and it will be given to you. A good measure, pressed down, shaken together and running over, will be poured into your lap. For with the measure you use, it will be measured to you.

This law applies when people are treated badly. If someone responds in kind they are simply multiplying evil, compounding and accelerating a process of destruction. On the other hand, if they return good for evil, they are setting up another process that will do more than stop evil: It will multiply good. Another way of saying this is that one cannot, in the end, separate virtue from its reward. Robertson writes,

I think that is an observable human phenomenon, and I think it is enunciated in the Bible, if we give of ourselves, we find benefits to ourselves [although] they may not be material. I think Mother Teresa has gained great benefits by feeding the poor and the needy of Calcutta, and she has become a world renowned figure by giving of herself to the most downtrodden group in the whole world. It's a moral law, and no more than that.[18]

The application of this law raises some difficult questions for government policy, and Robertson limits this law in one respect. When government restrains lawbreakers, it must enforce the law to maintain order, protecting the public from further harm. A thief must receive a just punishment. There is no turning of the cheek to the lawless or the moral authority of governments would break down.[19]

However, Robertson believes this principle of reciprocity can even apply to nations. For example, by treating Germany harshly after World War I, America and its allies reaped a terrible response from Germany under Hitler in World War II. But by giving Japan a generous and supportive postwar settlement after Tokyo had unjustly attacked America at Pearl Harbor, the United States won the favor and affection of the Japanese.[20]

Robertson recommends that the United States treat other nations very generously, up to a point. When another nation attacks American interests repeatedly and does not respond to a generous policy, he favors very tough measures that will force the enemy into line. He recommends that Washington be more generous to friends and tougher on enemies. He warns against a middle ground of guarded and cautious self-interest. Such restraint neither wins friends nor protects the nation from its enemies, and leaves America weak and isolated.[21]

At first glance, the Law of Reciprocity seems unlikely and impractical. There is something right about receiving the kind of treatment that one gives to others, but one wonders if life really works that way. Robertson is saying that it does, and that self-centered living is costly.

2. *The Law of Use* says that people who work hard and take risks will be productive and deserve to be rewarded, and those who refuse to develop resources will lose all that they own. This principle is stated in the parable of Jesus on the talents. "For everyone who has will be given more, and he will have an abundance. Whoever does not have, even what he has will be taken from him" (Matthew 25:29). Risk taking and effort are not simply commended because they work; they are the only right way to live. This gives a moral as well as a practical thrust to the Law of Use.

The Law of Use opens the door of prosperity and creativity to all who would honor their talents and ability with effort. This appears to favor the strong; however, Robertson says this rule is particularly good news for the weak because it shows them how to gain strength, promising them a sure reward for their initiative. On the other hand, he warns that if they do not invest their wealth productively, they will eventually lose it.[22] Robertson addresses the Law of Use primarily to the weak:

Christians especially show the symptoms of a defeated people. Many are sick, depressed, needy. They live in fear and confusion. Where, observers fairly ask, is the conquering army sung about in the great church hymns? Where is the blessing promised in the Bible from beginning to end? Was Jesus wrong when He said, "I will build my church: and the gates of hell shall not prevail against it"?[23]

The Law of Use and the other laws are all linked in Robertson's view to another principle that greatly increases their significance. This is the "exponential curve": Over time the results of obeying or disobeying these laws compound, or multiply, just like interest on a savings account in a bank. He says that great athletes and singers are excellent largely through the consistent exercise of their gifts that increases their talent. If gifts are not exercised, what little talent one may have will fade away. Undreamed of results are available, says Robertson, if individuals and nations will simply exercise the abilities given to them by God.[24]

3. **The Law of Perseverance** says that experience and the Bible teach the necessity of persistence and warns people away from any quick or easy solutions to problems. Life is full of struggle and delay; even prayer demands persistence, and this is so by design for growth and learning. He opposes the use of the supernatural as a substitute for effort.[25]

4. **The Law of Responsibility** says that success carries with it a duty to seek the good of others. America especially carries a burden to give from its strength to the rest of the world. To fail to help others, Robertson says, will earn this nation judgment in history from the hand of God.[26]

5. **The Law of Greatness** points to a desire within the human spirit to excel. Robertson does not see religion as the great leveler that reduces differences. Individuals and nations are each unique, and are meant to excel without oppressing others. He teaches that an open, humble, childlike learning attitude leads to achievement. Any nation that has high standards and serves others will experience true greatness and deserves special recognition.[27]

6. **The Law of Unity** is no longer commonly understood in America. Robertson believes that extreme pluralism with many groups going their own way will leave the nation in total confusion. He respects unity because it brings strength and underlies all creativity. When two people agree in prayer or fight as one against a common foe, they are much stronger. America needs more unity, a common core of beliefs in liberty and the purposes of government, as well as respect for diversity.[28]

7. **The Law of Miracles** seems to apply exclusively to people of faith. The confidence people have in God ought to be expressed concretely, he says, by acts of faith, praying boldly, and expecting God to act. Words of faith spoken with a forgiving attitude will release the hand of God to act. Robertson says little of how this would apply to government, but the Bible provides numerous examples of faith that led to supernatural miracles in the lives of public servants like Joseph and Daniel.[29]

8. *The Law of Dominion* defines the human task on earth as ruling. This teaching contrasted so vividly with Robertson's immediate experience that he wrote,

> You cannot help but juxtapose this desire of God with today's reality. The thousands of letters that pour into CBN, the pages of the newspapers, the screens of our television sets reveal anything but a people maintaining authority over their environment.[30]

He concluded that most problems he encountered through his "700 Club" ministry were caused by a loss of dominion. Designed to govern on earth, people have become addicted to what Robertson calls, "vegetables, flowers, and fruits." Medical care alone for dependence on alcohol, marijuana, and cocaine, he claimed, costs Americans more than $100 billion a year.[31] He is aware that his teaching would not be popular with substance abusers despite the obvious destructive power of drugs.

> Yet attempts to set men free from this slavery are often met with derision and hostility. It does not matter that death and degradation are the outcome. Men outside the Kingdom clutch their "pleasures" to their bosoms as if they were good, holy, and sacred rights.[32]

Genesis teaches "a sweeping and total mandate of dominion over this planet and everything in it."[33] The issue here is quite simple, according to Robertson: People either recover by breaking loose from drug captivity, or they are tied to a "cycle of despair, cruelty, bondage, and death." There is no middle ground.

Christians and drug users face the same indictment from Robertson: One group is passive and the other rebellious, but both end up victims because they each fail to master their world. Robertson wants people to shake themselves free of doormat religion or addiction. He sees mankind all too often either taking dominion "arrogantly, or not at all," either abusing the earth or being abused by it. He also states there is no excuse for people destroying the earth or themselves with technology. He says, "God gave us dominion over the earth, but it was to be a gentle dominion. We are to be very gentle stewards of this fragile planet."[34]

Robertson is fond of quoting God's words describing the builders of the Tower of Babel—"nothing they plan to do will be impossible for them." He said this in reference to their unity and ambition. However, the Tower of Babel was a unity without honor for God, and so God scattered them by confusing their language. Generally the Bible teaches respect for human limits and the danger of pride, but Robertson is concerned about lack of unity, about failing confidence in the face of apparently insurmountable problems. He believes that nations can harness science to meet these challenges as they submit to God, discovering a true basis for unity.[35]

> Without in any way advocating fanaticism, I believe God would enable man, under His sovereignty, to deal successfully with the conditions that threaten the world with catastrophic earthquakes. Scripture makes plain that God uses natural disasters as judgment upon mankind; but I am convinced that were man to turn from his wicked ways and seek the Lord, he would be able to take dominion over the faults in the earth's structure and render them harmless. For the words of Jesus spoken to the tumultuous waters of Galilee still echo down through history with great power and authority: "Peace, be still."[36]

The laws of *The Secret Kingdom* are a prescription for success in life and a standard by which the church and government are judged. If Robertson was previously concerned about the direction of religion and politics, the Kingdom teachings that he discovered substantially increased his discontent. He found no excuse in them either for a weak church or a government that cannot pay its bills, or for such a divided world.

Robertson's eight principles reflect his central concern: the recovery of strength and leadership for people of virtue. His perspective has nothing to do, he says, with "Christian Reconstructionism" or a world ruled exclusively by Christians. He has been accused of a belief that Christians can bring in a utopian Kingdom. Only Christ can do that, he believes. He states that he believes in Kingdom principles, which always work for everyone, because God is the Master of Creation and the source of all truth.[37]

For some Christians, the Kingdom is only a standard of perfection that no earthly regime can hope to match. For Robertson, it is an invisible and powerful presence close at hand that gives hope that by natural and supernatural means great good can be done, in the church and the world. Furthermore, in his rediscovery of biblical principles, his thinking seeks practical answers for guidance in all of life.[38]

Reciprocity encourages good deeds with rewards.

Use promises great growth through exercise and risk taking.

Perseverance maintains confidence during struggles.

Responsibility connects success to the obligation to help others.

Greatness develops everyone's gifts.

Unity provides support for decisions.

Miracles make receiving help from God possible.

Dominion establishes significant mastery over one's environment.

Convinced of the truth of these principles, Robertson is impressed by how easily intelligent people lose sight of them. They become "clouded," he says, when they refuse to acknowledge the reality of God. These laws are guaranteed to provide deliverance from selfishness, laziness, impulsiveness, unreliability, shame, division, lack of faith, and despair. Robertson has utter confidence in their practicality and utility for individuals and for government.

In his view, the mere study of human affairs without respect for the Bible will never restore a nation to good sense or prepare it for the great tasks and opportunities ahead. A scientific understanding of human problems without the guidance of moral principle produces volumes of information, but few answers, Robertson says. His concern is to help America to find the "reliable remedies" for its pressing needs. In conclusion, Robertson says that nothing short of spiritual revival will bring America to a full recovery of these laws, and the strong and virtuous leadership needed for the future.[39]

· 10 ·
What Kind of Revival for America?

♦ *How is revival at work in other countries?*
♦ *What good would a revival do?*
♦ *Would revival be a threat to liberty?*

Iran and Israel are two modern examples of nations changing under the impact of religion. Pat Robertson is particularly interested in them because his prophetic perspective tells him that both are important to the rest of the world.

Iran serves him as a model for religion gone mad. Few in the West, certainly not Robertson, will defend a religion when it encourages terrorism, declares holy wars, and considers death in battle a guarantee for eternal life. Iran's clergy-dominated politics threaten to unhinge the entire Middle East.

Israel by contrast is a democratic nation with increasing religious influence in its politics. This example of a Jewish religious revival interacting with contemporary politics throws light on Robertson's views. A Council on Foreign Relations study group met in New York and Chicago between 1982 and 1984 to study the future of Israel. Their report, *A Changing Israel*, written by Peter Grose, traced developments in Israel back to a "milestone date" in 1967, when Israel recovered Jerusalem and won the Six-Day War. In that year, "Sephardi" Jews in Israel, who had come to their homeland in the late 1940s from North Africa or from the Middle East, outnumbered for the first time the "Ashkenazi," those Jews who came to Israel from Europe.[1]

The Ashkenazi voted largely for the Labor Party with its pragmatic and Socialist programs. The Sephardi on the other hand were more traditional, had greater respect for authority, were generally more observant in their religion, and voted for Menachem Begin's Likud Party, a conservative coalition. Begin lost eight national elections before he finally won on his ninth attempt in 1977, becoming Prime Minister of Israel. Behind this remarkable story of human persistence lie some interesting facts. Israel, once a largely secular nation, is increasingly religious in its public life. This shift has political implications, and something similar may be taking place in the United States.[2]

Today, these two groups, the Oriental Sephardi and the European Ashkenazi, are merging. Education, army life, and intermarriage combine to establish relationships that encourage national unity. Grose believes that within two generations the large cultural gap between Jews of Oriental and European origin will disappear. Meanwhile, Grose stated, "The most important differences between the Ashkenazi and Sephardi cultures involve attitudes towards the Jewish religion and its role in society, and toward the meaning of the Jewish homeland."[3]

There is a serious battle today in Israel between secular and religious forces. There is also a struggle between political parties for the control of Israel's government. As the Labor and the Likud parties compete for dominance in politics, more radical religious groups are no longer unimportant, because they hold the balance of power between the parties. Far stronger politically than their numbers would indicate, these religious groups within Israel today have great influence, especially in Jerusalem. Furthermore, the appeal of religion has not diminished. Grose wrote,

Zionist intellectuals had assumed that the zeal of the observant would gradually fade away in a modern state society, that their "superstitions" would be smothered by the modernization of a secure Jewish life. The opposite happened; the appeal of religion seems to have grown, not diminished.[4]

Grose said that younger people are drawn to religion, and he reported that among recent American Jewish immigrants coming to Israel, most seem motivated by personal religion rather than by patriotism or by ambition. By 1981, religion had become so important in Israel that Grose called it a pivotal factor. This disturbs him deeply.

Militant religious fundamentalism is a powerful force once it is unloosed, and it does not bode well for any process of conciliation, coexistence and mutual toleration. Secular Israelis are troubled by the appeal of the narrow, traditionally religious Jewish radicals, particularly to the young.[5]

At stake is the issue of who will finally be responsible for "settling the norms of public life" in Israel, secular or religious groups. In one brief decade between 1967 and 1977, the Labor Party lost half of its strength in Israel's parliament, refusing to make room for the Sephardi in its organization or religion on its agenda. Grose wrote of the Labor Party, "The more the leaders talked about the good old days of Socialist idealism and pioneering, the more they repudiated the expression of Judaism in favor of the secular 'modern' voice, the more they cut themselves off from the former underclass which now found itself in the majority in the state of Israel." This turned out to be a nearly fatal political mistake for the Labor Party, he says.[6]

Menachem Begin, himself an Ashkenazi, made the most of this opportunity handed to him by Labor. Speaking in simple, clear-cut terms about Israel and its identity, he cut through complex issues in a way attractive to voters, especially to those outside the Labor power structures. Begin and the Likud were able to make room for Sephardi outsiders with their religion and connected their concerns to a more conservative vision for Israel.

From the perspective of leadership in America, represented most notably by the Council on Foreign Relations, nothing could be more dangerous to American interests or to world peace than an Israel dominated by the religious. These people cannot easily be persuaded to compromise. Furthermore, from this American perspective, religious Jews, especially the more observant, are difficult to understand. For this and for other reasons, Grose predicted that conflicts in the Middle East will intensify. He advised Americans not to rush in with quick solutions to problems better dealt with slowly and intelligently over time.[7]

Religious revival is not unique to Christianity or to America. It can be totally disruptive, as in Iran, or be largely contained within democratic structures as in Israel. In America, Robertson argues, belief in God provides the self-restraint that makes freedom and democracy possible.

Revival means two things to Robertson: It can mean simply the revival of religion, particularly religion that believes in the God of the Bible. This broad understanding encompasses Islam and Judaism.

Revival also has a more specific meaning to him related only to Christianity and its impact on society. He supports both kinds of revival in the world and in America, as long as the fundamental rights of human beings to "life, liberty, and the pursuit of happiness" are respected. In fact, he believes that theistic religion provides the only firm basis for liberty.

Robertson's belief in revival assumes a basic trust in people. If God communicates personally to all human beings and entrusts them with great decisions, then merely human leaders need to learn to trust them too. In the past, in America, revival and democracy supported each other, and in Robertson's view the nation must maintain confidence in both the spiritual and political will of the people. The alternatives, he concludes, are to be ruled by an oligarchy of elites, or even worse, by dictatorship.[8]

What Kind of Revival for America?

Religion's Contribution to Democracy

Americans traditionally learn their first lessons in citizenship in religious communities. Robertson claims religious people are less likely to take drugs, to violate laws, or to pull down the general norm of public order. They are more likely to work hard, to raise children, and to contribute positively to community life. In short, religious communities, says Robertson, help to hold America together. Furthermore, the truths of religion limit government. The absolutes of the Bible restrain and direct public officials and the law on issues like abortion, pornography, and education. Robertson states that we must not lose the contribution that faith in God makes to America if the nation is to secure the future of its children.[9]

One does not have to be a Christian or even to believe in the God of the Bible to agree with Robertson on this point. The French writer Jean Jacques Rousseau argued centuries ago that a belief in an afterlife with future punishments and rewards was needed to stimulate good citizenship. He even proposed a religion without the Bible to serve as a foundation for politics. Christianity was too specific, too narrow, and too limiting to get a nation to accept its claims, he thought, and he looked for a substitute for Christianity. Other people agree with him but find their answer in forms of secular humanism.[10]

Robertson is persuaded otherwise. He believes that faith in God, in the Christian and Jewish sense of a biblical Creator, is still adequate for America and indeed for the world. He thinks America needs the same basic religious foundations it had from the start in 1776 and 1787, and that having more Christians in America will help to make room for all people regardless of their race or creed. The chief danger for America now in his view is that in its wealth and pleasure it is becoming selfish and egotistical with no common purpose, with no love of country.[11]

Nowhere is the danger of individualism more tragically evident, in Robertson's opinion, than in the church. Francis Schaeffer, Christian writer and theologian, addressed this problem with him in a series of "700 Club" programs made in 1982 and aired again in 1986. Schaeffer criticized a false spirituality that limits religion to Sunday forms, personal morals, and the afterlife, and has not taught Christians to respect their civic obligations. All of life is sacred, he said, and withdrawal from politics is foreign to the true spirit of Christianity. This teaching session of Schaeffer's impressed Robertson deeply.[12]

Schaeffer taught the "700 Club" viewers that if government was not based upon principles taught by the Bible and limited by other institutions, then government would go its own way and take for itself what he called "autonomous authority." Sooner or later it would claim the right to do what it pleased without respect for human life or for moral principles. Robertson, who emphatically agreed with Schaeffer on the "700 Club" show, says that understanding religion's rightful place in America and in the world is the first part of the solution. Christians also need to be proud of the positive influence of their religion.

As long as Christians are ashamed of their own community of faith and its teachings, they cannot be "salt" and "light" in the world as they were meant to be. For Robertson, lack of confidence and ignorance have placed Christians at a disadvantage in America.

He also envisions a day when large numbers of American people embrace the Christian faith and go into government service. But it will take revival for all of this to happen, and he waits for it expectantly. Encouraging graduating seniors at Oral Roberts University in 1986, he said,

> And this means that institutions are going to change. They will reflect the faith of the people that are coming to the Lord and they are going to reflect the faith that you will share which means that the parade is already marching down Main Street and all you've got to do is get at the head of it and look like a leader and you are going to be carried along to heights you never dreamed of. It isn't the way it was twenty or twenty-five years ago. There is a new wave, a new

day to be alive, a new day to go out into the world, for the world is going to change in accordance with the plan of God.[13]

Looking at the church in modern America, Robertson is aware that what he is saying sounds preposterous. How can religion preserve democracy? Rather than waver, he warns, "Despise not the day of small things." These words came originally from the lips of the prophet Zechariah encouraging the people to rebuild the walls of the temple in Jerusalem; rebuilding projects can be tougher to finish than the original construction because the past often seems irrecoverable, and Robertson knows that people need encouragement to get involved.[14]

Robertson's Understanding of Revival

Robertson's conviction is that in the midst of political and social problems so great that government cannot begin to solve them, there is help available, sent by God. Before the National Religious Broadcasters in February 1986, he said,

> When the enemy comes in like a flood, the Spirit of the Lord will raise a standard against him. And we are seeing juxtaposed with these problems and with these evils, the greatest spiritual revival in the entire history of the world.[15]

Revival cannot be imposed by anyone, Robertson thinks, not even powerful evangelists. Perhaps in the supercharged atmosphere of a mass meeting a crowd will respond, but not a whole community. Thirty years ago he learned that preaching by itself simply does not produce revival. A woman who prayed with a small group of women for revival in Billy Graham's original Los Angeles meeting in 1949 taught Robertson the meaning of revival. Speaking to him in New York in 1957, she said,

> Revival is a moving of God among his people, and an awareness of God laying hold of an entire community. In a successful evangelistic

campaign, many are brought to a saving knowledge of the truth, and the church will be enlarged, but in revival the fear of God lays hold upon the community, moving men and women who until then had no concern for spiritual things, to seek after God.[16]

Instead of religion being the preoccupation of a few people, a revival opens the way for it to be an accepted experience or vocation for anyone and everyone. Revival then for Robertson comes when religion is accessible to ordinary people.

He writes that the young people of America especially need this experience. Without much purpose or direction, they begin to look elsewhere. Without a faith in God there is a "loss of vitality" which damages family values, the work ethic, and basic respect for themselves and their future.[17]

Revival succeeds where the regular work of religion fails. Robertson sees many if not most Americans alienated from Christianity, not comfortable with its culture or practices. Revival finds these people and gives them a genuine religion with fresh forms of expression, very different from humdrum ritual. Talking one day to a businessman with whom he was negotiating to buy his first television station, Robertson was able to frankly discuss this problem. The businessman said,

I like Christianity, but have been turned off by Christians. I've developed a pretty bad reputation as a businessman. A lot of folks think I'm unscrupulous, but I really do love Jesus Christ in my heart, and you've touched me with what you're telling me about a God of miracles and supernatural power. Most guys like us believe that God is like that. But when I used to go to church, I'd hear some preacher say that miracles aren't for today. You're telling me they are. You're telling me God is still in that miracle working business. And I believe you.[18]

Americans need revival, says Robertson, partly because formal religion has lost touch with both the common people of the world and God. He wants people to understand that when he speaks of it he is concerned with everyday life and not just the afterlife.

> It helps people care about their families, it makes them honest, not to cheat on their income taxes, to be better citizens, to be loyal members of the body politic, kind, gentle to one another. That is the outworking of revival, instead of cheating and lying. We've had thousands who were drunkards, bums, in jail, on drugs, they had all these problems. They say they met Jesus Christ in their life and they are changed. The way society will be changed primarily will never be through government. Government can't do what is needed. Society, man and woman need in their inner beings to change, to want to do better, to serve God and man, and that's what spiritual revival brings on.[19]

Revival then is not just more religion; for Robertson it means God-centered, not church-centered living. Solid relationships beginning with God and extending to the family, neighbors, and the larger community result.

Robertson even expresses this understanding of revival in the architecture of his buildings. In his Portsmouth studio built in 1968, and in his current Virginia Beach facility dedicated in 1979, there are unusual prayer chapels that Robertson designed to be "alive with symbolic meaning." The rooms are circular, and suspended in the middle of each is a cross. There is no pulpit or outward sign of authority giving special place to a preacher or to a priest. Robertson writes that his purpose was to focus attention "heavenward." People sit on simple circular benches and meditate on God who he believes is at the center of life, holding it all together. The only other symbolism present in the new facility are statues of angels ringing the room, giving a sense of invisible help close at hand.[20]

In fact, Robertson rarely attends a local church on Sunday, defending this by saying that his presence as a famous public figure tends to disrupt services. He rests on Sundays and takes a complete break from work and even from campaign activities. He may not follow the Apostle Paul's instruction to meet regularly for church, but it is consistent with Robertson's concern that churches commonly package religion too neatly, excluding people who are not attracted to a four-walled religion.[21]

According to Robertson, revival tears down inappropriate barriers that separate the secular from the sacred, and opens people up to all of life. It goes beyond religious leaders and political control. It influences people in many ways and creates a climate of health for government as well as religion. Revival sustains politics by teaching people self-control and neighborliness. Robertson, in the end, claims that without a powerful revival, America will experience more chaos and anarchy, and then tyranny, as government clamps down to maintain order.

> Either we're going to have a powerful revival, where the Holy Spirit descends from heaven, purges sins, convicts men of sin, brings this nation to its knees in revival—a religious revival such as John Wesley saw in England—or we are going to have the purging of God's judgment, which will involve bloodshed and disaster and chaos and anarchy. . . . It's going to be one or the other. . . . We've lost the central organizing core that made this nation great. We've gone away from it.[22]

Revival is a religious answer to cultural and political decline. It works on a mass scale, with persuasion rather than coercion. Breaking the walls of isolated religion, it also attacks secular individualism and greed. Such religion brings people together for common community purposes preserving their personal right to a free conscience, according to Robertson.[23]

Revival and Religious Liberty

On the evening of September 17, 1986, a black choir sang, "Let everything that has breath praise the Lord" (Psalms 150:6), launching Pat Robertson's coast to coast appeal for supporters to back his candidacy. In a religious atmosphere, testimonials followed, with comments like, "This nation without God is nothing," by former professional football player Rosie Grier; "Our Constitution is made only for a moral and religious people," by Beverly LaHaye of Concerned Women for America; and "Separation of church and state does not mean a separation of God and government," by Southern Baptist leader Reverend James Draper. Entering Constitution Hall moments before Pat Robertson appeared, evangelist Oral Roberts said, "We are going to touch the people where they hurt." Everything looked and sounded as much like a religious revival meeting as it did a political rally.

But the Reverend Harald Bredesen, Robertson's close friend of over thirty years, had the last word. His statement was that only the man "at whatever the cost . . . who hears and obeys God, can lead us in this hour." Such words inspire trust in some minds, terror in others, and sound just plain foolish to many. They require that Robertson deal with the issue of revival and religious liberty in America.[24]

Television reporter Marvin Kalb on "Meet the Press" asked Robertson about the issue of a Christian America. "Is it your far out hope that one day America will be Christian? Is it your vision as a politician, your mission to make this a Christian nation?" Robertson responded: "I don't think that's the intention of anyone today. If it is, I'm not aware of it." He went on to explain that the real issue is one of jurisdiction. The government has no authority in the area of conscience, because the Constitution clearly draws a line protecting individuals from the "coercion of the state." Robertson believes the government does have authority over conduct when persons or property are damaged, but none over what people think or believe. If he were president his duty would be to uphold freedom of religion and good morals.[25]

Before the Nieman Fellows of Harvard University, he was questioned about his frequent references to "the good Christians of early America" and what this meant for "Jews and other non-Christians" who might suffer if there was a massive Christian revival in this country. The questioner reminded Robertson that Jews were not considered citizens in Massachusetts until 1821, "forty-five years after the Declaration of Independence." The questioner recalled Protestant oppression of minorities.

Robertson's answer was to link revival historically in America, in the First and Second Great Awakenings, to the release of minorities, not to their oppression. He predicted increasing freedom for all people, showing that while religion can be oppressive, true revival liberates. He recalled his Baptist ancestors in Virginia and their fight with the Anglicans to establish a place for themselves. Religious liberty in Virginia was the result. He concluded by saying,

> I know of no sentiment whatsoever, to in any wise impose some kind of religious orthodoxy on anybody. I know the people I am involved with myself, would fight to the death for religious freedom for all people, because all we are interested in is a level playing field. . . .[26]

In fact, he draws a sharp distinction between his work in religious broadcasting and the duties of a president. In a press conference in New Orleans he was asked to explain his statement that Christians had been disappointed by recent presidents. Did this mean that only a very religious person could successfully occupy the White House or that Ronald Reagan was a failure in Robertson's eyes? He quickly responded:

> Just the contrary. I think that Ronald Reagan has made an incredible beginning. But politics is the work of the possible, not the impossible. The work I'm presently in is the work of the impossible. But politics is the work of the possible. And he has done what was possible. There were certain things that were impossible given the political climate of our nation.[27]

Revival cannot be imposed by government; it is a sovereign work of God, and even as a broadcaster he could do little to bring it about. He calls the efforts by Christians to create revival "an impossible task." Politics is different, severely limited by the "political climate" of the nation. What Robertson did not say in this interchange was that he thinks revival alone can actually change the climate that will make solid leadership in the White House possible.

> It is questionable whether any purely political leader can overcome the enormous lassitude which has seized a population taken over by free sex, widespread narcotic and alcohol use, and personal selfishness. Widespread religious revival is the only answer, and this is why spiritual values and government cannot be separated.[28]

A combination of spiritual vitality and political liberty has given America its distinctive place in history, according to Robertson. He does not believe Americans need to apologize for the phrase "Manifest Destiny," since this nation, even with its evident failures, has been a bulwark for liberty and a "lighthouse to the world." Threatened as the nations are today by great evil, Robertson sees America legitimately serving a dual role: Some people will carry the Christian message to the world, and government will help to protect liberty. Robertson argues that from their earliest beginnings the American colonies dedicated themselves to be both a civilizing agent and a spiritual light to the nations.[29] He quotes from the original Virginia Charter given by James I:

> We would vouchsafe unto them Our License, to make habitation, plantation, and to deduce a colony of sundry of Our people into that part of America commonly called Virginia. . . . We greatly commend . . . so noble a work, which may, by the providence of Almighty God, hereafter tend to the glory of His Divine Majesty, in propagating of Christian religion to such people as yet live in darkness and miserable ignorance of the true knowledge and worship of God, and may in time bring the infidels and savages living in those parts to human civility and to a settled and quiet government.[30]

In simple terms, Robertson stands for the separation of religion and government when it comes to the rights of conscience. Beyond that, he sees religious liberty giving Americans the opportunity guaranteed to every person by law, to think for themselves in matters of religion and to choose whether or not they will follow Christ. Liberty makes room for religion, and religion in return supports and helps to define that liberty.

Revival and World Events

Robertson does not think that revival is a vain dream simply because one has not occurred on a national scale in recent American history. He thinks they come periodically or in cycles. He has studied the history of revival in America and points out several critical revivals that he believes preceded or prevented terrible national calamities and helped the nation to meet them: The Great Awakening preceded the American Revolution, and the Second Great Awakening occurred before the Civil War, preparing America for its great battle with slavery. In England a great revival led by John Wesley motivated that nation to deal with slavery, child labor, and prison reform. Robertson believes England's revival spared them the fate of France which experienced a bloodbath and dictatorship under Napoleon.[31]

In recent years, he has found evidence of a growing revival on a worldwide scale. Where one might least expect good news, in nations like Argentina and the Philippines, Robertson reports widespread Christian movements, and he believes this is related to recent improvements in the politics of those nations, where governments are becoming more democratic and respectful of human rights.

> I don't think it is coincidental, for example, that Mrs. Aquino came into the Philippines. She is one of deep faith, and a woman at the same time who believes deeply in personal freedom, and the oppressive dictatorships of the right and the left are going to begin to crumble . . . In Argentina last year there were 500,000 professions of faith in Jesus Christ in one year. I'm broadcasting myself in nine cities in Argentina, and the church is very strong, the Catholic church is reviving, the Protestant church is reviving, and along with that will come, hopefully, democratic institutions and stability.[32]

Reviewing the history of Christian revival, he concludes that it always leads to social concern and more healthy government. In his discussion of this subject with Francis Schaeffer, Robertson states that if a culture denies God, having once known Him, they will soon throw off the restraints of reason and tradition and lose their liberty. To reverse this process, he believes a once largely Christian people must recover the "Lordship of Christ in the totality of life" and then recover liberty for the nation as a whole, and to fully recover, the nation must go all the way back to where it lost its way.[33]

The general opinion of modern educated people is that religion only produces conflict and intolerance; Robertson thinks that the opposite is now largely the case. The rejection of religion leads to these very things as well. But he believes religion is on the move everywhere.

> I am very optimistic about the world. I think that God has got His hand on it. What I see immediately ahead of us is a tremendous spiritual revival. Now, at the same time, I also see the failing of Soviet communism and socialism around the world. And I think long range, there is a move in Great Britain towards God, in America, in the Middle East, in South America and Africa, and in the Far East. In other words, we're seeing a worldwide spiritual revival, which will bring about freedom and liberty and a breaking up of some of these outmoded systems.[34]

He considers religion a force of the future bringing hope, and atheist political systems from the past as tyrannical and obsolete. Robertson recounts how he won an argument with a Chinese Marxist official, when he pointed to the oppressive system in the Soviet Union and asked him why this was so if communism was true and led to freedom. When the Chinese official had no answer, Robertson commented later,

> And anything that goes against the freedom that you and I yearn for, that is common and shared by all mankind everywhere, is

ultimately doomed to fail. And that's why, in my estimation, the conservative movement is growing. Even as we get further insight into what seems to be a magnificent spiritual revival that is taking place in our world, we are also looking more and more to a time when I see the ultimate downfall of the Communist system which is going against nature, and more and more triumph of the conservative system which is in accordance with man and nature. That's why the election of Ronald Reagan in 1980, and again in 1984, was not an aberration of history.[35]

Robertson believes that the study of the past and events in the future will confirm his confidence in the staying power of liberty supported by religious revival. He enjoys recalling the comments of Alexis De Tocqueville, an astute French observer of America, who traveled in this country in the early 1800s and compared what he saw in America to France and Europe. He quotes De Tocqueville,

> I went into her halls of legislature, and the greatness of America was not there. I went out into the fields of her agriculture, and the greatness was not there. I went into her places of industry, but I could not find the greatness of America . . . I went into a little church, and there I heard the simple preaching of the Gospel of Jesus Christ. Then I knew why America was great. America is great . . . because she is good. If she ever ceases to be good, she ceases to be great.[36]

Atheism is the great enemy of all religion and a terrible threat to mankind when linked to radical politics. Yet, in one respect, Robertson's views on revival are in tension with Christian evangelism. He supports belief in God first. This precedes in a sense his commitment to the Christian faith. He is for basic theism, a belief in a personal, infinite, loving God, whether one is a Jew, a Muslim, or not attached to any specific religion. Revival of any healthy religion, be it Christian or not, is progress in the right direction, and ought to be encouraged, from his perspective. Robertson then calls for cooperation among religions within the nation and internationally. In America, he considers secular humanism the chief threat, and around the world atheistic communism the greater menace.

Robertson's commitment to evangelism fulfilled his mother's dream. She wanted to "evangelize the world for Jesus," which Robertson calls an impossible task. His father had lesser goals for America as a senator.[37] Revival is more than pure religion and more than conservative politics. It combines the high spiritual walk of his mother with the practical concerns of his father. In his lineage there are a number of ministers and political leaders. Having fulfilled in some measure his mother's aspirations by establishing CBN, Robertson can now turn to the unfinished agenda left by his politician father. "Regardless of where God leads me, CBN had a mandate to fulfill: that of spreading the Gospel of the Kingdom, of bringing the knowledge of God to the ends of the earth, of being part of a great company who would help to usher in the very second coming of Jesus."[38]

Politically, revival serves a dual purpose in America. It rescues citizens from total preoccupation with their private lives, pointing them toward public service, and it helps to deliver religious people from shame. Religious institutions benefit and the nation is helped by an active citizenry. Robertson thinks that revival is needed to equip Americans for self-government.

Once the "sleeping giant" of inactive Christians begins to wake up, he predicts widespread Christian activism. The church must either remain in a defensive position awaiting further persecution, or become more involved and let the chips fall where they may. Robertson's concern is that Christians are slow to take up responsibility; they are more ready to suffer than to govern in this world. His desire is to mobilize them and inspire in them a sense of who they are—persons designed by God for service and rule.[39]

What will happen if Christians get involved in politics? The long-term implications for America are disturbing and hopeful. Coping with resurgent religion will strain the political parties as it did before the Civil War. These parties are the engines of accommodation in a two-party system. To have the support of enough votes to gain the nomination, and certainly to win the general election, requires that a candidate push to the middle of public opinion, looking for an electoral majority. Robertson's candidacy, extreme as 't may look to some observers, represents more moderate forces in religion and a willingness to compromise somewhat in politics.

There are dangerous elements of the population that would like to capitalize on impending national troubles, according to Robertson. His desire is to give the United States leadership in what he says will be turbulent times. Religion represents, to him, oil on troubled waters, a return to stable structures and beliefs.

◆ 11 ◆
Prayer: Robertson Depends on It

◆ *Does Robertson believe he is God's candidate?*
◆ *How does he get divine guidance?*
◆ *How would he pray in public?*

P at Robertson believes sincerely in a personal God whose ways can be followed and whose directives can be received and understood.

His introduction of God's will into the campaign has caused problems. A few days after returns were announced in the complicated Michigan delegate selection process in August 1986, Robertson appeared in Washington, D.C., at the Off the Record Club. He claimed victory in Michigan—a first-place finish or a strong second, depending on the final outcome. Before this audience, Robertson said:

> Our goal in Michigan was to do two things. Number one, we wanted to show that the evangelical Christians, those who care for traditional values, would enter into the political process, get involved in precinct politics. The second thing we wanted to show was

that some of them would know how to cope with the hustle and bustle and hurly-burly of politics, and get elected![1]

Not surprisingly, after such comments Robertson was asked if he claimed religious authority for his candidacy. Robertson responded that no candidate could claim God's mantle: "A person should be evaluated on the basis of their integrity, their intelligence, their knowledge of government, and their public policy solutions to real problems." As for God's guidance, he said, "Eighty percent of the American people think God has a plan for their lives." A Gallup Poll conducted for him in February 1986 confirmed that as many as 69 percent of the people were confident that God "guided" them in their decision making. If God has a plan for each person's life and wants each to discover it, then, said Robertson, it only makes sense to search it out. Previous candidates like Eugene McCarthy prayed about their decisions, and, like them, Robertson had a "peace" that this was the right course.[2]

When asked, "Did you ever know if you were God's chosen candidate?" Robertson responded that he did not know anything more than that it was right for him to run. "We try as best we can as fallible mortals to do what we feel is God's will in our lives." He would not claim that God supports him for president, but he feels he has God's support for his candidacy.[3]

Robertson says he is not the only contemporary leader to seek guidance. He relates that Corazon Aquino, the president of the Philippines, prays before making decisions and looks for a peace within before acting. Robertson expects God to guide him through circumstances, by relevant Scripture passages, or with an inner calm and confidence that he is doing the right thing.[4]

Receiving guidance might appear to some as an insult to human intelligence, but Robertson does not think so. He is convinced that if we examine the complex issues of our day without God's help, we will eventually lose our way. Guidance takes into account our limitations, as Proverbs 3:5, 6 advises: "Trust in the Lord with all your heart and lean not on your own understanding; in all your ways acknowledge him, and he will make your paths straight."

These verses, given to Robertson years ago by Reverend Cornelius Vanderbreggen, the man responsible for his religious conversion, are the basis for his view of guidance. They do not mean to him that he stops thinking when problems get too difficult, but they do warn against overconfidence and self-sufficiency, and encourage humility in the face of human ignorance. He states in his book *Beyond Reason:*

> After nearly 300 years of high-flying faith in the limitless capacity of man's mind, we find that there are limits to our brain power. We find that we don't live in a closed system that can be completely understood if smart humans just work hard enough at it. On the contrary, the real universe is open-ended in a frightening sense that we can't begin to comprehend. Things are not at all what they seem.[5]

Guidance, in Robertson's experience, is more of a struggle to get free of false answers than an easy way out. For example, when he started a Christian television station and things did not work out as planned, his sense of guidance allowed him to doubt his decision without giving up too easily. If God led him to start a television station, then there must be a way to do so. But if all efforts failed, then he would turn to some other work. Guidance sought in this manner encouraged Robertson to act in the face of enormous difficulties without taking away his personal responsibility for decisions made.[6] He said,

> Prayer is not playing magic games, spinning prayer wheels, reading off a list, or asking for things to be done. It is a communion. "Deep calls unto deep," the Bible says. In prayer the depths of your spirit are in communion with the depths of the Spirit of God. Out of this can come instruction, guidance, or a burden to pray for certain things.[7]

Seeking guidance for his ministry following seminary, he discovered the instruction of Jesus to the rich young ruler to sell all that he possessed before he could follow Jesus (Luke 12:33).

Robertson applied this verse to his life directly and immediately. He sold virtually all he owned, gave the money to the poor, and moved into a slum in Brooklyn. Soon after obeying this "rich young ruler" principle, he made the key decisions that launched his television ministry.[8]

Robertson practices fasting to give him a clearer sense of guidance, as he directs energies normally spent on everyday tasks toward the pursuit of instructions from God. Still, prayer and fasting are not a guarantee for understanding God's guidance, nor does he claim that prayer alone makes one wise enough for leadership.[9]

Robertson concludes his account of God's leading in his early ministry with a story of failure. Bunker Hunt, the Texas millionaire who later would play a supporting role in his political ambitions, is part of the story. Robertson was told through a third party that H. L. Hunt, Bunker's father, was going to substantially fund his television ministry. Circumstances and apparently supernatural events confirmed this mistaken belief. Eventually, Robertson discovered that the Hunt story was a hoax and the supposed guidance an illusion. Robertson learned from this not to follow any supernatural signs if they take him beyond the simple and reasonable principles of the Bible. Guidance that provides a shortcut to success should be rejected—guidance flows from the Bible's principles for living.[10]

From some viewpoints, Robertson's statements on guidance are a foolish superstition or a political game. Confident in the heat of battle and buoyed with a strong sense of providence and purpose, Robertson can say of his candidacy:

I thank God that I'm an American. I thank God, more than anything, that I'm a Christian and that I know Jesus Christ. And I thank God that we can speak for all Americans, not just Christians but our Jewish friends, for all people everywhere. We have love, we have compassion, and we pledge ourselves to fight for freedom and liberty of all men and women everywhere, and to preserve the great traditions this country has been founded on.[11]

Robertson believes that his political efforts are blessed by God and feels led to run for public office. As will be seen later in a discussion of his views of prophecy, he believes strongly that God speaks directly to people today, giving them comfort and guidance. But he makes no claims to be "God's candidate," nor does he say that God actually told him to run for president. In any event, his own evident desire and ambition would cancel his credibility if he did claim that God had spoken to him.

Public Prayer

Robertson's unapologetic approach to prayer puts a gap between himself and the other candidates. Like an ancient king who was credited with controlling the weather and providing good crops, Pat Robertson prayed on television for a wall of protection from Hurricane Gloria in November 1985. The hurricane turned and diminished, later hitting the Northeast, doing limited damage. He took this as a sign from God for his entering the presidential race, but he did not pray alone; he said, "There were probably a million people praying" during the hurricane. If the hurricane had struck a devastating blow, perhaps Robertson would not have entered politics. He wanted some assurance that faith worked in facing natural disasters before he took on the challenge of running for president.

Recently he was asked in Washington, D.C., "Are you concerned that some people think you may pray a wall of defense against missiles?" Robertson's response was to recall President Franklin Roosevelt's public prayers for America during World War II, Abraham Lincoln's call for prayer during the Civil War, and George Washington's personal piety in the founding period of the nation. He sees nothing contrary to sound public policy in his prayer.[12] Asked if prayer worked on the hurricane, Robertson responded:

And so does God answer prayer? Yes, He answers prayer. And was our region spared? Yes, it was spared. And was it an answer to prayer? I think it was, because that hurricane was aimed right at us and it would have devastated our region. . . . I can't imagine anything wrong with praying that God would keep a tornado or hurricane or some disaster from people's homes and lives, or that He would bring rain to farmers who were going out of business because their crops were parched.[13]

Praying for the weather is something Robertson has done for years. Once, in the mid-fifties, he prayed for rain to keep a group of young people in a building so that he would have the opportunity to preach to them. In a recent book defending weather prayers, Robertson writes: "Yet there are times, especially in dire emergencies, when humans who have a deep relationship with God can exercise extraordinary power over the land, the seas and the weather." Assuredly it is a common experience for people in the path of a hurricane to turn to prayer.[14]

When Robertson's father, Senator A. Willis Robertson of Virginia, lost his election in 1966, Robertson explained this as the consequence of a hot day at the polls which kept the senator's supporters home. A hot day, he wrote, was God's way of settling this election.

Weather is unpredictable and dangerous. A few changes in wind, rain, and temperature can disrupt farming, destroy homes, and take lives. Yet Robertson teaches that weather is under the control of God. "In Biblical terms, God's blessing is associated with rain and bountiful harvests. His disfavor is revealed in drought and poor harvests."[15] Robertson wrote to his supporters in the harsh winter of 1977:

For a brief period factories were closed, economic life halted, agriculture demoralized and government taken by surprise. This winter could well serve as God's warning to the United States that all our might is helpless to stand against a minor shift in the wind.[16]

Robertson is skeptical, however, that people learn from the weather what God is trying to teach them. He writes:

People never seem to learn spiritually from short term trouble. Like Pharaoh of Egypt as soon as the plague is over they harden their hearts and go back to their old ways.[17]

Civilization tends to shut God out, he feels, forgetting that He is the one who holds things together. Robertson is alert to what might dramatically disrupt human life and how completely dependent humans are—"only a minor shift in the wind."

Robertson sees a close relationship between his views on prayer and the concept of providence accepted by the founding fathers George Washington and Benjamin Franklin, who also supported public prayer. Robertson is convinced that most Americans pray, and he sees nothing incongruous about a political leader praying or calling a nation to prayer. Many people would agree that America needs a president who can pray.[18]

On a recent national television show, Robertson noted that according to a Gallup Poll, 7.5 million Americans have received a healing through prayer. When asked about his own prayers for the sick on the "700 Club," he repeated this story:

> There was a young man in a Contra hospital, a secret hospital as a matter of fact, in Honduras, whose leg was going to be amputated because of gangrene. He had a picture of Jesus on the wall; he had a cross. I felt so sorry for him that he was going to lose his leg at the beginning of his young life that I knelt by his bed and we prayed together. I got word from a friend of mine who was inside Nicaragua just a couple of weeks ago that a young man came up to him and said, "Please thank Pat Robertson," . . . It was that same man, God had healed him, and he was back actually fighting inside of the country. It was a remarkable thing. I was quite gratified.[19]

Documented for use on television, this account unabashedly combined prayer and healing in a political setting. Furthermore, Robertson's public prayers on television unveil his political convictions on some subjects more clearly and completely than his speeches or books. For example, in April 1985, he prayed confidently for God to oppose communism and to give relief to its victims. Christians and Muslims are singled out and supported in their struggle against Soviet oppression:

We see the cry of Christian people in Romania, Hungary, Czechoslovakia, East Germany, Poland, Estonia, Lithuania, Latvia and inside the Soviet Union and in other parts of the world where communism has spread. God, they cry out to You for freedom of conscience, for freedom to worship. And they're being persecuted and tortured physically and mentally and deprived of their education. They're being made second-class citizens because they want to tell about God. Lord Jesus, hear their cry. Hear their cry, our Father. And bring down this evil that has fastened itself on mankind. Bring it down, Lord God, by the power of the Holy Spirit. Do miracles, we pray, O God, and strengthen the hands of those who would fight for freedom wherever, around the world, Afghanistan, those Mujahedeen, whoever they are who would fight for liberty and freedom, Lord—that they might be strengthened against oppression. Lord, liberate the captives, we pray. Do miracles. Set them free. We break the yoke of oppression in the name of Jesus.[20]

At other times Robertson has prayed against specific leaders. His basic concern, however, is not with individuals but with the Soviet system.

We pray . . . bring down the rulers of the Soviet Union. Destroy international Marxism and dictatorship over conscience and over freedom that comes from this monstrous system of demonic evil . . . In the name of Jesus that system shall be destroyed.[21]

Robertson's political prayers assume that God and the devil are both fully involved in politics. Praying for America recently, he boldly stood against destructive supernatural forces operating in the cultural power centers of the land.

Father, in Jesus' name, we pray now for a spiritual renewal in this land that will sweep from coast to coast and border to border. We bind at this moment the power of Satan over this land. We break the hold of Satan in Washington; in the state capitals; in New York City, the financial capital; in Chicago, the commodities capital. We break the hold of Satan in Hollywood over the film and entertainment capital. In the name of Jesus we bind the strong man and spoil his house. Satan, you are beaten. And Jesus Christ is victor.[22]

In his prayers for America, none are more graphic than those for the Supreme Court:

> Father, in Jesus' name, at this very moment we pray that the power of God Almighty might be felt in the Supreme Court. And those who have set themselves on high—above the Constitution, above the people, above the president, above the Congress, above legislatures—God, that You who are above all might demonstrate Your power to them that they might see the error of what they're doing . . . Father, we plead our case to You. Little children are being denied the knowledge of Jesus Christ and denied the knowledge of God. Little children are growing up in a drug-infested world, in a world filled with pornography and sensuality without the weapons they need to protect their spirits, Lord. And the Court is taking away what few weapons are left. God, our society is being terrorized by crime, and these men have consistently taken away the protection we need to defend ourselves from hardened criminals. And, God, seventeen million babies—their blood cries out against some of these men on the Supreme Court. Lord God, hear the cry of the unborn dead, who have been slaughtered since the decision of the Supreme Court. Lord, hear and answer the prayer of Your people. Do not delay, Lord: move. And may Your will be manifested in Washington and the Supreme Court of the United States. In Jesus' name, Amen and Amen.[23]

Such aggressive prayers are highly offensive to some people because they sound like he is taking the role of a prophet. Robertson believes that he is being heard by God and that God agrees with him, and this is far more than most politicians and many preachers assume about their own prayers. On the "MacNeil Lehrer News Hour," MacNeil asked Robertson: "Do you believe that you are actually a prophet of God yourself?" He rejected the label, claiming instead that he spoke prophetically simply when he addressed serious problems as any true minister should, "in the name of God."[24]

Robertson is especially impressed with the significance of the April 29, 1980, "Washington for Jesus" rally when 500,000 Christians joined in public prayer for the nation. The high point of the day for Robertson took place about four o'clock in the afternoon when CBN host Ben Kinchlow rose to his feet to pray. Kinchlow had everyone point to the Capitol building that houses the Congress, and with his voice amplified by huge loudspeakers, he commanded the devil to leave. Robertson said later at a pastors' brunch in St. Petersburg, Florida, that these prayers helped to elect Ronald Reagan.

> From that day on, something wonderful began to happen . . . the election of Ronald Reagan in 1980 was not the triumph of a very, very highly personable actor . . . It was a sovereign act of God Almighty in answer to prayer.[25]

Prayer for Robertson is a flexible concept. It covers all situations of life from those we understand clearly, like a threatening hurricane, to politics—where we merely claim what is best for us without being specific about which candidate we want God to choose. He is hesitant to claim a political victory in prayer. He recalls that he has given benedictions for candidates of both parties and simply prayed that God would give His choice, providing a wise leader. Nevertheless, this open and expectant approach to prayer is unusual both in the average church and, of course, in politics. It is highly offensive to some and attractive to others.[26]

What is the political effect of this emphasis on prayer and the supernatural? For Robertson it undergirds his sense of integrity. As a religious person, he understands that without effective prayer, his credentials as a Christian candidate are incomplete. The secular world knows, perhaps better than the church, that for Christians to be consistent they must believe in and practice prayer. Certainly for Christians personal prayer is a common identity—pious people pray.

Moreover, Robertson thinks that prayer generally unifies people more than it divides them. He writes,

> The "700 Club" program obviously has universal appeal. When you pray for people, you make friends. It makes no difference who they are: Protestants, Catholics, Jews, Buddhists, even atheists—all are grateful that you care enough to pray.[27]

Robertson sees prayer as effective communication that breaks through to people when mere talk alienates. He feels that personal prayer is natural to every human being.

But for Christian supporters of Robertson, there are additional meanings. For Christians, prayer is a vehicle for God to help people, and the political process needs help. A good president strengthened by prayer will make a better president. In fact, prayer is a visible part of Robertson's political meetings, but what does prayer mean in the national context?

Some politicians and many others are offended at Robertson's prayers, particularly when he claims that they are answered. One candidate for Congress in Oklahoma, Tulsa University Law Professor Gary Allison, is reported to have said that Robertson's claims about Hurricane Gloria are "blasphemous" because "that's an act of God and he is taking credit for it." Robertson had appeared the day before at a fund raiser for Allison's opponent.[28]

But the political choices of those opposed to Robertson are few when it comes to prayer. One can attack prayer, which is close to political suicide; one can ignore the issue; one can line up some prayer power of one's own, or one can say that prayer belongs outside of politics. Allison chose to attack Robertson's prayers—perhaps the most self-defeating way to handle this volatile issue, especially in Tulsa.

Robertson knows that he is relatively safe politically when he prays. If the press or his opponents dare to ridicule his prayer, he is convinced this "will backfire." Clearly prayer is back in politics.

This is a strategy that puts people who oppose him in a vulnerable place before much of the American electorate. Other candidates may not pray for miracles like Robertson does, but many will consider it wise to at least pray before political functions.[29]

Robertson's visibility on prayer and the supernatural is a liability and an asset. Many will write him off for being strange. Others will see in his willingness to be different a strength and a promise of something more in politics. He can afford to offend both opponents and party leaders on the prayer issue—it is the party primaries and caucuses where the people vote that make his candidacy possible.

Presidential Prayer

Robertson was asked by the press if he would speak in tongues in the White House. He answered directly, "Well, if I pray I wouldn't question the fact that I might pray in the Spirit. I see nothing wrong with that. It's a form of prayer." Robertson understands the significance of the independence of leadership in the White House. The moment he stops being himself he has lost the edge that sets one apart in a position of authority. But to be set too far apart is to lose your following altogether. He reported that about 135 million people worldwide pray in tongues. This kind of prayer is spoken in unintelligible syllables, and it is believed to be an expression of worship by those who use it, that God understands. He defends this practice based on the New Testament account of early Christians and his own experience, saying that it provides "a marvelous sense of peace and communion with God."[30]

Robertson recounts a conversation between Herb Ellingwood, former aide to President Reagan and now administrator for Americans for Robertson. Ellingwood asked Reagan, then governor of California, "Governor, are you going to run for president?" Reagan's response was, "If God wants me to run for president, then He will have to make the people want somebody like me, because I'm not going to change." For Robertson this example is deeply comforting, because Reagan eventually won the presidency without pandering to public opinion.[31]

However, Robertson says that his public prayers will be different in his role as a political leader. There is a sharp difference between pastoral prayers and that of public officials. His model for public prayer in America is George Washington who used terms like *providence* and *Creator*. Such language is acceptable to people who believe in God, and it expresses the basic terms of the Declaration of Independence. Some will perceive this as compromise. Even a newsman criticized him for not using religious language on one occasion. He responded, "I'm not sure I have to invoke God to tell Republicans how to win elections."[32]

A strong confidence in prayer can strengthen leadership. Furthermore, prayer is also a release for frustration when restraint is needed. Often, leaders are tempted to act when it would be wiser to do nothing but wait patiently for clarity or for events to unfold. One staff member of Robertson's suggested that Ronald Reagan's White House acted in the Iran-Contra affair largely because they felt helpless to move events. He thought that prayer might have kept them from making such a mistake.

Christians have claimed benefits from prayer for centuries. Prayer can enable the strong to wait, curbing restlessness. Prayer is also encouraging in the face of enormous problems. Prayer is beneficial to the active mind that must seek solutions beyond one's immediate ability to put them into practice.[33]

But some people are afraid that a president who prays will be dangerous. The Associated Press Editorial Board asked Robertson, "All your advisers tell you one thing, and you converse with God, you pray, and you get an answer, that's what religious people do, right?" Robertson countered this objection to his candidacy by recounting his experience in building and running organizations.

One cannot get along in that environment with so many possibilities and confusion without listening to advisers and learning to make wise decisions on the basis of available information and the advice of people. In a multitude of counselors is wisdom, and I believe that the key is who your counselors are.[34]

Perhaps the real issue between the press and Robertson in this instance has more to do with genuine leadership that can overrule the counsel of subordinates or critics. The press rightly senses that Robertson would pray and chart his own course; if Robertson was not a praying person but simply an independent thinker, they still might be alarmed.

The most recent instance of prayer playing a vital role in diplomacy, says Robertson, was in the Camp David accords involving Egypt's President Anwar Sadat, Israel's Prime Minister Menachem Begin, and President Jimmy Carter. This achievement required tenacity by all three leaders and a willingness to go the second mile in negotiations. Robertson writes:

> At the beginning of the Summit meeting, the three leaders issued a joint call for prayer. As he announced the conclusion of the talks, President Carter declared that the prayers of many had been answered. One little-known fact in all this was the role of CBN board member Harald Bredesen, who brought the concept of the united Christian, Jewish, and Muslim prayer for peace first to President Sadat and then to the White House. During the talks, the facilities of the White House were made available to Doug Coe of International Christian Leadership, who dispatched thousands of messages requesting prayer for the talks to religious and political leaders around the world.[35]

For Robertson, prayer goes beyond creeds and political convictions. Prayer is the response of one's heart and mind to God at the deepest levels of one's spirit and person. Prayer is an everyday experience for Robertson and his staff. For example, one day in the spring of 1987, Robertson was flying to a political appointment. Feeling very tired, he called Herb Ellingwood, his administrator, and asked Herb to gather together the Americans for Robertson staff to pray for him. Robertson had been up until after midnight the night before and needed strength. Herb immediately called the staff to prayer.

What would a staff member at Americans for Robertson do when called to prayer if he did not believe in God or had no religious convictions? Perhaps he would pray anyway, to the "unknown God" if necessary (Acts 17:23).

Robertson reports that there was a prayer meeting in 1953 in which a prophecy was given that "God is going to establish a center in this Tidewater area, and this end-time message will go out all over the eastern seaboard and spread throughout the country." He reports an even earlier Tidewater prayer meeting, in 1607, when this land was dedicated to the purposes of God. He finds in these prayers and the remembering of them a basis for confidence in the ongoing presence and activity of God in history. Despite the failures of people through the centuries, when prayers seem fruitless, God is able to make them come true, when we least expect it, at a later time, even in another generation.[36]

For Pat Robertson, prayer links people with the past and the future. Prayer makes both history and the future alive. His thinking in the late seventies and even today is influenced by a sense of destiny related to prayer.

Can prayer be placed in the middle of politics without overheating it to the point that people require prayer before they will listen to a leader? Robertson is calling the spiritual strength and integrity of Republican and Democratic politicians into question. He is also challenging the relative isolation of politics from religion. Moreover, if Robertson is successful in politics, what will Americans expect of his successors?

Robertson handles this problem by saying that he will pray like a George Washington or an Abraham Lincoln. But can he make such a transition from the "God anointed prayers inspired by the Holy Spirit" that he is used to praying, to a more formal and remote invocation of providence? There is a difference between his powerful and explicit prayers as a religious broadcaster and what he says that he would do as president. His temptation and that of his followers will be to have contempt for limited prayer.

King David was the great prayer warrior of the Bible. His prayer songs certainly have had a greater impact on history in the long run than his greatest military triumphs. People do long for a reunion of prayer and politics, because they have become so separate that prayer seems otherworldly, and politics unrelated to God. Robertson promises an appropriate and restrained restoration of prayer to American public life.

·12·
Prophecy: Robertson Defends It

♦ *Is Pat Robertson a prophet?*
♦ *How does he understand biblical prophecy?*
♦ *What predictions has he made?*

Pat Robertson frankly claims to receive words from God. He also believes in a "word of knowledge" where God shows someone another person's need for the purpose of bringing help or healing to them. This is a distinguishing characteristic of his religion. Yet to hear from God means different things to different people, depending on one's experience and perspective. Robertson's theology teaches that God has communicated in the past and does so in the present as well in a variety of ways. What does this have to do with politics? Inevitably a great deal, because leaders are accountable for their decisions and must be able to give rational explanations for their actions.[1]

Prophecy in the Bible and in Christian tradition has at least three forms. First, it is a word from God requiring that justice be done and that people live morally; this is customarily delivered in a sermon based on Bible teaching or occasionally in a pastoral rebuke of public officials. A second type of prophecy interprets the Bible's predictions of future events and attempts to understand the meaning for today. A third form is receiving a message that one claims comes from God, that predicts future events; its truth is judged simply by whether the events take place as prophesied and by its significance measured by the Bible and by Christian teaching. All three forms are in the Bible. However, present-day prophecy is not accepted by all Christians; some believe that God stopped speaking directly to people after the Bible was written. Robertson respects all three forms of prophecy.

He is bold about prophecy because he considers it an essential part of historic Christian teaching and experience and has seen prophecies fulfilled. But this is a delicate matter to handle in public, even among Christians. It would seem to be politically prudent to conceal or to minimize this conviction. However, this could weaken his leadership by undermining his integrity.

Robertson calls for more respect for prophecy. How this will affect his politics is a serious matter. What would a "prophetic" political role mean for a president in contemporary America?

Robertson has been something of a critic of church and state. Now he seeks political office, without denying his past role as a "prophetic" gadfly. In nonreligious terms, a journalist wants to be president.

Shame

To believe that God communicates is to invite difficulties, but to be defensive about it, denying his beliefs, Robertson thinks would be self-defeating, and it would also violate the Scripture that says, "Despise not prophecy." He believes that Christians often have a lack of respect for their own religious community and its teachings, and this cuts them off from the rest of society. No one wants to associate with a people who have contempt for themselves and lack respect for their sacred beliefs. The problem is not necessarily that such Christians are hypocrites, but that good people who live consistently nevertheless lack the courage to be openly different. Robertson works to inspire Christians to overcome this weakness.

Robertson was raised in a Southern Baptist church and experienced little persecution related to his religious beliefs, though he says his mother's religion embarrassed him until he had a conversion experience in his twenties. He relates that in his southern upbringing he was taught "always to be gracious, even at the expense of the truth." To speak the truth when you know it will offend someone was considered poor manners. But basing his religion on what he believed was the truth, and not any longer upon southern customs, required that Robertson free himself from his upbringing and learn to have independent opinions. With God's help, he says, he learned to respect the truth.[2]

In his first book, *Shout It From the Housetops,* Robertson recounts a most embarrassing moment at his own conversion. He had been somewhat religious and was even contemplating becoming a preacher at the time, like his grandfathers before him. But when he encountered Dutch evangelist Cornelius Vanderbreggen in a posh Philadelphia restaurant, he had to face his own resentment of Christians as a despised group before he could even begin to deal with the facts of the Christian gospel and whether, in fact, he could believe in it.[3]

Vanderbreggen in a most natural way handed the headwaiter a gospel tract. Robertson relates, "I couldn't believe my eyes. The man was handing the waiter a gospel tract. I was mortified beyond expression and quickly shifted my eyes back to the menu again." Things got worse. Soon the preacher pulled out a Bible and began to read it aloud. Robertson was convinced that the headwaiter would shortly descend to throw them out. He remembers vividly his response:

> I knew I had no choice but to sit there and act like I was listening. I could feel the moisture in the palms of my hands now, and little rivulets of perspiration running down my face. I tried to smile, but sensed my mouth had the shape of a crooked stick. I could feel a

hundred pairs of eyes staring at us from all over the room while Vanderbreggen continued to read in a soft voice, accenting his thoughts with occasional gestures.[4]

The waiter did descend. He came discretely up to the table and asked them for another tract. Having given the first one away to a lady at another table who was eavesdropping, he wanted one for himself. While he observed the ensuing conversation between Vanderbreggen and the headwaiter, Pat writes, "I was aghast. Right here in the middle of this plush restaurant these two men were carrying on a conversation about Jesus Christ!" This experience of religion without shame changed him.[5]

After this conversion, the religion of his childhood became the center of Robertson's adult life. What had been insignificant to him in his youth—the faith of his mother—now commanded his full attention. He began to identify with Christians in public no matter what his friends and business partners might think. He also embraced the Bible with its teachings and its supernatural events. After this public humiliation in a Philadelphia restaurant he was born again in more than a spiritual sense. He realized that he had been subject to the opinions of other people. He faced his temptation to have no genuine convictions of his own, to falsely maintain his reputation as a free thinking and independent man, when in fact he thought like everybody else. He learned to delight in being distinctively Christian in public, partly because of the freedom it brought him as a person to think his own thoughts and form his own conclusions about life.

Yet Robertson soon understood that religious traditions, too, could crush the freedom to think and to innovate. Robertson became acquainted with one of the most unusual preachers of his day, Reverend Harald Bredesen. He was ordained in the Lutheran Church and a leading pioneer in what came to be called the charismatic movement. Believing God spoke through prophecy by the Holy Spirit and did miracles, Bredesen brought his message and his supernatural experience to the major denominations of America including Episcopalians, Presbyterians, and Roman Catholics. Robertson recounts how God spoke to them in the "early days," in 1959.

> It seemed as if a heavenly teletype machine had mysteriously been activated. We pieced the message together: "How long will you be bound by fear of men who themselves are the slaves of Satan? I am doing a new thing on the face of the earth. How long will you be silent? Declare the whole counsel of God. Hold nothing back. Hold nothing back!"[6]

This message stirred Bredesen and Robertson to break out of their partly self-imposed submission to church traditions that denied miracles. Their first response was to contact the wife of well-known preacher Norman Vincent Peale, Ruth, and tell her of their experience of the Holy Spirit. Soon the charismatic movement and its young leadership became a subject of public discussion in America and around the world, in religious circles and in the secular press. Its spread largely hinged on the freedom of its leaders to be open about their experiences and beliefs.

After fasting and praying for a week in 1959, Robertson made his major decision to found a Christian television ministry in the Tidewater region of Virginia.

> Despite all the outward problems, I knew that He would not let me down. Now He showed me what the Apostle Paul meant when he wrote, "Hope maketh not ashamed; because the love of God is shed abroad in our hearts by the Holy Ghost which is given unto us."[7]

Shame weakens initiative and dissolves strength, according to Robertson, but a person who innovates takes risks that expose him to the possibilities of failure and then of shame. To act boldly one must face the possibility of ridicule and overcome the thought of it in advance. He believed it better to risk all and to lose than to remain secure and to win nothing.

In Robertson's understanding, shame takes two forms that are equally devastating to a religious community's relationships. First, there is a group shame, when a minority group with a way of life totally different from a secular majority is tempted to withdraw, to avoid persecution and to preserve its own identity. Of course, when a group dominates a nation as Protestants once did in America, there is a temptation to be arrogant and oppressive. But when a group survives at the margins of public life, rarely speaking out on issues, it becomes defensive and eventually shameful. Looked down on by those outside, it begins to look down on itself.

Second, the problem of group shame becomes even worse when group members believe that they have workable answers for the nation. When they believe that they understand what people desperately need, and yet have no adequate platform from which to speak, and face ridicule by others, shame grows. In religious communities, defensiveness grows directly in proportion to the gap between knowledge and responsibility. If this problem is not dealt with, eventually the community will be tempted to despise its own beliefs and teachings. Increased responsibility and the opportunity to influence others reduces this second form of shame.

Robertson has not lost his hatred for shame. Instead he has learned to deal with it by going public. To retreat, to be less distinctively Christian because he is afraid of what others might think, is worse to him than to face their contempt. To be publicly identified with Christians may seem dangerous for a politician, but for Robertson it is essential to his self-respect. To deny his religious beliefs and to shun Christian brothers and sisters means not freedom but enslavement to false opinions. He describes this problem:

> Yet vast numbers of Christians have been intimidated about carrying a Bible on the street or bus or subway. They're afraid of being categorized as religious freaks, or perhaps old-fashioned and out-of-step with the world. They are nervous about being discovered in prayer or other attitudes perceived as different. As for authority— whether it be over Satan or over the natural order—their timidity is overwhelming. And yet, as we have noted before, the Bible says, "God has not given us a spirit of timidity, but of power and love and discipline."[8]

Understanding the Times

Robertson does not hesitate to think prophetically. He believes that events in our world are accurately foretold in the Bible, and that Christians can still receive prophecies. Nothing in his thinking could be further from secular analytical approaches to knowledge.

Robertson has studied Bible prophecies about the last days of history and teaches about them in his book *Answers to 200 of Life's Most Probing Questions*. Whatever troubles lie ahead for the nations of the earth, he believes the church will go through them too. He does not think Christians are going to escape hard times by some miraculous "rapture" or deliverance. He also teaches that Jesus Christ could physically return to this world at any moment, as He said He eventually would, and subsequently set up the rule of God on earth which is to last for a thousand years, a "millennium." Yet Robertson believes that only Jesus Christ here in person can establish the Kingdom of God and usher in the millennium.[9]

These conclusions limit Robertson's optimism about what government can accomplish by itself. He does believe that godly people will help to rule the earth after Christ's return; however, there are difficult days ahead, he says, and no amount of human effort by itself is sufficient, in the end, for rescue.[10]

The key Bible prophecy that Robertson says has been fulfilled in our day is the return of Jerusalem to Israel in 1967. In Luke 21:24, Jesus predicted, ". . . Jerusalem will be trampled on by the Gentiles until the times of the Gentiles are fulfilled." This prophecy has great significance for him. He says, "Since the time of the Babylonians under Nebuchadnezzar, Jerusalem has always been under some kind of foreign domination."[11]

The meaning of Jewish control of Jerusalem is only partly evident to him. He believes that it indicates the ending of a 2500-year era of history and the start of something new. He also believes that it means the second coming of Christ is near. Meanwhile, Robertson advises, the basics of life will continue apparently unchanged, with people "eating and drinking, marrying and giving in marriage," and then Christ will come.[12]

The most significant prophetic book for Robertson in recent years is the Book of Joel. This minor prophet predicted a great outpouring of God's Spirit and was quoted by the Apostle Peter at the Pentecost birth of the church. Joel's words helped the early church to locate its place in history. Now, almost two thousand years later, Robertson sees in Joel a road map for charting the course of events today, revealing what will happen in the future. In chapter 2, verse 17, Joel laments a great injustice, the mistreatment of godly people.

> Let the priests, who minister before the Lord, weep between the temple porch and the altar. Let them say, "Spare your people, O Lord. Do not make your inheritance an object of scorn, a byword among the nations. Why should they say among the peoples, 'Where is their God?'"

Anticipating a worldwide revival of genuine faith as prophesied by Joel, Robertson is grieved by the thought of these people becoming the doormat of civilization, treated with contempt. Such a future until the end of time would appear to be a heartless fate. He believes instead that the Luke passage is to be coupled with Joel, promising unprecedented relief. Jerusalem will not be trampled upon anymore—". . . Jerusalem will be holy; never again will foreigners invade her" (Joel 3:17), and neither will Christians have to suffer under the feet of those who misunderstand or hate them. He believes the domination of a godless culture over the reputations and lives of religious people will stop, at least for a time.

> If you read those prophecies a little more carefully, you'll see that something precedes all that judgment. And that something is that God is going to restore to His people the years that the locusts have eaten and that He is going to prosper His people. I think the Book of Joel, when understood properly, gives a . . . timetable on world events that is quite accurate. There's a part in there that I'd never seen until about a year or so ago, when I realized that there is an incredible financial prosperity coming to the people of God. And following the incredible financial prosperity is a revival of enormous

magnitude, when God pours His Spirit upon all flesh, and whoever will call upon the name of the Lord will be saved, which means mass evangelism beyond anything you've ever dreamed. And in that context—after that—maybe some problems begin to happen. But we haven't seen this tremendous outpouring of the Spirit. And we really haven't seen the exaltation, if you will, of God's people worldwide, that Joel speaks of, when He will take away the reproach. There isn't quite the reproach there once was to say, "I'm a born-again, Spirit-filled Christian," but there are still plenty of people in their little closets that are laughing and making fun of those "holy jumpers" or whatever—you know, all those religious people. Well, the day is going to come when all that reproach has got to be gone.[13]

According to Robertson, the Book of Joel is not written just for the nation of Israel, for the early church used it. For him, the end of foreign domination of Jerusalem means the beginning of a whole new set of relationships among nations and peoples. Repeatedly Joel says, "Never again will my people be ashamed" (2:19, 26, 27), "In those days and at that time, when I restore the fortunes of Judah and Jerusalem" (3:1) and will gather all nations for judgment.

Robertson claims that the world's economy and politics are truly on the brink of disaster. America can for good reasons expect a "general collapse." But in the midst of this disarray not all will suffer equally. He thinks that Christians in particular will begin to experience new strength coming from God and from right living.[14] They will have a clear understanding of what is needed for the good of mankind.

And to God's people God will give wisdom. He's going to give solutions to them just like He did to Daniel and to Joseph and those people who found favor in God's sight. Those who found favor in God's sight are going to be given wisdom, and we will understand the solutions to the world's problems. "You've got something we don't have." But in order to do something, I believe the call upon the church in 1984 is earnest prayer. Get your own house in order.[15]

Robertson sees new responsibilities and promotion coming for godly people of excellence. He is convinced that the basic covenant promises once extended to the people of Israel are valid for today, both for the historic nation of Israel, and for the Christian church. This is the basis of his new optimism concerning the future. Out of revival, new leadership will arise. On January 1, 1985, Robertson said,

> You know, God said we were supposed to be the head and not the tail. We're supposed to be on top and not on the bottom, and I think the long-range trend is that God's people are going to move into positions of leadership—I mean in all kinds of areas. I mean, there's going to be general growing prosperity and blessing for the people of God. Now that's my opinion. But I think that's going to happen. It's going to get better and better and better, and God's going to begin to thrust His people into positions they never dreamed they were capable of taking on. They're going to move into new areas of responsibility in the next few years.[16]

Robertson said people will search out Christians for public service because there will be a strong contrast between their lives and those who reject God. He is acting on this directly by encouraging Christians to get involved in law and politics, and by doing so himself. Perhaps he sees in his own candidacy a fulfillment of this prophecy.[17]

Predicting the Future

Between February 1977 and the fall of 1982, Robertson made some interesting predictions about world events. His newsletter, "Pat Robertson's Perspective," written and signed by him and published eight or ten times a year, contained financial advice and commentary on politics and economics, connecting current events to Bible prophecy. In 1981 he prophesied a drought:

> One historic measure of divine judgment is poor weather leading to poor crops. Famine serves as a warning. We can expect further

drought in 1981 and a reduction in grain output. By 1982, unless there is a further turning to God in our land, we may well experience alarming drought and crop shortages.[18]

Soon after this statement there were famines in Ethiopia and elsewhere. A global weather disaster, El Niño, "a dislocation of the world's largest weather system, flung high winds, rampaging floods, and the misery of drought around the globe."[19] Destruction costing nations an estimated $8.5 billion took America's weather forecasting system completely by surprise and caused much suffering in Africa, North and South America, Australia, and Asia.

The trade winds faltered, and the equatorial current reversed direction across the entire Pacific. Sea surface temperatures rose as much as 14°F above normal, until a great tongue of warm water stretched 8,000 miles along the Equator.[20]

It is Robertson's perspective that life is precarious in the best of times, and nature itself is unpredictable and certainly uncontrollable. Human reason and technological power are both prone to fail because of the instability of our environment. He writes:

The disintegration of communism, the world population outstripping food supplies, a serious shift in weather cycles, the dependency on cartel-held oil supplies, a highly fragile world financial order, and the high probability of war have all served to lift the world's problems beyond the reach of man's finite abilities.[21]

Robertson predicts unprecedented changes ahead and says that these are not the times to hide one's head in the sand. Nor does he recommend simply falling back on the eternal truths that never change. Americans, and especially Christians, he says, need to become interested in events, and to see them as part of a meaningful unfolding plan, not just as random accidents, and to be prepared to act.

The Bible tells us that the wise man sees the danger and hides himself, and the foolish goes on and is punished. Christians must stay alert both to the dangers and the opportunities of our age. We are living in the fastest-paced era of history. There will be wide swings in the next few years: In finance, in life-style, in government policy, in evangelistic opportunities. Dramatic changes will leave us breathless. It is imperative that we know the voice of God and can recognize what comes from His hand and what does not.[22]

In 1977, Robertson predicted that President Sadat of Egypt would seek peace with Israel and that Israel's other Arab neighbors would eventually also make peace. He also warned that a coup could well take place in Iran placing the whole Persian Gulf in jeopardy. Sadat did seek peace shortly and the Shah fell with disastrous results. There was some truth to his prophecy.[23]

But in the December 1977 "Perspective," he said that a severe economic depression was probable within five years. In the next issue, he said, "I do not see any major war or dislocation of the U.S. economy—at least not in the next three years." Readers had to wonder about such changeable guesswork. In 1979, Robertson grew concerned that the end of the world was approaching. In later speeches he regrets his pessimism and states jokingly, "Under Jimmy Carter a lot of us thought that the end was near, and I've gotten more optimistic in subsequent years than I was in 1979."[24]

Robertson claimed credit for five accurate predictions in his December 1977 "Perspective," but by the early eighties he was also aware of his prophetic limitations. He claimed that some of his predictions came from God and others were based on evidence and argument. How he helped people to keep this straight when he made predictions was not so clear.

Dealing with the expectancy of new developments that his approach to prophecy encouraged, Robertson warned his readers not to stop the basics of everyday life, reminding them that in all this change the basics of worship, work, and marriage were to continue. When Robertson first broke ground for his new television station, on June 5, 1967, the day the Six-Day War began in Israel, he read aloud the Luke 21:24 Scripture concerning Jerusalem. For more than twenty years he has remained consistent in his view that this generation is like no other because of the fulfillment of this prophecy.[25]

However, from 1977 to 1982, Robertson viewed this verse through the lens of Ezekiel. Not until 1983 did the Book of Joel add to his perspective. Ezekiel prepared him for conflict in the Middle East and for an economic depression. He wrote a special edition of "Perspective" in February 1980, entitled "Prophetic Insights for the 'Decade of Destiny,' " and called his predictions tentative, "not something set in stone brought down from the mountain," but intended to provoke thought.[26]

He focused on Ezekiel 38 and 39 and talked about the events following the return of the Jews to Israel. At the heart of this Bible passage is an account of an invasion of the defenseless unwalled villages of Israel. Based on his interpretation, he believed that the neighbors of Israel (Egypt, Syria, Lebanon, and Jordan) would not attack but would remain at peace with Israel, but more distant nations (Iran, Ethiopia, and the Soviet Union) would become involved directly. America would either be neutral or help Israel in this scenario. He went on to predict the downfall of the Soviet Union, the rise of an antichrist, perhaps in Europe, and the coming of Christ. These events seemed imminent to him in 1980, and again in 1982.

However, by 1983 the Book of Joel helped him to reconsider his belief that the end of history as we know it was upon us. Ezekiel was too pessimistic taken by itself. Joel and Ezekiel together gave Robertson a prophetic balance, encouraging him to engage more in politics and to construct fewer prophetic scenarios.[27]

Robertson also says that some of his predictions have not yet happened. In 1983 he recalled saying fifteen years earlier that there would be a severe financial crash in which only government securities would be safe, that a struggle would develop within the Soviet government endangering the rest of the world, and that Cuba's Fidel Castro would fall. He recently reminded his viewers that these events have not happened yet, but he is watching for them with a sense of expectation. He believes any personal prophecy must be tested by the Bible, by the church, and by events.[28]

For Robertson, God's presence and wisdom is demonstrated through specific prophecies that mention names, dates, and places. The Jerusalem prophecy of Luke would not mean much if it were not a specific place with a name. Robertson connects his own destiny to names, dates, and places, and he attributes significance to them. This gives him a sense of continuity in a very uncertain world.

For example, because CBN is located near Cape Henry where the first permanent European settlers landed on April 29, 1607, Robertson connects this event to the establishment of CBN many years later. In 1977, he deliberately dedicated the CBN satellite earth station on April 29. In 1980, the "Washington for Jesus" prayer meeting held in the nation's capital met at his suggestion on April 29. A similar rally will meet on April 29, 1988. He believes that the celebration of meaningful dates helps people to connect the past and the present with the future.[29]

Robertson reported that he first sold copies of his book *America's Dates With Destiny* in September 1986, in New Orleans. Later when Republicans announced New Orleans as the site of the 1988 Republican Convention, he saw a connection between these two events—the first sale of his book and the location of the convention in New Orleans. His book is meant to help Americans recover their liberty, and he believes that the convention can also be a part of that recovery. One wonders if in his mind New Orleans may also connect him to the presidency.[30]

The significance he sees in names, dates, and places is a hidden purpose at work connecting things providentially. It is a way of investing meaning in events, to make them say something. Certainly, by doing things the right way and at the right time he hopes to receive God's blessings. In Robertson's thinking, the world is simply alive with meaning and if we would only open our eyes we would see the invisible connection of things. He connects his own actions to what he believes God is doing and acts in the faith that he is a participant in providential history, trusting God to control the outcome.

Two "prophecies" of a sort seem to relate directly to American politics and to the 1988 campaign. In one of his more recent predictions, discussing Reagan's cabinet shake-up in January 1985, Robertson gave what in 1987 appears to be an accurate assessment of the second Reagan administration:

> If you'd like a prediction for the next couple of years, I think that Ronald Reagan is going to wind up being somewhat discredited in this second administration, second term—a lot of it because of policies that are not of his own doing . . . and his policies will no longer be at the center of it, and he's going to wind up with his Teflon image tarnished a bit. And it's regrettably so, but it will not necessarily be his policies that will do it. But it will come upon him.[31]

Robertson also makes room for God to speak through people who may or may not know that they are speaking the truth about the future. He enjoys quoting a warning prediction made by Paul G. Kirk, chairman of the Democratic National Committee. In a fund raising letter, Kirk warned Democrats against Robertson:

> P.S.: The price is now too high. Don't let 1985 become a year like 1979 when we all said Ronald Reagan can't possibly win. Because when Pat Robertson finishes his scripture reading and begins to televise his State of the Union Address, it'll be too late.[32]

Robertson says, "I will be hesitant to give Mr. Kirk the title of prophet, but who knows?" Giving the Democrats credit for prophesying his victory would be an opportunity for generosity and vindication, especially after he has suffered so much grief over the prophecy issue.

Robertson's prophetic sense of the future, whether stated in terms of reasoned expectation or as supernatural revelation, generally deals with impending trouble. When he steps out of this role he gets uncomfortable, not trusting his optimism. After all, good-news false prophets are more popular than the negative doomsday types. When he does say that good things are ahead, as he did in 1986, he says that he "could be totally wrong . . . I'm out of character right now." Perhaps he sensed as he spoke that in his new role of politician he could not speak any longer with such confidence about the future because his words would be self-serving.[33]

Robertson's view of prophecy changed dramatically in the early eighties. Prior to that, he used Ezekiel to construct prophetic scenarios, fitting pieces of the geopolitical puzzle together. With his discovery of Joel and his recovery of optimism during the Reagan years, he adjusted his thinking. Not so inclined to make predictions, his prophetic perspective today pays more attention to general trends and to specific regions of the world, such as the Persian Gulf, than to specific events. Prophecy now gives him insight into the times rather than an advance look at tomorrow's headlines. The one perspective served him well as a television commentator, the other will be much safer in politics.

Prophecy gives Robertson a sense that he lives in momentous times. He believes that the future is dimly perceived at best, even with the help of prophecies that are given to encourage responsible action, and events are not simply fated and inevitable. Jerusalem's return to Israel in 1967 confirmed his belief in the reliability of the Bible, and he thinks this one event ought to encourage people's respect for prophecy.

Because Robertson believes in a future millennium of the Kingdom of God on earth, he must resist two dangers, according to theologian Larry Hart. This belief can lead one to abandon politics while waiting for Christ's return, as evangelicals have been prone to do in recent American history, or one can be tempted to launch utopian experiments, hoping to establish God's rule by human initiative. Robertson says that he rejects both of these extremes, preferring to work for reasonable improvements in politics, confident that with God's protection, human life will continue even through the hard times prophesied by the Bible.

Robertson is aware that his approach to prophecy makes people uncomfortable, and they will not trust him if his views are eccentric and his actions unpredictable. To counter this impression, he speaks of prophecy in a relatively low-key manner and hopes that the Bible and his beliefs will be measured on their merits. Prophecy steadies him, for no matter how bad circumstances are, there are good reasons to persist in hope that God cares and things will turn out all right.

In Robertson's mind, the most significant question in the 1988 election is the willingness of Americans to have candidates speak the unpopular truth. If they genuinely want candidates with convictions and a real understanding of what the day requires of them, they must look for politicians who are willing to offend some voters to help the nation. He says the American people are now aware of this problem.

> I think they're tired of politicians. You know the definitions. A politician looks to the next election and a statesman looks to the next generation. And they're saying, "Give us some statesmen. We're tired of these guys who are making deals and always trying to cut something just to win a few votes in the next election."[34]

Politicians and preachers would often rather be popular than speak the whole truth. After all, both must appeal to people for their support or for votes. It is tempting to leave them comfortable and give them no great challenge, asking for no sacrifices. Yet if leaders only tell citizens what they want to hear, refusing to address questions of justice and righteousness, politics as well as religion suffers, and eventually leaders lose the respect of their followers.

The dilemma of every religious and political leader is how much truth can be delivered without losing public support. In simple terms, leadership, whether political or religious, must be wedded to the art of telling people only so much, not to deceive them, but so that the people will not be overwhelmed, trusting their lives into the hands of leaders. They must make real decisions on behalf of the people, knowing the practical implications. Robertson has been dealing with the public for over thirty years. He knows religious rejection and the difficulty of being candid in a public place.

In 1959, when he arrived in Virginia to begin his adventure in Christian broadcasting, Robertson found that other Christians were reluctant to associate with him because of his emphasis on the Holy Spirit and miracles and his risky pioneering television idea. He had to face the odd looks of bankers and newspaper reporters. He writes of overhearing two reporters "convulsed in laughter" after hearing him speak of his television venture. These reporters agreed to run a story on him saying, "Tell you what, Mr. Robertson, since you're the son of Senator Robertson, we will at least get a photograph, and then if we decide to run a story we can use up most of the space with your picture." It was bad enough to be thought of as a religious nut, but to be known as the son of a respected senator as well was indeed a strange combination. Perhaps this young Yale Law School graduate thought, as he listened to those reporters laughing, "I'll show you yet I'm worthy of respect."[35]

Robertson may never gain the respect of journalists or bankers. He has been honored by some preachers, and he may win the respect of politicians. Perhaps politicians, like preachers, understand shame more intimately than do bankers and journalists.

In practical terms, the prophecies from the Bible that mean the most to Robertson today deal with revival. Finding reason to hope for revival in the Book of Joel gives him confidence that genuine religion will not die. He thinks that spiritual recovery will lead to a renaissance of democracy and to a more secure world.

· 13 ·
Robertson
Meets the Press

♦ *How is the press handling Robertson's candidacy?*
♦ *What do interviews with him reveal?*
♦ *What limits press coverage?*

In view of the renewed interest in religion, the politics of Robertson take on additional significance. Religious candidates are judged not just for their politics but also for their faithfulness to their beliefs. No one loves a hypocrite, especially in public life, and a religious broadcaster will most certainly be scrutinized closely. Secular writers, journalists, and politicians, some of whom are learning to respect the Bible, are critical of Robertson, judging how accurately he follows the Bible. It seems ironic that he will be held accountable to biblical standards by the press and by qualified though sometimes irreverent critics, much like Abraham was corrected by foreign kings.[1]

Robertson's early steps into politics brought a quick response from the media, led by the networks, the *Washington Post,* and the *New York Times*. Requests for interviews poured in, averaging over two hundred a week. Well over two thousand articles, including six major cover stories, dealt with Robertson between January and September 1986.[2] Coping with this deluge, Joe Gray, CBN's vice-president of public relations, estimates that he himself averaged at least one interview per day. He says that the initial group of reporters he spoke to were against Robertson and his candidacy.

> I can recall one young lady with a major news network who was absolutely hostile, not that she didn't like Pat, but that we were Christian. Before she left we noticed a complete change in her attitude and she was actually friendly after spending the better part of a day with us.[3]

Some reporters appeared fearful when they visited CBN. They wondered if Christians were going to "lay hands" on them and pray for them while speaking in tongues. Instead, shown courtesy and respect, most overcame their preconceptions, according to Gray, and did a good job reporting the basic news story. Others were not fair, acting cordial and positive while at CBN, and then doing "a real hatchet job." When particular reporters earned a reputation for false journalism, misrepresenting Robertson and refusing to change their stories, he would not have any further interviews with them. But the majority, says Gray, were excellent and professional in their work.[4]

Initially, reporters concentrated exclusively on Robertson's religion, ignoring his politics. The news was that a faith-healing, tongues-speaking television evangelist was running for president. The sheer incongruity of the prospect of a charismatic president fascinated the media. The most-repeated questions were, "Will you speak in tongues in your White House speeches?" "Will you turn to the Bible for answers?" "How about moving hurricanes?" Fearing something unnatural or bizarre, equating tongues with magic or trances, reporters wondered if he would remain in control of his faculties.

Finding Robertson sane, bright, and articulate helped to allay some fears, but it also raised questions. They wondered, perhaps, if his religion was just a front—a window dressing that hid a hunger for power.[5]

Another concern of the press and the CBN public relations staff was the accusation of a lavish life-style. Reporters were given access to information on Robertson's house, cars, airplane, and income. He reported that he gave CBN more money from his book royalties than he received as a salary. More recently, during the scandals involving the PTL network, CBN worked with the National Religious Broadcasters to strengthen reporting procedures for CBN's income and expenditures. Gray reported that CBN complied fully with the NRB financial-reporting requirements.[6]

Robertson thought that he would be ignored or trivialized by the press because they opposed him. Asked when this would change, he replied, "I told them that in 1989, when I had my hand on the Bible and was being sworn in, they would finally take me out of the underdog category, and they probably won't until then."[7]

One way to handle the press's disrespect is to discount its importance. Robertson said, "There was one Republican in the White House a few years ago who said, 'Don't worry about the press, people wrap fish in yesterday's newspapers.' " It is when the story is totally untrue that he takes action; otherwise he thinks it is better to ignore any mistreatment.

Robertson often turns his religious identity into a political asset:

There is clearly a bias against evangelical Christianity in the secular press. I had eight hundred interviews last year, so I am aware of what I speak. . . . I think one thing people like is somebody who has firm beliefs and doesn't back down from them. I have learned that anytime I soften a position concerning religious matters, the press come like barracudas for blood. The answer continuously is, "I am not ashamed of my testimony of Jesus Christ. I am a believer in Jesus. I believe in the Bible. I'm not ashamed of my strong Christian faith. You're going to take me like that or you won't take me at all. That's the end of it." And when that is said in that kind of vein, there's no more argument, because we are a religiously tolerant people. If I don't make fun of the customs and deeply held beliefs of the Muhammadans or the Jewish people or the Catholics or other Protestants or of any other religious group, then they shouldn't make fun of the way I worship God. I believe that any attempt to do that will result in a backlash. I've already seen a favorable backlash.

People say, "Now wait a minute, this isn't American." It's un-American to make fun of the way a man worships God. This is a question of individual conscience, and we have to respect a man and his beliefs. That's what I learned early on in the process . . . I can't change now, regardless; I wouldn't want to.[8]

Considering the press to always be at least potentially hostile allows Robertson to be bold about his faith. He counts on the public's basic sense of fair play and respect for religion to protect him from extreme harassment. A certain amount of abuse can even turn to his advantage, winning sympathy and respect from voters.

The press is something of a new aristocracy, and while giving them a measure of deference, Robertson is enough of a country gentleman himself to resist intimidation with courtesy. He is also enough of a rabble-rouser to care little about their opinions. He says, "I am no longer fearful of jousting with the press. I have talked to some of the real tough journalists, and I think that they have given me a fair hearing. Through God's grace, I have been able to hold my own."[9]

When Robertson was invited to discuss politics with the editors of the *New York Times* he enjoyed their hospitality. The editors pressed him to support higher taxes; he favored cutting federal spending. They served him an elegant lunch, he said, with "eighteenth-century Queen Anne furniture, British sporting prints on the wall, lovely linen on the table, beautiful crystal china, and finest silver."[10]

Understanding the Press

The press itself is subject to scrutiny and increasingly vulnerable to attack. A recent study of journalism, *The Media Elite*, looks carefully at the working press in the leading television networks and newspapers. This study uncovered considerable evidence that reporters by and large share a bias based on their common experiences. Although reporters rarely falsify information, their individual perspectives and common experiences color what they write.[11]

The reporters are better paid, better educated, and more well-known than most of the people that they speak or write about. Most grew up in large cities, were educated in the best eastern universities, and voted against Reagan. They are far more liberal politically than the general population, and are suspicious of authority, wealth, and power; yet they are quick to protect their own interests and reputations. Business elites draw their contempt and envy, as do politicians.

News coverage of presidental elections in recent years has been especially negative. *The Media Elite* found that the press felt obligated to be critical of President Reagan partly because he was so popular with the public. By one estimate, in 1984 Walter Mondale had nine times more positive reporting than Reagan. The media are harder on a front-runner, and this can work to the advantage of a candidate like Robertson who rates low in general polls. If his candidacy is deemed unworthy of criticism, he escapes for a time, but if he is successful in elections, he will no longer be ignored.[12]

Either way, the press is not equipped to understand Robertson's religion or politics. Of the reporters studied in *The Media Elite*, 86 percent never or seldom attend religious services; yet 20 percent said that they are Protestant, 14 percent are Jewish, and 12 percent are Roman Catholic.

> Most have moved away from any religious heritage, and very few are regular churchgoers. . . . Most place themselves to the left of center and regularly vote the Democratic ticket. Yet theirs is not the New Deal liberalism of the underprivileged, but the contemporary social liberalism of the urban sophisticate. They favor a strong welfare state within a capitalist framework. They differ most from the general public, however, on the divisive social issues that have emerged since the 1960s—abortion, gay rights, affirmative action, etc. Many are alienated from the "system" and quite critical of America's world role. They would like to strip traditional power brokers of their influence and empower black leaders, consumer groups, intellectuals, and . . . the media.[13]

The evidence points to an intense conflict ahead prompted by a press that will use its elite position to attack anything it considers threatening to a more open and tolerant America.

Robertson's religion upholds the conservative moral and political standards opposed by the press. Though he calls himself a member of the press, he respects those in authority even when being critical, and he favors competition that allows strong individuals and corporations to succeed. At worst, his religion is incomprehensible to reporters, his morality scorned, his politics and economics rejected, and his candidacy treated with derision mixed with fear. At best, he will be given a chance to express his views.

Larry King Interview

During the unholy "Holy Wars" of 1987, CNN's Larry King interviewed practically every Christian participant who wanted to make a statement to the nation. Having a somewhat irreverent Jewish host lent credibility to the guest by providing neutral ground. King's sharp questions raised the issues, allowing guests to make their cases without sounding like propagandists. Being a sympathetic but detached bystander, King refereed the "Holy Wars" contest impartially, entertaining the public and serving the larger interests of clarifying truth. The direct but always respectful attention that King gave to Jerry Falwell, Oral Roberts, Pat Robertson, and others was not as dangerous, it seemed, as letting newsmen write the news. Giving viewers a chance to call in and ask questions also helped to create a fair and open climate.

No Christian public figure distanced himself farther from the religious television scandals than Robertson. He wanted nothing to do with the PTL debacle and regretted statements made by Oral Roberts. Appearing on "Larry King Live" in the middle of the revelations about Jim and Tammy Bakker, he commented,

> I must say, well, I am a little surprised and obviously dumbfounded at what is coming out; but nevertheless, I don't see it hurting me because people understand that I'm different, and that Billy Graham

is different . . . God's cleaning house, that's necessary and I applaud it. If something is in there that shouldn't be, let's get it out and get rid of it . . . I think Jerry Falwell has been very statesmanlike in the way he has worked.[14]

King asked him if he could forgive Bakker. Robertson responded that God had not called him "to be a judge." He would forgive Bakker, but there would be consequences—money might have to be paid back, and they would live with a terrible disgrace that could not be gotten rid of simply by forgiveness.[15]

Robertson's own war record in Korea came up for discussion next. Accused of shirking combat duty in Korea by former Congressman Paul J. McCloskey of California, Robertson had sued him for libel in the Washington, D.C., Federal District Court.[16] King asked him why he sued McCloskey when this would draw more attention to these charges. He replied,

> Well, I was faced with a real dilemma. I have done a lot of things when I was young that, if somebody wanted to charge me with them, I would have to say, "You are absolutely right." This just does not happen to be one of them. I did not use any influence in the service. I went where I was ordered. I was in the headquarters of the first marine division on the border of North Korea. The marine corps called that combat. So I was doing what I was told to do, and I came home and was discharged honorably.[17]

King asked him if he had documents that he could produce in his defense. Robertson replied that the accusations were based on hearsay and all the evidence that he submitted in court pointed the other way.

One of the strengths of public one-on-one interviews is that a series of questions can be asked and answered in a sensible order, unlike press conferences where many reporters ask unrelated questions. In his interview with Robertson, King asked carefully prepared questions designed to probe his relations with other Republicans. He wondered whether Robertson would consider it a victory if he finished second in Iowa and in New Hampshire. Robertson said that he fully intended to win both of those races but that the press would call a second-place finish a huge success.

He questioned Robertson's alleged takeover of precincts in the South Carolina Republican Party. Robertson responded that his supporters in South Carolina had been taken advantage of by Bush forces, particularly in Richland County.

> Our people won that going away. We got one hundred black people into the precincts . . . it had never happened before in the Republican party. Seventy of them became precinct delegates, and all seventy were disqualified. I am a Southern Baptist, and when you hear somebody calling a Southern Baptist a Nazi, you begin to wonder who it is that's running things down there. The rest of the state has been very cordial. We are working beautifully with the Republican Party all over the state.[18]

Asked if Republican regulars were afraid of Robertson, he replied that they were not so much afraid of him as positive toward Bush. He did not acknowledge in any way a divisive impact on the party although there is evidence of sharp conflict between party regulars and Robertson supporters in some states. He claimed that he was a loyal Republican who abhorred discord within the party and would support the Republican nominee no matter who it was, unless that person had used "dirty tricks" against him in the campaign.

During questions on "Larry King Live," a viewer called in and commented, "About a year ago or so, you said that a critic of yours died of a heart attack because he criticized you, and you said God struck him down." King asked, "Could you conceive of saying that, Pat?" He responded that he had been criticized so often by so many people—"I am talking about tens of thousands of people"—that he could not imagine someone dying because they attacked him. He said he had never said such a thing.[19]

A person called in from New York claiming to be an editor of *Playboy* magazine. He had attended a Robertson rally in September

1986, he said, and had observed a Robertson campaign worker grabbing a protesting homosexual and shouting, "Shut up, Satan, that is why you are all dying of AIDS." He claimed this person clearly represented Robertson. Robertson denied any responsibility. "That's nonsense, how can I be held responsible for some usher in New York?" He simply regretted the alleged happening.[20]

These questions from Larry King's viewers presumed that Robertson's religion would be divisive, making it difficult if not impossible for him to gain the Republican nomination. The conventional wisdom of the press was that he could represent a religious minority in politics, but not all Americans. In short, these people thought that Robertson's religion gave him enough political followers to enter the race, but not enough to win.

Commenting on this after Senators Gary Hart and Joseph Biden dropped out of the Democratic race, columnist Jeff Greenfield wrote that religious candidates like Robertson and Jackson, while not acceptable to most Americans, could remain in the presidential race with their character flaws and political stumbles because their supporters would continue to back them blindly, despite sins and errors that would torpedo another candidate. He suggested that there was, in effect, a double standard operating to favor religious politicians. He claimed the press was not as tough on Robertson and Jackson, since they believe that they cannot be elected, and that any press exposure of their weaknesses would be minimized or ignored by their religious constituents.

> Since the press does not expect either to be a serious Presidential contender, neither the press nor the political establishment has thus far held either to the standards by which a conventional politician would be measured.
>
> So what do you suppose would happen if the press published highly credible reports that the Rev. Pat Robertson had materially distorted his accomplishments and background? And what do you suppose would happen if the press published highly credible reports that the Rev. Jesse Jackson had a track record of utterly chaotic financial mismanagement throughout his public career?

We don't have to guess at the answers. The fact is, both of these men of the cloth have already been subject to highly critical reports dealing precisely with such transgressions. And the best guess is that neither of these political mavericks will suffer much because of them.[21]

The net effect of close scrutiny of candidates, Greenfield concluded, was that "The way things are going, by next summer they may be the only two people left in the race." He may have meant that the press was being too critical of candidates or that Hart, Biden, Robertson, and Jackson are all equally flawed, and that the only reason the latter two survived was that their supporters protected them. No doubt the lack of strong loyalty from millions of people made Hart and Biden more vulnerable when their faults were exposed by the press. But what must be looked at more closely is the assumption that Robertson's moral character and behavior is no better than the unfortunates, Hart and Biden, and the belief that the press would go easy on him and his supporters would protect him.

Ted Koppel Interview

On the same day that Greenfield's analysis appeared, the *Wall Street Journal* revealed that Robertson's first son had been born ten weeks after his marriage to Adelia "Dede" Elmer, now his wife of thirty-three years: "They were married secretly on August 27, 1954, in Elkton, Maryland, known as the venue for quick marriages."[22] Robertson concealed his marriage and the birth of his son from fellow law school students and they did not live together as a family until Robertson moved to New York, the *Wall Street Journal* claimed. This revelation brought the issue of his personal integrity to the fore.

Robertson defended his action as a legitimate protection of his family and their reputation, and said he had done the honorable thing. He had not lied about his wedding date, but had concealed the fact that his first child was conceived out of wedlock. The *Washington Post* reported,

In an interview with the *Washington Post* late last July, Robertson indicated that he had gotten married on his birthday, March 22, in 1954. He was asked then, "When and where did you get married?" He replied, "We were married, we began I'm trying to think, it was thirty-three years ago, March 22, we celebrate, my birthday."

Asked about this yesterday, Robertson said, "I did give (the *Post*) an honest answer." He said he and his wife have always considered March 22, 1954, the day they were married because "our son was conceived on that day." He said he has always celebrated his anniversary on that day. The couple's legal marriage on August 27 "to us, wasn't any big deal," he added.

Robertson said he has not previously revealed the actual date of his marriage because "this was a man trying to protect his family." But he said that when he decided to run for President, he expected the information would come out. He said he has no complaint with the *Wall Street Journal* because "they said exactly what happened."[23]

However, as reporters began to pursue the account the next day, Robertson blasted the press for an invasion of privacy.

It is outrageous to intrude into a man's family and to try to do damage to a man's wife and children under the guise of journalism . . . To dig back to somebody's family 33 years ago and try to resurrect some skeleton is in my estimation outrageous because the skeleton isn't there.[24]

When the press suggested that this concealment was part of a pattern of dishonesty, that he misrepresented facts about his past accomplishments as well as hiding his faults, Robertson categorically denied the charges, saying, "this isn't going to have one bit of impact negatively on me because the people who support me understand forgiveness."[25] This reinforced the opinion that religious public figures will be let off easy and won't suffer consequences like other candidates.

As the nation pondered the news of Robertson's earlier wrongdoing and considered the issue of his honesty, conservative religious people did, in fact, seriously question the significance of this press criticism. If Robertson could be morally discredited, even his most loyal followers would find it hard to continue their support, and without them his candidacy would be over.

Knowing that he was possibly at a make-or-break point, Robertson welcomed the public forum he had found earlier during the PTL scandal—an interview with a tough and reputable journalist. This time it was Ted Koppel of ABC, on the October 8, 1987, "Nightline" program.

Koppel suggested that the issues raised could end Robertson's campaign. "Nightline" correspondent Jeff Greenfield narrated film clips highlighting Robertson speaking on moral, family, and religious values: "We must bring back the old-fashioned concept of moral restraint and abstinence before marriage." Then Greenfield reviewed charges that Robertson himself had distorted facts about his past:

1. A Robertson claim that he is on the board of directors of a local bank. In fact, he is on an advisory board.
2. A claim that he is a tax lawyer. In fact, he flunked the bar exam and never practiced law.
3. A claim that he made sixty thousand dollars a year from CBN; in fact, he made much more . . . his full income has never been disclosed.
4. Most seriously, former Congressman Paul McCloskey has charged that during the Korean War, Robertson used the influence of his father, a United States Senator, to get out of hazardous combat duty. Robertson is suing McCloskey for libel. His biography no longer calls him a combat veteran.[26]

Koppel accused Robertson of preaching high moral standards while concealing his own less-then-honorable past and asked him directly, "Don't you feel like a hypocrite?" Robertson replied that for years he had spoken publicly of the sins of his youth, saying he had "lived a rather raucous life."

I was engaged in wine, women, and song on a number of continents. I have freely acknowledged that over and over again, but I've also acknowledged that I had an experience with Jesus Christ, we call it being "born again," that radically changed my life, and I have said that to the press on a number of instances. But for the last thirty-one years, I'll take my stand that I have lived a life of extraordinary probity, and I've been an extraordinarily faithful husband and father.[27]

There was nothing hypocritical or dishonest, he thought, about covering his marriage date for his family's sake. Later in the interview, Koppel commented, "I would have done exactly the same thing to protect my children or my wife."

Robertson's claims about his Korean War record were then examined. Koppel quoted Robertson's campaign biography (Americans for Robertson) saying, "In 1951, he was sent to the Far East where he served as the Assistant Adjutant of the First Marine Division in combat in Korea."

Robertson responded, "That's exactly right," and Koppel objected that Robertson's division was in combat but that Robertson was not. Robertson was assigned to the forward headquarters of the division that was about three miles away from the enemy lines. The Korean Service Medal and the three bronze battle stars which he had claimed were given him were actually awards given to the entire unit and not to individuals.

Robertson agreed with these basic facts but would not agree that he had distorted them in his biography. Koppel pressed him on whether he had been in the trenches, as a definition of *combat*. He stated that since he was attached to the headquarters of a combat unit, he was in combat as the marine corps defined the term and saw no reason to withdraw his claim. Robertson wanted his war record recognized.

Robertson's campaign biography listed him as serving on the "Norfolk Metropolitan Board of Directors of the United Virginia Bank, an 8.7 billion dollar banking institution." Koppel said this was not true. Robertson responded that he was on the board of the

Norfolk branch of the United Virginia Bank. Both claimed to have talked to the bank that day for clarification. Koppel objected that the branch bank was not worth $8.7 billion. Robertson said the parent institution was worth that much, but called this "hair splitting" over different interpretations of the same words.

Koppel then questioned Robertson's claim that he had attended graduate school at the University of London. Robertson had attended a summer art and architecture course after graduating from college, but he was not taking it for credit toward a graduate degree. Robertson said that both undergraduates and graduates attended the class:

> There was a special course set up for American students to study the arts in Britain today. It was a wonderful summary—T. S. Eliot read his poetry to us, we went down to Coventry Gardens and saw the ballet, we studied architecture, we studied art at the National Gallery, we learned about Britain, it was a marvelous course, and it was study for me as a graduate student.[28]

He could not understand, he said, why the press was attacking him on such fine distinctions.

Koppel explained his reasons for concern. Robertson "is known as a man who holds himself and everyone else to the highest standards." Therefore, when his campaign résumé made it appear that he was in combat, on the board of directors of a large bank, and had attended graduate school in London, there was a pattern of inflated claims and inaccurate campaign hype that deserved to be exposed. Since Robertson had tremendous accomplishments he could be justly proud of that he thought qualified him for consideration as a presidential candidate, there was no reason to "puff things up a little bit," Koppel said.

Robertson saw it differently. He stood by all the facts in his résumé, but he said, "I didn't set my résumé up to be analyzed under a microscope . . . and if it isn't accurate, I'll be glad to change it." He said the accusations of the press revealed more about the nature of the press than about his character.

You play this game of "I gotcha," and I want you to know that the sharks are starting to have a feeding frenzy but the blood just ain't in the water. I'm not going down on this one, I have no intention of it, because frankly, in my estimation, this is ridiculous.[29]

Koppel responded that Gary Hart and Joe Biden probably felt the same way when they were attacked. Was Robertson's position any different?

Robertson replied, "I have tried to live a life of extraordinary integrity," and said he cared deeply for even small points of truthfulness. Then why did Robertson remove some material from his biography, *Shout It From the Housetops*, Koppel asked, when it seemed that it might damage his candidacy? Robertson defended himself by saying that the old complete edition was still being given out by CBN and Americans for Robertson, and that there was, in fact, no cover-up taking place. The old version of the book "is a very good book," he said.

Koppel then raised the question of whether these issues and the revelation that he was not married when his son was conceived would make it difficult to gain support among the general population. Robertson thought the opposite was in fact true; the news of his earlier moral failure would make it easier for people to relate to him.

People will now look at me and say, "This man has been through some of the problems I've had," because people in America are hurting, and I have a vision that would encompass the hopes and dreams of all Americans. . . . So I see, frankly, instead of what has come out and been very painful, instead of it hurting, it's going to help, because it will help broaden [support], because people will say, "He has been where I've been."[30]

When asked if he would have left the race if he'd done what Hart or Biden had done, Robertson said he would have. Current sexual immorality and flagrant plagiarism were not excusable for any candidate. He had not lied to protect his family, he had simply covered this earlier disgrace, he said, and he had not lied on his résumé and could only be fairly accused of being less precise than some wanted him to be. He counted on the good judgment of the American people to protect him from this unjustified effort of the press to undermine his record of integrity.

The "Nightline" interview demonstrated that the press will hold Robertson to the highest possible moral standards. If he says anything that appears to be self-serving exaggeration, whether intended or not, he will be held accountable. Doubtless, other questions about Robertson's record will be raised. In fact, two of the issues mentioned—the right of Robertson to call himself a tax attorney and the salary and benefits paid to him by CBN—were not dealt with by Koppel.

Robertson will not escape scrutiny because he is religious. He may even benefit from attacks by the press, especially if he is given a chance to defend himself as he was by Koppel. If Robertson had lied about his marriage, war record, business career, and education, his candidacy would have ended on the night of October 8 under the direct questioning of Koppel. Only the truth protected him in such a public arena. His followers, no matter how loyal, would not have made any difference.

Robertson used deliberate silence, ambiguity, and word choice to make his record appear as strong as possible. This was not dishonesty, Koppel concluded, so much as self-flattery born out of his defensiveness about his lack of experience in government—Vice-President Bush and Senator Dole did not need to use these tactics. He advised that Robertson's record would stand without the slightest overstatement if it was as demonstrably superior as Robertson claimed.

Koppel had begun his questioning by quoting from the Bible passage that Robertson had used as the title of his book *Shout It From the Housetops:*

> There is nothing concealed that will not be disclosed, or hidden that will not be made known. What I tell you in the dark, speak in the

daylight; what is whispered in your ear, proclaim from the housetops.

Matthew 10:26, 27

Koppel viewed this as an ironic prophecy of sorts that was fulfilled when Robertson's delayed marriage was discovered by the press. Why should Robertson be upset, he said, when journalists did what the Bible said must happen?

What Koppel failed to mention was that these words of Jesus were meant to encourage the people of God to boldly proclaim the truth even under persecution. The passage said everything concealed would someday be made known, and in the interview, not only his weaknesses but Robertson's strengths in debate and his past record were put on display in a way that in the end shone to his advantage. He will, it is hoped, get rid of any self-serving lack of precision that shows up "under the microscope," as Koppel advised.

Greenfield had thought Robertson's behavior no better than Hart's or Biden's. He also saw the media failing to press its case on these issues and Christian fundamentalists protecting Robertson from criticism. None of these assumptions were correct.

Robertson's résumé represented him adequately if not perfectly. The press, in its coverage of this story, gave Robertson a beating. If there is a double standard in press treatment of Robertson, it is that he will be measured against his own ethical standards, which are far tougher than the usual political rules. Koppel said at the end of his interview, "You're very courageous to come here tonight and let me bang away at you, and I appreciate it, and I'm sure we will be talking again as the campaign goes on."

Sympathetic Christians were not willing or able to insulate Robertson from this heat, but rather considered the evidence to form their own conclusions. Any candidate caught lying in the campaign to serve his own personal political ambitions will certainly lose the respect of those taught to hate deceit.

The assumption that no one will be able to endure the searchlight of truth for very long must also take into account the role of mercy in politics, as Robertson pointed out. "Mercy and truth are met together; righteousness and peace have kissed each other" (Psalms 85:10 KJV), the Bible says, and politics has always had an element of hyperbole. This leaves room for an active press, a sympathetic public in need of leaders, and less than perfect candidates.

Robertson has one thing to overcome that is far more difficult than the investigations of the press. If his character and record are as solid as he thinks, his performance on "Nightline" demonstrated that he can defend himself well and keep his perspective. What is much harder to deal with is the way the press can ignore him and what he advocates if it chooses to do so. For many years, religion has been considered a dying irrelevance by the media. Shaking that presumption will take nothing less than unusual circumstances and a truly remarkable political campaign.

Press Coverage

CBN television and the "700 Club" have the task of providing coverage of the presidential campaign for their viewers without becoming a partisan instrument of the Americans for Robertson organization. Like all religious television, CBN is protected from censorship by the free exercise of religion and the freedom of the press provisions of the Constitution. CBN can support Robertson editorially, yet the network is also regulated by the Federal Communications Commission. CBN News plans to cover the presidential election—the primaries, the conventions, and the general election; however, the "700 Club" obviously will be under pressure to restrain its coverage to protect its own operations from criticism and possible regulation.[31]

The first significant test of CBN's Robertson coverage occurred following the report of his late marriage date. For the entire week the "700 Club" had been dealing with the theme "Families in Crisis." On Friday, Dede responded to the news reports. Hostess Susan Howard asked her how she was handling the pressure. Dede answered,

When I went to bed on Wednesday night, I wanted to go live on the third floor for the rest of my life, and then I got up Thursday morning and I began to feel this buoyancy and this joy that I had lost. I had even questioned the Lord, "Lord, why did You allow this to happen? You told us You'd protect us, and yet You've let this happen." Actually this is probably the greatest protection He could have given us because now we have nothing to hide.[32]

When Dede first found out that she was pregnant thirty-three years ago, Pat had responded, "It can't be!" She said it had been hard coping with "being married to a man who didn't really want to be married to me," but following their marriage and after experiencing a spiritual rebirth, he had done a "total about-face."

Silence had protected their family reputation—now disclosure released her to deal with this painful subject in a positive way to help other women in similar circumstances. This felt to her like a "chastisement from the Lord," but was meant, she thought, for their benefit and that of others in the long run.

Undoubtedly, this "700 Club" program, though not explicitly political, benefited Robertson's campaign. It showed him working out of a difficult situation, turning his early marital failure into a stable family with healthy relationships. His son Tim co-hosted the program on which his mother appeared, and his mere presence testified to his father's faithfulness.

Columnists not known to favor Robertson's politics or religion noted this and boldly defended him. Mike Royko wrote:

This isn't something Robertson or his wife wanted anyone to know about. They don't believe it's anybody else's business. It's not something I wanted to know about, because I agree with Robertson—it's none of my business. Or yours, or the *Wall Street Journal*'s.[33]

Robertson, Royko said, had made no secret of his early rebellious years. Royko argued that Robertson is not a hypocrite for advocating sexual chastity, and both the marital difficulty and his later handling of it is in no way comparable to the Gary Hart case. There is something quaint, he thought, in having Robertson so attacked "in an era when hundreds of thousands of unmarried couples openly live together."[34]

Others in the press were not sympathetic to Royko's position. In fact, the *Richmond News Leader* called on Robertson to leave the campaign. Not disclosing his marriage date, the paper argued, provided further grounds for disqualifying him from the candidacy.[35]

The contribution of a secular press in handling public controversy is especially important to religious political figures. There must be settings for healthy open discussion if Robertson is to flourish in politics. Winning the support of skeptical people requires a neutral forum. On the other hand, finding a respectful neutrality like that provided by Larry King and Ted Koppel will not always be possible. Robertson will have to take what he can get in the adversarial relationships that usually characterize dealings between politicians and reporters.

Robertson's switch to politics generates humor. The seeming incongruity of his running for public office inspired one of the better cartoons done by Berke Breathed in his *Bloom County*.[36]

Hodge Podge the rabbit, Portnoy the groundhog, Cutter John the paraplegic, and Opus the penguin are playing "Star Trek," riding in a field in their wheel chair.

Hodge Podge:	"Our mission: To seek out and destroy new and amoral life forms."
Portnoy:	"Sounds wishy-washy."
Cutter John:	"Analyze, Mr. Spock."
Opus:	"Wishy-Washy is an emotional term. I am a being of *pure logic*."
Hodge Podge:	(pointing a gun at the grass) "Something's hiding in the grass! You there! Who are ya?"
Milo Bloom:	(dressed in a red devil costume with his hands up) "Just a L'il Ol' Secular Humanist."

Robertson Meets the Press

Hodge Podge:	"Hands up! Watcha up to, Humanist Heathen?"
Milo Bloom:	(with his hands up)
	"Been infiltrating the government, schools, and
	textbooks with our evil hidden agenda."
Hodge Podge:	"Conspirators! What's that agenda?"
Milo Bloom:	(with hands up)
	"World Socialism, public education,
	feminism, big shoulder pads for women,
	unisex bathrooms and a godless society
	based solely on pure logic."
Hodge Podge:	(confused) "Pure Logic?"
Hodge Podge:	(turning and pointing the gun at Opus)
	"Hands up, Spock!"
Opus:	"Me? I'm illogical! I'm illogical!
	I love Pat Robertson!"

· 14 ·
Public
Responses

♦ *How has the Jewish community dealt with Robertson?*
♦ *What are other groups saying?*
♦ *Is the general public open to him?*

Robertson faced numerous unexpected obstacles launching his candidacy in 1987, enough to have sunk his ship several times over, yet the *Washington Post* commented, "Robertson Campaign Persists." The "Holy Wars" broke in the spring, the IRS investigated CBN, Robertson sued Paul McCloskey for libel, the petition signature campaign stalled, contributions dropped at CBN, and polls showed a larger than usual percentage of the American public hostile to him. Despite these shocks, the *Post* noted that Robertson's organization continued to win enough support for a serious race. Bush's own regional directors, assessing the progress of their campaign in March, judged that Robertson was the best-organized candidate in the South, and he did well in Michigan and South Carolina.

"The Robertson forces came on like gangbusters," said John Courson, a South Carolina State Senator and GOP national committeeman. "It was like a hurricane coming in from the Caribbean. We were blindsided."[1]

The *Post* reported Marc Nuttle, Robertson's campaign manager and strategist, saying that the voter turnout in 1988 could be so low that any candidate who relied solely on the party regulars to elect him, without personally loyal supporters, would be a sure loser. "If your base is the party, you're in trouble," Nuttle said. Robertson, on the other hand, had a solid core of support, was well-known by the general public, in that most recognized his name, and most liked him. Nuttle thought the memory of Jimmy Carter, the first "born-again" president, would hurt Robertson more than the "Holy Wars." People would not vote for Robertson just because of his religion.[2]

Jewish Responses

Jewish responses to Robertson are generally negative. He supports Israel and defends the separation of church and state, but his broadcasting record of evangelism even among Jews, his identity as a minister, his close relationship with the New Right, and his support for religion in public places, especially in schools, makes his political task in the Jewish community extremely difficult if not impossible. The simplest Jewish response is to dismiss Robertson as someone who does not belong in presidential politics at all, and to hope that he returns quickly to religious broadcasting. Separation of church and state protected the United States from most religious persecution, and many Jewish people think that Robertson's candidacy undermines this separation and endangers their community.[3]

The National Executive Council of the American Jewish Committee (AJC) invited Dr. Herbert Titus, a close associate of Robertson, to address their 1986 annual meeting. The Council also invited Dr. John Buchanan, the chairman of People of the American Way, and a vigorous opponent of Robertson, to share the platform with Titus. Buchanan opposed teaching creation in public schools because, he said, it is a religious doctrine and not science. Titus addressed an entirely different subject, namely, the belief in creation as an assumption of the American founders undergirding their belief in liberty. Like ships passing in the night, these two presentations addressed separate issues. Titus said that belief in God supported liberty, and Buchanan believed that creation should not be taught in public school science classrooms.[4]

The discussion following these presentations confirmed one important fact. The American Jewish Committee is aware of significant new questions about religion and its rightful place in American public life. At one time it appeared that banishing religion from politics and government protected Jews, but this is no longer so evidently true. There are "many vexing and profound questions that surround these issues," said Rabbi A. James Rudin. But his concern was not so much to recover a place for religion as to limit its influence.[5]

In the November 19, 1986, *Wall Street Journal*, a former vice-president of the Minnesota chapter, Elliot Rothenberg, took the national organization to task for opposing Robertson. Rothenberg objected to a fund-raising letter sent out by the American Jewish Committee singling out Robertson as "an exemplar of a larger and, from our perspective, dangerous trend," threatening "the very foundation of our democracy." The American Jewish Committee letter made no reference to anti-Semitism by Robertson, but it did accuse him of advocating instruction on creation in schools and of having reactionary views on both the Constitution and women's rights. Rothenberg asked what these issues had to do with the Jewish community or democracy. The committee, he claimed, was simply defending a liberal agenda that Robertson happened to disagree with.[6]

American Jewish Committee leaders denied Rothenberg's charge that they were promoting a private political agenda in the name of separation of church and state. Pointing out recent abuses by the religious right, they warned:

Fundamentalist candidates claim to know God's will and work to change social policy to conform to it. To an unprecedented degree, the 1986 elections were characterized by office-seekers identifying themselves with divine guidance and their opponents with Satan. Political philosophies and programs ought to be debated vigorously. This can't happen when one group claims divine sanction.

Fundamentalists advocate the doctrine of "original intent," which purports to understand the thoughts of the Founding Fathers and declare any judicial evolution since then as illegitimate. This would roll back decades of gains on civil rights and religious pluralism. Even more serious is the fundamentalists' attack on the schools. They support censorship of books with which they disagree and introduction of sectarian religious observances.[7]

In the troubled farm economy of Iowa, the Committee also noted, there were new evidences of rising anti-Jewish sentiment Some bankrupt farmers blamed eastern Jewish bankers for their fate. Given Iowa's importance in the coming presidential election, there was a strong desire in the Jewish community to halt this poison before it spread further in American politics. Robertson's position, blaming banks for their contribution to the nation's economic woes, could conceivably encourage others to blame Jews. In difficult days, politics will turn ugly.[8]

Standing before an Anti-Defamation League meeting in Boston, Robertson was asked about comments attributed to one of his CBN staff that Jewish reporters somehow have less of a handle on the truth. Robertson refused to defend the alleged statement. "Thank the Lord, I didn't say that one. I was not even misquoted; I did not say that, so I can't defend it." Pressed to denounce the alleged statement, he refused to comment. He said that after ad-libbing in public for ninety minutes a day for twenty years, he had enough mistakes of his own without having to handle the comments of others. Certainly, he thought, getting the facts straight, as every reporter must, had nothing to do with religious faith.[9]

Not satisfied with this reply, someone said, "I am a Christian. Do I have a better shot at getting at the truth than my Jewish friend beside me here?" Rather than simply saying yes or no, Robertson went on the offensive:

I'll tell you the words of Jesus, and you can argue with Him. He said, "I am the way, the truth, and the life." So, that was the statement of Jesus Christ. If a person believes that Jesus is Messiah, then that person believes that He is the embodiment of truth, because that's what He said. If somebody doesn't believe that, then of course they don't believe that He is the embodiment of the truth. But the orthodox Christian, if you will, would believe that Jesus Christ is the fullest expression of truth. The Apostle Paul, who was a Pharisee and was brought up at the feet of the great Rabbi Gamaliel, said, "In Him are hid all the treasures of the Godhead bodily." Now, that's New Testament theology.[10]

Still not satisfied, the questioner requested a further answer which Robertson then gave in simple terms:

My wife just had surgery. She had cancer. She had a mastectomy. The best doctor in town was Jewish. We got him to operate on my wife because he was the best. Now, I would much rather have a Jewish surgeon than a Christian butcher.[11]

Earlier, in Michigan, Robertson had praised Christians for their patriotism and hard work on his behalf. He had claimed they loved God and country more than others did. Picking up this statement, a questioner at the Anti-Defamation meeting asked him to repudiate it. He refused, claiming that in the context, praise for Christians in middle America who favored traditional morals and the Reagan agenda more than most citizens was not too radical and was not meant to cast aspersions on anyone. There clearly were people who were not as patriotic as these Christians.[12]

One listener commented that rabbis all over the nation attacked Robertson by name in their sermons for saying that non-Christians were termites that should be fumigated. Robertson quickly explained that when he had made a reference to termites he was talking about people who called themselves Christians, who were subverting their own religion. In particular, he was referring to a Baptist religion professor he had debated who rejected the Bible and the traditions of Christian theology and yet continued to teach in a Baptist college. Robertson said this professor did not deserve to teach in that school because he was violating its integrity. "Now, that's what a termite does. He moves into a house, lives off the structure, and undermines it." Robertson thought that such a person should leave and go to another school.

Throughout these interchanges before the Anti-Defamation League he kept his good humor. When asked, "How detailed is God's plan for your life?" Robertson could not resist saying, "I'll let you know in 1989." He looked for common ground, refusing to be kept on the defensive for long. Christians, he said, had a mandate to proclaim the Gospel of Jesus Christ and on this there could be no compromise. Jews lost more of their children to secular forces and to apathy than to Christian conversion, so he could not agree that his evangelism as a broadcaster was much of a threat; and as a Christian politician, he had

. . . one absolute mandate, and that is to defend to the death the right of all people to believe, to practice, and to proclaim whatever belief they have without any hindrance whatsoever. This is not a question of toleration. Toleration is not what we're talking about. It's an absolute right of all people to be free of government intervention in what they believe. And it would be absolutely repugnant to the evangelical position to try to impose any type of spiritual discipline, if you will, on the rest of the nation. We believe in pluralism, we believe in freedom.[13]

He appealed to them to consider once again the basis of cooperation between Jews and Christians. They faced common foes in secularism and in communism and needed to join together to make room for voluntary public expressions of faith in God. He also asked to be quoted accurately and in context and objected that every slip of his tongue was a weapon seized to end his political life.[14]

The outcome of Robertson's conversations and debates with the Jewish community is not yet clear, but this could prove to be an extremely interesting and fruitful dialogue. It could also degenerate, if either loses respect for the other. If he continues, his political career will place him before the Jewish community again and again, to allow him to be questioned and to work to reassure them of his intentions.[15]

Responses of the Clergy

Religious and secular papers have interviewed local pastors for their opinions of Robertson. Not surprisingly, they showed little unity in a New England sample taken in the fall of 1986. Some simply said, "If God has called him into politics, I'll support him," but those who opposed his candidacy thought him a better religious broadcaster than politician. There was considerable skepticism that his candidacy would be taken seriously or that it could go beyond raising significant issues. Reporters dealing with these responses saw no firm consensus. There was considerable resistance to the idea that evangelical Christians would support Robertson simply because of his religion.[16]

In Robertson's own backyard of Tidewater, Virginia, the responses of the clergy to reporters in the fall of 1986 were similar to those of New England. The pastor of Christ and Saint Luke's Episcopal Church, the Reverend James Samuels, was said to be open to a Robertson presidency but wanted it clear that his vote, no matter who he voted for, would not be a "Christian" vote but simply a political decision on his part. Some pastors focused on the danger of Robertson speaking in God's name or pushing his religion on others. A constant refrain was, "We need good moral leaders, but. . . ." There seemed to be respect for Robertson's character and his leadership, but little confidence, by then, in his decision to be a politician. Some of those surveyed, particularly a Unitarian pastor and a Conservative Jewish rabbi, boldly opposed the candidacy. The remainder appeared neutral, preferring to observe from the sidelines, uncommitted one way or the other. Clerical interviews uncovered something of a skeptical openness to

Robertson, a "show me and I'll think about it" attitude. Most responses were diplomatically stated to protect the pastor from criticism.[17]

Robertson has had little contact with the Roman Catholic hierarchy. However, conservative political commentator Joseph Sobran thought that he was finally giving Catholics what they needed—"some political leadership." He thought that Robertson demonstrated in Michigan his ability to activate conservative Catholics and evangelicals. His confidence and his desire to win was breaking a loser's mentality in American religious communities:

> I saw Robertson bring a crowd to its feet with one of his fervent, homey speeches. Tall, courtly, soft-spoken, he conveys deep feeling. He's also a brilliant man of many talents, all of the sort liberals find it hard to appreciate: in touch with people, skilled in business, able to defend ideas that are unfashionable though not unpopular. His obvious handicap is that he's typecast as the "fundamentalist" candidate.[18]

Sobran thought that Robertson genuinely desired leadership and was prepared to go out and do what it took to get it. This spirit of "do or die" combined with a gentle touch attracted people who have never found in the Republican Party the courage or the sensitivity to understand their needs or desires. Family issues are crucial to Roman Catholics, says Sobran, and Robertson got Catholic votes without having the support of their bishops.

In Louisiana, a reporter asked Robertson about anti-Catholic statements made by his supporter evangelist Jimmy Swaggart. He replied,

> Well, if somebody supports me, what it means is that they are embracing my platform, I'm not embracing theirs. I'm a person of harmony and moderation. I have put out a hand of friendship and

fellowship to Roman Catholics, to various Protestant denominations, because I think as Christians, the essential thing is to find those points in which we agree, and emphasize those, and not spend time tearing one another down on points about which we disagree. Obviously there are disagreements. I'm a Southern Baptist, and I have my beliefs and I'm going to stick with them. I'm very strong in my beliefs, but I'm not going to criticize some other denomination because they believe differently than I do. I'm going to do everything I can to love them and to find common ground with them. If people want to help me politically, they will be helping that kind of approach to government and to life, not a divisive one. I'm not that kind of a person.[19]

Robertson refused to deny Swaggart the right to his convictions on issues of theology but at the same time made it clear that his relationship with religious groups would be inclusive and cooperative.

Bridging gaps between denominations, getting them to work together, and respecting their differences is something Robertson has done for years at CBN. Using this interdenominational skill in broadcasting to bring political unity will be a further test of his skills and of the willingness of Christians to work with other groups. Asked if his Southern Baptist loyalties would alienate and divide, he replied,

I think that in 1960 when John Kennedy ran, there was a spectre raised that he would be a puppet of the Pope in Rome. He dispelled that concept with one speech in Houston, Texas. He was favored by the liberal press, and so that statement was given great credibility all across the country. I have made similar statements and will continue to do so, and I would hope that the press of our nation would give my statements the same weight they gave his.[20]

Response of the Black Community

The "700 Club"'s black co-host, Ben Kinchlow, joined Robertson in January of 1977. For over a decade he helped to end the ethnic isolation of Protestant white religion. A fairly large percentage of the guests and the coverage of the "700 Club" deals with subjects of interest to the black community.

For example, in 1987, Marine Corps Corporal Arnold Bracy, a black soldier, was accused of helping the Soviets spy on the American Embassy in Moscow, where he was stationed. Bracy denied this. Brought back to the United States and held in Virginia, he was released from the investigation for lack of evidence. CBN immediately interviewed him and afterwards he held a press conference on the premises of CBN. Talking to reporters, he stood directly in front of a huge oil painting, twenty-eight-feet long, depicting the flight of Joseph, Mary, and Jesus to Egypt as King Herod slaughtered the innocent children of Bethlehem. The obvious message of the painting was that political oppression was never far from genuine religion and though God allowed terrible suffering, He also would make a way of escape. CBN views its role very much in this light and uses its programs to help those who, like Bracy, face forces beyond their control.[21]

Robertson believes that his bridges to the black community are strong, unlike the rest of the Republican candidates who draw few black voters. His record at CBN with Operation Blessing speaks for itself. Republicans for years have had a minority party, winning presidential elections, yet unable to attract ethnic communities to its fold largely because of its poor record on civil rights. Robertson is ready to end this cultural isolation for Republicans, much as he helped to break down barriers between white evangelicals and the black community in America. Republicans need to begin to think and act for the whole nation again.

> I think that the election of Ronald Reagan was a trial of ideals, of the hopes, of the ambitions, and the aspirations of the great majority of the American people; and I don't believe the Republican party is any longer a minority party. We may be a party for minorities but never again the minority party.[22]

Robertson's entry into politics is often compared to that of the Reverend Jesse Jackson. Though quite different in their views and experience, the two are more identified with religion than they are as yet with politics.

When Jackson ran for the Democratic Party's presidential nomination in 1984, his particular concern was the mistreatment of the poor and ethnic groups in the nation, and he used his candidacy to help set the agenda of the Democratic Party. One of his positive contributions to the party and to the nation was the registration and mobilization of previously inactive voters. There is evidence that blacks, especially in the South, responded to Jackson's campaign.

Some observers see Robertson doing the same thing for the Republican Party, mobilizing new voters and bringing issues like abortion to the attention of the nation. Interest group politics with a religious flavor is hardly new, yet Jackson's candidacy carried within it a potential for division that stretched the patience of Walter Mondale in 1984 and complicated plans for Democratic candidates in 1988, much as George Bush and fellow Republicans feared that a Robertson candidacy would divide their party in 1988.[23]

When asked about Jackson, Robertson responded that although Jackson is an "attractive" leader, he is outside the "mainstream." This is true, says Robertson, not because he is black or represents minorities, but because his political views are not compatible with American convictions. As long as Jackson will not retract statements like the one he made in Cuba, "Long live Fidel Castro! Long live Ché Guevera! Long live the Cuban revolution!" Robertson does not want his own candidacy or views even compared with Jackson's. He calls himself a mainstream Republican candidate and does not believe he is a threat to the unity of the party, despite the fact that he is distinctively religious.[24]

Against a Democratic candidate in the general election, Robertson hopes to win from 25 to 35 percent of the black vote. Ronald Reagan won less than 10 percent in 1984. Endorsed by leading black ministers like E. V. Hill of Los Angeles, Robertson does well among blacks, who have a tradition going back to slavery of entrusting ministers with public responsibility. Gearing for the campaign, he hired George Vinnett, a black professional from Tulsa, Oklahoma, as Regional Press Secretary, and Ben Kinchlow carries more responsibility and is even more visible than before on the "700 Club."[25]

Conservative Responses

Contrary to common belief, not all Republicans are conservative; many Democrats are. Not all conservatives are religious and not all evangelicals are conservatives. Not all Christians are conservative or evangelical. Robertson is Christian, evangelical, conservative, and Republican, and is not always well received by Republicans or conservatives.

At the National Young Republican Convention held in Seattle in 1987, Robertson received a chilly reception. Monitoring applause for the speakers, the *Washington Post* reported Congressman Jack Kemp the winner with Senator Bob Dole second and Vice-President Bush third. Other candidates received lukewarm responses, except for Robertson. The *Post* reported that the audience was inattentive and almost rude in its treatment of him.[26]

All the Republican presidential hopefuls except Bush spoke at the 1987 Conservative Political Action Conference annual meeting in Washington. Kemp received a standing ovation, and former Governor Pierre DuPont got an enthusiastic greeting. Robertson's words on the family and the crisis in moral values apparently elicited little response from the crowd. Conservative leaders may agree with him on issues, but he is an outsider and a liability because of his religious opinions.

These encounters illustrate the fact that Robertson will not be fully at home in any single group. To Republicans he is a newcomer, to conservative leaders he may be a liability, standing as he does for strict morality and for the supernatural. From

Robertson's perspective this is probably not all bad. He is jealous of his independence, and politically, he does not want to be the prisoner of any specific group or ideology. He would be loyal to his affiliations but never controlled by them.[27]

One problem that many political conservatives have with Robertson is that his brand of politics is tied to Bible teachings about right and wrong. He is not a libertarian who believes sexual conduct is simply a matter of personal choice, a view some conservatives espouse.[28]

Responses of the General Public

In an earlier generation, parents or grandparents who called themselves Republicans or Democrats voted a straight ticket for one party or the other, and their children followed them. But gradually over the past fifty years, people have voted as individuals and have often split their vote, voting for both Democrats and Republicans in the same year. For example, in the South, voters generally vote Republican in the presidential election and Democratic in state races. This largely explains why the Congress is controlled by Democrats even in years with landslide Republican winners such as Nixon in 1972 and Reagan in 1984.

Democrats are not trusted in the White House. Republicans have appeared more capable of leadership and seem less likely to get the nation into trouble. Between Eisenhower's victory in 1952 and the 1984 election, only once, in 1964 with Lyndon Johnson, did Democrats win more than 50 percent of the votes. The continued skepticism of voters is reflected in their split-ticket voting, giving votes to both parties. A genuine party realignment among voters that would give one party dominance in government for a generation, like Margaret Thatcher in Great Britain or Franklin Roosevelt in the thirties, awaits a set of crises that require leaders ready to give the nation direction. Robertson predicts the crises of a generation, in both the economy and foreign relations, and except for the real possibility that he is right, his political ambitions would be futile.[29]

When the *Wall Street Journal* and NBC News polled voters in 1987 on what kind of leader they wanted for their next president, 48 percent wanted someone with a "vision and plan for the country." A record of competence ranked second with 24 percent, followed by strong moral character at 17 percent, and agreement on major issues, 9 percent. Voters look for a president with the positive spirit of Reagan, but perhaps with new tougher policies. Asking people to look several years ahead, this poll found that 60 percent thought the nation was headed into troubled times and only 33 percent were confident of good times in the immediate future.[30]

In another poll taken in the southern states in the spring of 1987, voters ranked their concerns. At the top were social issues like alcohol and drug abuse, followed by morals, health, economics, government, and finally foreign policy. In this poll Robertson was the preferred choice of 9 percent, with Kemp at 10 percent, Dole at 17 percent, and Bush at 53 percent.

However, a study done independently by political scientists John Green and James Guth at Furman University found that Bush's lead was deceptive because his supporters were not as loyal as Kemp's or Robertson's. "Only 54 percent of those favoring Bush said they felt 'very close' to him, compared with 85 percent for Kemp and 97 percent for Robertson." Perhaps, the authors suggest, Bush scored high in the polls because voters had not united on an alternative to him. Rich, better educated voters in the South leaned toward Bush; the poor and less educated tended to favor Robertson. Other candidates like Kemp and Dole had their support spread evenly between groups of voters [31]

Green and Guth say that polls do not predict who will vote in the party caucuses and primaries. They give an indication of the public mood, but tell little about actual outcome because so few people vote in the party nomination process. Strong Robertson supporters are very important to his hopes for winning the nomination, because they will show up at the polls. Robertson has a substantial obstacle in the fairly high percentage of people who oppose his candidacy. As many as 20 percent of the Republican Party contributors surveyed say that they could not support Robertson if he won the nomination. However, the study shows that the Bush lead is especially vulnerable and is ready to be taken from him by any of the Republican challengers.[32]

· 15 ·
The Surprising Campaigner

- ♦ *Can Robertson mobilize evangelicals?*
- ♦ *What is his political strategy?*
- ♦ *Where will he go from here?*

Robertson's substantial support among Democrats, especially in the South, gave his campaign manager, Marc Nuttle, confidence as he outlined a basic strategy. Independent voters number at least one-third of those registered to vote in thirty states. Most voters, whether Republican, Democrat, or Independent, think of themselves as middle-of-the-road, halfway between liberals and conservatives, when in reality their views are significantly to the right and conservative.

Robertson's opinions are very close to average Americans', much closer than the moderate or liberal Democrats. If he is able to win the Republican nomination, Nuttle says, the final choice for voters will be either Robertson or a more liberal Democrat; or the Democrats could nominate a southern conservative like Georgia's Senator Sam Nunn, who has, however, declined to run. Nuttle hopes Democrats will select a moderately liberal candidate, giving Robertson an excellent chance of winning the presidency if nominated.[1]

Political parties no longer provide services, jobs, or entertainment to people as they once did in the cities and small towns of

America. For decades, party reformers sought to encourage participation in activities, particularly in the selection of candidates. Primaries, which are statewide elections of party nominees, and caucuses, where small groups of registered voters gather locally to vote for the candidates, were the simplest and most effective ways of including voters in this important political task. But generally, voters remain outside the process until they vote in the November general election. By taking his cause to the people early in the nomination process, Robertson has stirred the waters considerably.

The last popular candidate for president known in history for his piety, besides Jimmy Carter, was William Jennings Bryan, the Democrat who ran and lost three times—in 1896, 1900, and 1908. Bryan is famous for his "Cross of Gold" speech, delivered to the Democratic Convention in Chicago (1896), and for his role in the 1925 Scopes "Monkey" Trial in Tennessee dealing with teaching evolution in public schools. Destined to be a great loser, Bryan left his mark in American history. But Robertson is not just a repeat of Bryan. Much has changed in America since the turn of the century, and to the surprise of many, religion is increasing in importance again. Robertson is determined to encourage this process and to make a unique contribution.

What makes the 1988 campaign so unusual, at least in the beginning, is the absence of a clear front-runner in either party. The nomination is open in both parties, making predictions extremely difficult. Furthermore, the Reagan legacy is a hard act to follow for two reasons. First, he was a popular figure and a gifted communicator. Second, he leaves behind a set of tremendous problems, not of his doing especially, but potentially the undoing of his successor. There is speculation that some well-known politicians chose not to run in 1988, expecting an impending depression.

Anticipating troubled times, Robertson hopes to lead America through them and on to better days. If he should lose in 1988, undoubtedly he will prepare for 1992, using every available moment to lay his foundations organizationally as Reagan did in 1976. The single most practical qualification for a candidate seems to be unemployment, so that one can campaign full-time, as did both Carter and Reagan. Robertson will most likely try for the presidency until he wins or retires. This means he may have two or at the most three opportunities. He is clearly launched on a political career for the next decade at least. The transition to politics has been made, whatever the outcome.

Robertson is confident that he will do well in the 1988 campaign largely because of the loyal dedication of his supporters and the political apathy of Americans. About 10 percent of the eligible American voters participate in the nomination process of either party. A very few people control party nominations—as few as five thousand voters in a Congressional district can win the district for a candidate. Robertson's minimum goal is to get 5 percent of the traditional Republican vote, and Marc Nuttle thinks that he may get 10 percent. The rest of his support they think will be new blood from the outside, people who usually do not vote in Republican primaries or caucuses.

The increasingly Republican evangelicals are voting in record numbers, and were one of the largest voting blocks to support Ronald Reagan in 1984. In 1986, Nuttle states that they made up about 25 percent of the electorate, the largest single grouping other than male and female. He attributes 75 percent of the Republican growth between 1972 and 1986 to an increase of evangelical voters. Nuttle, a nationally known attorney and political consultant from Oklahoma, joined Robertson's staff in January 1986, largely because he was convinced that with the evangelical vote, Robertson could win. No Republican can win without this block of voters. This may deter Robertson's rivals from attacking his religion.[2]

Mobilizing Christians

Mobilizing millions of evangelical voters for Robertson is not a simple task, because some Christians are deeply opposed to his entry into politics, viewing it as a compromise of his ministry or a conflict of interest. He felt this conflict in 1979. After briefly supporting a Democrat in a state contest, he pulled back "to focus on the spiritual mission of reaching people for the Lord Jesus

Christ," and "to avoid anything which could cause confusion on the accomplishment of that mission," and many wonder why he is entering politics again.[3]

In September 1987, this issue reemerged when journalists discovered that the 1986 edition of *Shout It from the Housetops* had omitted a statement from the earlier 1972 edition: " 'I have called you to my ministry,' he spoke to my heart. 'You cannot tie my eternal purposes to the success of any political candidate.' " Robertson said he had not intended to leave out these words, which referred to his father's 1966 Senate reelection effort. They expressed his conviction at the time that he ought to remain in religious broadcasting and not get heavily involved in partisan politics. They also warned that religion deals with far more important matters than government. Today, Robertson considers his decision to enter politics not a betrayal of his earlier ministry— he has fulfilled his call to establish CBN—but rather a legitimate way to integrate his religion-based convictions with a public role.[4]

At stake is the place of religion in politics. Not surprisingly, at least some conservatives want Robertson in politics because he brings vitality and voters to their cause. But there are Christians who fear that Robertson's religious supporters are being exploited by those who have no real love of God, respect for the church, or a sense of where to draw the line between church and state. Some of his most vehement opponents are separatist evangelicals who see in his politics the making of a religious sellout to naked ambition and a secular agenda. One such opponent, Richard Goldstein, writes,

> Undoubtedly Christians have the right to help make civil laws, and God uses these laws to help keep order, but the New Right wants more than law and order. They want their Christian consensus at the heart of a new civil religion intended to bring morality back to America. Yet they can no more make America moral by passing laws than they can make a myna bird Jewish by putting a skull cap on its head and teaching it Hebrew. That's why no matter how much political clout the New Right amasses, no matter how many parties

they take over or judges they appoint or laws they pass or conservatives they elect—even putting Pat Robertson in the White House—the New Right's plans for a moral America are doomed. They're attempting God's work with man's methods.[5]

Robertson is somewhat cautious in his approach to this sensitive subject. But he believes that the Bible teaches Christian involvement in civic affairs, and that God is working in the world for the good of nations. Nevertheless, keeping a clear distinction between one's faith and one's political role, to maintain the separation of church and state, is very important to him.

I think the President is the President of all the people. Because he has at his disposal certain coercive powers, he must exercise great restraint in what he says and what he does. A minister, on the other hand, is the head of a voluntary association. The minister's job is to tell people how to find the way of salvation and how to live as they're on the way to heaven. He is dealing in a voluntary matter of the spirit. The President is dealing with the compulsory matter of the sword. We must render to Caesar what is Caesar's, to God what is God's. We should not use the sword of Caesar to coerce what must be a voluntary decision of the spirit brought about by reason, by the Scriptures, and by the Holy Spirit Himself.[6]

There is no law against clergy serving in public office. In fact, the Constitution forbids any religious restriction, but Robertson respects the significance of keeping church and state functions separate. To avoid confusion on this matter, he resigned his Southern Baptist ordination before formally seeking the Republican nomination.

In Connecticut, two Robertson supporters sharing his views have integrated their Christian beliefs and their political activism. Gordon Curry, a salesman, and Richard Lappert, a psychologist for the State Department of Education, collected signatures for him primarily because he stands for traditional values. They think the breakdown of the family, drug use, and illiteracy demand more attention from government. Remembering how Ronald Reagan was abused by the press and accused of being a wild-eyed radical, they expect to elect Robertson in the same way, by appealing directly to the good sense of their friends and neighbors. Their religious beliefs are related consciously to their political activity, but they do not necessarily use them to win votes.[7]

Robertson says the motivation and program of evangelicals are not the same as interest groups that are looking for government assistance. Not asking for any special favors, he believes they are ready to give to their communities and want government to maintain order and decency in the nation. Since evangelicals are not asking for money or for extra privileges, he says they ought to be respected and their concerns for the nation's welfare given careful consideration. Few other groups have the public interest in mind or are prepared to make personal sacrifices for it, he says. This is the only kind of Christian-political activism that Robertson supports; any other religious agenda that would take advantage of political audiences by trying to convert them or seek special privileges akin to support for a state church would not be appropriate, and would compromise biblical principles.[8]

This concern, that evangelicals dare not act simply as an interest group, is expressed by Charles Colson, convicted Watergate conspirator, founder of Prison Ministries, and author of *Born Again*. Colson advises Robertson to use his candidacy and political involvement to teach Christians their broader civic responsibility. When someone says, if "24 percent of the people are born again, 24 percent of office holders should be born again," they are using interest-group tactics that are out of place, says Colson, and Robertson needs to restrain these overzealous Christians:

> The Robertson Campaign puts Evangelicalism to its toughest test in decades—for if the triumphalism continues, the backlash will intensify, diminishing Christian influence in society. On the other hand, the exposure could provide an opportunity for Christians to articulate a responsible view of political involvement.[9]

Evangelist Jimmy Swaggart was slow to support Robertson because he wanted no compromise with the world and what he considers its doomed power centers. After meeting with Robertson in September of 1986, he changed his mind and added his endorsement enthusiastically, perhaps because a Robertson presidency seemed such a foolish and remote possibility. He compared it with Christopher Columbus's venture, and to the "ragtag army" of George Washington that overcame the invincible British redcoats. He delighted in the thought of an underdog taking on the whole system at its own game and winning. Swaggart believed that Robertson could indeed represent all Americans and Christians:

> Pat Robertson is one of us. I believe he is a man who will bend over backward should God place him in a position of which we speak, to be leader of all the people, irrespective of whom they may be, that no freedoms ever be curtailed respective of that individual's religious persuasion or whoever they may be. Honesty, integrity, and character, that's what America needs.[10]

Few things anger Robertson like the suggestion that Christians should stay out of politics. If there is a single issue that he would like to put to rest, it is the idea that religion disqualifies someone from public office. Yet he believes this issue smolders in the minds of many, especially those who resist religion and traditional morality.

> People are terrified that we will get organized and understand what to do politically. They are terrified. And they're saying, "Separation of church and state. Get back behind your stained-glass windows. Don't you dare get in the process. We know how to run all this. You stay home and you worship Jesus and let your old folks sing hymns and have their knitting parties and their church suppers, and leave the government to us."
>
> Listen, my father was in politics for thirty-four years. He was a senator and a member of the House of Representatives. I grew up with those folks. I learned "mommy," "daddy," and then I learned "constituent." I have seen the governor of Virginia, or heard him when I was at Washington and Lee, go into a fraternity party, get so

drunk that he fell into a hedge coming out, and they had to carry him and throw him in his limousine. I've been with a senator from California in Denmark who was so drunk he couldn't stand up.[11]

Another idea that Robertson adamantly opposes is the argument that his candidacy deserves no respect because he cannot win. The argument is a cover, he thinks, for the opposite fear, namely that his candidacy will be victorious. He quotes a professor at the University of Michigan, a Democrat, who claimed, "Pat Robertson will probably never win the Republican nomination." The professor then said, "But if he does, he will get 25 percent of the black vote, and the Democrats will have to fold their tents for the next forty years."[12]

The Reverend Jerry Falwell supports George Bush. Robertson respects this commitment given to Bush several years ago, but he wants people to know that Falwell and he are on good speaking terms. Despite their political differences, they are agreed on most public policy issues and share a concern for the nation.

Between 1980 and 1986, Falwell was very active in politics, endorsing candidates and speaking on their behalf. He gained friends in politics, but he also made enemies by his blunt outspoken ways. In 1986 he pulled back, first, he said, to nurture his own pastoral ministry, and second, to reconsider his political involvement. Thus, he was free to help in the PTL troubles of 1987. Politics, however, is more complex and devious than he ever imagined, and he wants to gain perspective and consider whether to get involved in partisan politics again as a preacher. He has stated that he will not participate in the campaign. Falwell's endorsement of Bush actually helps Robertson partly by diffusing the charge that Christians are involved in a conspiracy to take over the Republican Party. [13]

The *New York Times* reported that Robertson's chances in New Hampshire depended heavily on evangelical voters who numbered between ten and twenty thousand in the state. It would take approximately fifteen thousand more votes to win if all these Protestants back him in what is reported to be a predominantly

Roman Catholic state. New Hampshire Senator Mark Hounsell, one of the few Republican regulars to back Robertson, hoped that his broadbased political views would win him the needed additional followers. The task of mobilizing evangelicals has to be carried out without offending other voting groups.[14]

Observers of New Hampshire see some surprising developments. Reverend Keith Marsh was a Dartmouth College senior when he became an evangelical Christian. After graduating, he lost a bid for a delegate position at the 1986 state Republican convention. Undaunted, he continues his political activities, now for Robertson. Marsh was one of the few pastors in the area willing to abandon the traditional political neutrality of ministers.

> Back in '80 and '84, we knew (the election) was important, but I didn't know anybody who did more than vote. There's been a lot of going back to the Constitution, going back to our roots as Christians, going back to our roots as Americans, and seeing that, hey, Christianity had an awful lot to do with the founding of our nation . . . This isn't some kind of new Jerusalem . . . but it's very hard to look into the life of George Washington or any of these guys and not see how they are deeply affected by their love for God and their love for the Scriptures . . . Evangelicals are not interested in Christianizing the nation, but in exercising their right to participate in the electoral process.[15]

Other local pastors encourage their flocks to vote, but have refused to do more for Robertson. How religious voters respond to the mixed signals and differences among pastors remains to be seen. Speaking to a group of pastors, Robertson encouraged them to catch a vision for what could be done with a minimum of political effort. He described the task of getting involved in elementary steps: His methods worked in Michigan where the petitions simply called for active moral involvement in politics.

> All you have to do is take a piece of paper, which I'll give you, and go out in your precincts, that's the neighborhood where you live and the folks around where you live, and get twenty signatures of people

who say they would like you to be a precinct delegate. Then you get it notarized at a notary public and bring it back to our office, and we will file it for you . . . So they went out and did it. It wasn't a very big deal. It was a relatively simple process, but they did it. On filing day, May twenty-seventh, those people, mostly evangelicals and those who cared about traditional values, with forty-eight hundred precinct delegate petitions all filed and notarized (for the) Republican party, (and) several hundred petitions for the Democratic party . . . You say, does that mean anything? Well, it's 50 percent more than the Republican party had ever had in its entire history, that's why it meant something. This was nothing for the churches to do and the Christians. They just went out and did it and brought the things back, and suddenly it was headlines all across the nation.[16]

Robertson urged the pastors to put aside doctrinal and ecclesiastical differences and to seek a practical unity that would give them real influence for good in public life. With this unity he assured them that they could mobilize enough people to protect the future of America.[17]

Grass-roots Christian political activity is so new and unusual in recent years that Robertson supporters like Bob Snelling of Sarasota, Florida, make newsworthy stories in their own right. *New Business*, a Florida-based magazine, ran a feature article on the president of Snelling and Snelling, the "World's largest employment agency franchise." The Snellings read about Robertson in the *Saturday Evening Post*, and wrote him a letter volunteering to help. Bob travels with his wife, Anne, giving speeches and holding meetings for Robertson. "We're up to our ham hocks," says Snelling, "traveling all over the country trying to get a ground swell."[18]

Newspapers are intrigued by the Robertson volunteers—they've never seen anything like it. In North Carolina, Carl Horn, a thirty-five-year-old Roman Catholic attorney who ran for Congress in 1984 and lost, is helping to lead the Robertson effort. Horn was the subject of a story run in the *Atlanta Journal*. He is especially concerned about abortion. A Yale law graduate, he is reaching out beyond the Protestant community and counsels Robertson to avoid the phrase "born-again Christian.' He does not want to see the campaign suffer by being attached to a label or to a terminology that fits only a minority of the religious people in America.[19]

The *Fort Worth Star* carried a story on Karen Cameron, the Texas State Director of Americans for Robertson, who campaigned for George McGovern in 1972. A mother of four, Cameron got involved in the "Right to Life" movement in 1974, shortly after the Supreme Court in *Roe v. Wade* (1973) refused to uphold a Texas law against abortion. Initially afraid to talk in public, she soon overcame her shyness, speaking to university classes and larger groups. In her role as a spokeswoman for Robertson, she stresses his training in law and economics, and his experience in business and broadcasting. She hopes he will lose the label "televangelist" and reach beyond the religious community. Cameron is optimistic about the campaign in Texas, even though George Bush is from that state. She says, "I don't see the enthusiasm for Bush that Pat has among his supporters. Enthusiasm is contagious."[20]

In an age of declining local political party activity, the Robertson influx has brought renewed involvement. For example, in Sumner County, Tennessee, at the Americans for Robertson meeting held at the local community college, the paper reported that no regular members of the County Republican Caucus were present. Beginning with prayer and Scripture reading, the group of volunteers got down to business, organizing to collect 1,659 signatures on petitions for the "Draft Robertson" movement.[21]

Robertson's strategy has had some difficulties. In fact, the 3-million-signature drive caused great difficulties for the pre-campaign. By the summer of 1987, over a million signatures had been collected with a second million promised. The logistical problems of securing that much support were immense, and workers resorted to all kinds of extra efforts. Robertson commented, "Some have sent petitions to friends in Christmas cards. A Manassas, Virginia, couple sent petition forms out with three hundred wedding invitations." Workers called in neighbors for "video parties" where they played the video of Robertson's September 17, 1986, announcement.[22]

Under the pressure of a self-imposed deadline, Americans for Robertson resorted to a telephone campaign to solicit endorsements for the candidacy. Those responding positively were then contacted by mail. Some doubted that 3 million people could be mobilized in so short a time. A valid petition with a million signatures would indicate substantial support, but 3 million, if they are not carefully validated, could undermine somewhat the integrity of the petition. Some criticized Robertson for setting too high a goal in the petition drive.[23]

On September 15, however, he announced that he had met his goal and had 3.3 million petitions. He said that he hoped to get 4 million more by the start of the primaries and caucuses, giving him a support base of 7 million. By stirring interest and assistance for his campaign through the simple device of a petition drive, Robertson will receive credit for being an innovator.

Political Strategy

Working to establish his campaign organization, Robertson raised money—over $7 million by May 1987, according to *Fortune* magazine, compared with $4 million raised by his nearest competitor, George Bush. Because he was not a declared candidate, he did not yet report his campaign funds to the Federal Election Commission. By September of that year he claimed to have raised over $11 million. Candidates can receive federal matching funds of up to a maximum of $9 million, one dollar for every two they raise privately, limiting them to $27 million in all and restricting the amount they can spend in each state for the nomination battle. His early goal was to raise $30 million by July 1988, so that he would not have to use any federal matching funds and could spend as much as he needed in any state, however he may settle for matching funds.[24]

Robertson contributors are generally not wealthy. According to one study, only one-third of the contributors to the early campaign of Vice-President Bush, Senator Robert Dole, and Congressman Jack Kemp made less than $100,000 a year, while more than two-thirds of Robertson's contributors made less than that amount. He prefers to "raise a little money from a lot of people. I'm not beholden to anybody, nobody owns me, I don't have to cater to anybody." During 1987, before Robertson declared his candidacy, he did not report either the sources or the amounts of his contributions. He has also raised much of his money in hundred-dollar-a-plate dinners grossing more than $25,000 in an evening and recruiting campaign volunteers.[25]

Robertson's organization in 1987 included Herb Ellingwood, former aide of Ronald Reagan in California and the White House, and several other staff with White House experience. Gary Lawrence, his pollster, was a former partner of Richard Wirthlin, Reagan's pollster. There were Roman Catholic, Mormon, and Jewish representatives on his mainly Protestant team. However, the backbone of Americans for Robertson, laying the groundwork for his campaign, were state and local workers.

In the winter of 1986–87, Americans for Robertson had sixty-five paid staff, about twice as many as the other campaigns. By summer he had over seventy-five paid staff and by fall well over a hundred. In addition, volunteers were used extensively, some of them working full-time. Robertson remarked in the early spring of 1987, "In New Hampshire, right now, people tell us that I have more volunteers working in the field than Ronald Reagan did when his victory was over in 1980." In Iowa, in the winter of 1986–87, almost two-thirds of the counties had workers. Organizing this state and local effort in more than twenty states was Mary Ellen Miller, Chairman of M. & M. and Associates, a political consulting firm in Austin, Texas, specializing in Republican campaigns. Miller, a proud grandmother, considers the Robertson effort her last, and she plans to go out a winner.[26]

Michigan, Iowa, New Hampshire, and South Carolina are key states for the election because their delegate selection processes come early. Minnesota, where conservative Republicans are strong, may also have an impact because it rescheduled its caucuses for one week after New Hampshire's. Twelve southern states and eight other states are targeted because of "Super Tuesday," March

8, when their primaries are held. Conservative politics are popular in the South where evangelicals are strong. Texas is especially important because it is Bush's home state and because any candidate that wins at least 50 percent of the vote gets all 109 votes of the state delegates. California is also critical because of its size and "winner takes all" delegates rule.[27]

Local politics is not a picnic. Hardball tactics used by all sides influence the outcome. Robertson staff teach their people to expect rough parliamentary moves designed to stop their efforts to win delegates. They have been instructed on occasion to use tough parliamentary procedures and delays to obtain majorities in caucuses and to elect their people.

Conflicts between Bush and Robertson forces occur frequently.[28] One reason there is such conflict is that about one-fourth of the delegates to the Republican Convention will be selected under a "winner takes all" rule. Whichever candidate wins the most votes gets all the delegates and the losers get none. The only statewide primary with this rule is California; however, in other states this rule applies at the Congressional district level in the primaries. An additional 31 percent of the national convention delegates are selected by a caucus process as in Michigan and Iowa. If Robertson can mobilize enough people in caucuses and in states with the "winner takes all" rule, he will have a strong chance of winning the Republican nomination.[29]

Few Republican Party regulars have supported Robertson's cause at the outset, but he expects they can be won over after he has proven the strength of his voting support. His own volunteer base gives him an independence the other candidates lack. This was demonstrated for the first time in Michigan. In the spring of 1987, at the Republican State Convention, Robertson supporters took thirty-four of the State Committee positions, with Kemp winning thirty-one and Bush thirty-three. A Robertson-Kemp coalition won control of twelve of the eighteen Congressional district chairmanships. Robertson said that Bush had endorsements from 635 Republican officials in Michigan, spending over $1.5 million there, and still lost. Robertson claimed that he spent less than $60,000 in Michigan; volunteers at the precinct level made the difference. He projected these results would mean capturing forty to forty-four of the seventy-seven Michigan delegates to the Republican national convention.[30]

The second test of Robertson's grass-roots strategy occurred in South Carolina. Precinct caucuses meeting on March 10, 1987, selected delegates to the state convention. Robertson won about 40 percent of the delegates to the state convention. Most of his workers had never been active in politics before.

One of his local leaders in South Carolina, Don Gibson, lost his own campaign for Congress in 1980 and dropped out of politics for seven years. He reentered politics to work for Robertson, talking to small groups of people locally who showed up in enough numbers at the county convention to elect Gibson chairman of the Charleston County Republican Party.[31]

In South Carolina, a plan to join with Kemp forces to control the state convention failed. Robertson won strong support in South Carolina, but not enough to dominate the state. The final decision in South Carolina will come down to how the primary election goes in March 1988.[32]

Grass-roots methods worked for Robertson in Michigan and in South Carolina, and he hoped that they would work again in Florida. Florida is a strategic state on the road to the presidency because it is both large and southern. Bush should have had it wrapped up except for Robertson's supporters. Kemp and Dole wrote Florida off as a lost cause, according to experienced political columnists Jack W. Germond and Jules Witcover. The delegates to the Florida State Convention cast a presidential popularity vote in November 1987 and Bush expected to win easily. Governor Bob Martinez is cochairman of Bush's campaign and Bush's own son Jeb works in an influential political position under Martinez. State Republican rules allocate 40 percent of the delegates to the state convention to party office holders and their friends and supporters, giving Bush virtually total support from this group. The 60 percent that remain are picked at random drawings held at county party caucuses. To be eligible for the draw, a Republican simply had to send his or her name on a postcard to party headquarters in Tallahassee by August 1, 1987. Robertson decided to work the luck of the draw.[33]

The Florida director of Americans for Robertson, Richard Pinsky, gave thirty thousand cards to his workers for distribution. He hoped between three and four thousand were sent in, out of a total of eight to ten thousand received. By the laws of chance and the allocation rules, he thought Robertson could get from 15 percent to 40 percent of the delegates picked by the draw.[34]

There is nothing complicated about sending in a postcard, but apparently most Republican candidates didn't try in Florida. The winners in the Florida Convention will have to win again in the state primary which selects the delegates for New Orleans; however, a symbolic victory in Florida's November Convention poll sets the stage for the main events of January, February, and March in Iowa, New Hampshire, and the South. Germond and Witcover thought that Robertson's people once again, as in Michigan and South Carolina, might slow the Bush charge for the nomination. They predicted that Florida is "no fire drill" and Bush "could really get singed" by postcards.[35]

Robertson won the Republican Iowa straw poll held on September 12, 1987, in Ames, Iowa. Advertised as the "Calvacade of Stars," the Iowa Republicans paid twenty-five dollars a person to listen to speeches by presidential candidates and to vote their preference. The crowd, nearly double the size of what was anticipated, gave Robertson "thunderous cheers" when he spoke. He received 33.6 percent of the 3,843 ballots cast, compared with 24.9 percent for Dole, 22.4 percent for Bush, and 13.5 percent for Kemp. Iowa Republican regulars were "impressed" by this Robertson victory and the support and organization that it demonstrated. The Associated Press reported,

> Robertson called the straw poll the "major test that everybody went for," and dismissed suggestions that he's not electable. "I've won four out of four and if that isn't electable, I don't know what is,"

referring to votes in Michigan, South Carolina, Florida, and now Iowa.[36]

Three days later he announced that he had 3.3 million petitions and would announce his candidacy on October 1. Competing for press attention with Pope John Paul's national tour, the nuclear arms negotiations, and the confirmation hearings of Judge Robert Bork, Robertson's Iowa feat made national news. No longer was his candidacy considered a religious sideshow.

In late October and early November, Robertson won straw polls in southern Illinois and in Maine. More importantly, on November 14 in the Florida straw poll 37 percent of the voters cast ballots for him. The postcard strategy had worked. Bush controlled the party apparatus and won 57 percent of the voters, but Robertson clearly won the contest to mobilize interested voters.[37]

Active women volunteers—mothers, housewives, and career professionals—are the power behind the Robertson campaign. Forty percent of his contributors in the early campaign were women, three times the proportion of other candidates.[38] He also has appointed women to his paid professional staff: Connie Snapp, Director of Communications, handles press relations, and Mary Ellen Miller is the brains behind the field force. Speaking of this grass-roots constituency, he comments:

> They know exactly where I stand, and they obviously agree with me on these issues, so it's not just that I'm a "celebrity." But obviously it helps that I spend time in their home every day, it makes me part of the family.[39]

Robertson has no credibility problem with his "700 Club" women supporters. He is well known to them. Being a "part of the family" and actively supporting conservative groups like Concerned Women for America gives him instant appeal. Visiting New Hampshire, he met with over five hundred women for a dinner. "The place was packed, and the women were on their feet whistling, and I have never been in a place where women are on their feet whistling." Flattered, and perhaps a little frightened, Robertson may well be riding the wave of a fully woman-powered candidacy, the first in American politics. Historically, when women figuratively or literally take to the streets in politics, governments tremble.[40]

Activists who want a conservative Republican to win the presidency give Robertson high marks, except they doubt he can win. Respecting his leadership, they are not sure how he will be received by voters.[41] In the 1988 campaign, Robertson will have to lead the way with his volunteers and supporters. Only if he succeeds at the polls, and perhaps not until after he wins the nomination, will the professionals back his campaign. This will be healthy for Robertson and for government because it leaves the big political choices in the hands of the American people who control his political destiny.

Campaigning for president is a strenuous and complex task. For example, the election candidates spend a great deal of time in New Hampshire where significantly less than fifty thousand votes could win, because this race comes early and affects what the press says and what voters do in other states. Campaigning in New Hampshire is a much more personal process than it is in larger states.

> I was in New Hampshire the last few days. We had roughly seven hundred people in a meeting. Each one of them that I shook hands with will go and tell five other people, and then they will go out and begin to have home parties and show videos. It's a very slow process, but it needs two major primary or caucus states at the beginning. In Iowa and New Hampshire we have the leisure to do that, and those, then, take on enormous proportion.[42]

Robertson visits people in homes, small groups, churches, and local newspaper offices. Across the nation he holds large rallies of four to five thousand people. As the 1988 national campaign approaches, he intends to use thirty-second spots on television in major cities. He hopes that by then the larger public will want to examine his credentials more closely and hear what he has to say.[43]

Implications

Robertson's candidacy, whether he wins or loses, will serve to teach his supporters further lessons in their civic responsibility. If he wins, they will learn how they are to treat the losers and even more importantly they will become part of a much larger coalition of forces. If he loses, they will need to continue to respect government. There is a delicate balance between encouraging Christians to participate in partisan politics where they try to elect their favored candidates and teaching them to respect those who win the elections when their candidates lose.

Recently the Reverend Fred Price, a black pastor and television preacher, spoke of the Christian's civic duty at the largest mayor's prayer breakfast in Los Angeles history. Before Mayor Tom Bradley, a liberal black mayor, and a crowd of 1,700, Price taught on prayer for government leaders.

> Many Christians are unaware of their duty to pray for government, as both Romans 13 and 1 Timothy 2 outline . . . God doesn't hear prayers simply because we have needs . . . Think about all the people all over the world who are starving. Don't you think that God, in all His omniscience, knows they're starving? And yet He's letting them starve, because it's not His problem—it's ours. We have to do something about it. When we begin to do something, God will work through us.[44]

Price asserted that God would work through whoever was in authority. He praised the mayor for publicly speaking of his religious convictions. "A man that will dare to say that Jesus Christ is his Lord and Savior deserves our support." He did not ask his listeners to vote for Bradley, and certainly Price and Bradley would disagree on much, but he gave him the basic respect all mayors deserve according to the Bible. As the religious participate more in politics they will need the restraint and the affirming spirit modeled by Reverend Fred Price, as well as the new activism taught by Robertson.[45]

Respecting the institutions and leaders of government is not enough, Robertson believes. He does not respect the "horse trading" and mismanagment of politicians. His defense of Constitutional principles, his concern for families, for the economy, and for America's security, and his hope for greater prosperity and liberty in the world make him a disturber of the peace. Simply honoring government is far too passive an approach for Christians in our day, he believes.

It is apparent that religion affects Robertson's handling of public issues in several ways. First, it helps him take seriously certain facts that warn of long-term threats to the national welfare. The deficit, issues of constitutional theory, and pornography are only recently issues of concern to voters or to public servants. Only those with a long view became involved with these concerns early on.

Second, it helps him to be confident that he understands what the issues are—the deficit is bad, religious liberty is good, and family morals are a necessity. In every case, he is convinced that governmental leadership is partly to blame for either ignoring or causing problems.

Third, Robertson is sure his solutions, which require a return to simplicity—living and working within one's means, respecting the Constitution, and protecting community morals—can be communicated to the public and put into practice.

Fourth, Robertson's religious approach to public policy goes beyond self-interest. He calls this "a new vision for America." It would be a mistake to say this is just nostalgia. Simply a return to better, less complex times is not Robertson's idea of progress. This is a global vision centered partly in American initiative, and he says it is not utopian dreaming. He believes he is realistic about problems and cautious about the resources and abilities of the nation.

Finally, prizing liberty above all, Robertson believes that it will take unity and revival to preserve it. He is confident that world history is moving toward more personal freedom based on the concept that liberty is a gift of God, as the Declaration of Independence declares, or that oppressive regimes will prevail. Courage and consensus in democratic nations will insure their survival and will lead, he thinks, to the expansion of liberty to nations now suffering under dictatorships. Robertson thinks religious revival will help to protect and expand democratic influence.[46]

In short, Robertson understands his task to be: (1) to identify the problems, (2) to find the solutions, and (3) to communicate, in simple terms, what is needed to get his program across to the American people. As a religious broadcaster, Robertson studied current events. He said,

> I have the advantage of being a television analyst, and on my program, I have the opportunity to talk every day to the leaders of our country. I talk to senators, governors, scholars and journalists. I talk to people who have had tremendous experience. So I'm just being fed, just an absolute wealth of material, first from our news people, who gather for me the factual data and the statistics on whatever problem I'm dealing with, and then firsthand sitting down, person-to-person, for fifteen to twenty minutes to interview somebody, either in a studio or on satellite. During an average year, I will range over just about every social problem, and just about every foreign policy problem or domestic problem that is in the news.[47]

Issues are complex and don't easily compress into the minutes or seconds of television coverage. Robertson says that after years of experience he has an inner time clock that helps him to express his thoughts clearly and quickly. He knows "what is good TV and what is bad TV."[48]

The advantage of these years of television discipline is breadth of understanding—the disadvantage is shallowness. He compensated for this problem by specializing in key areas: in politics, he examined leadership; in economics, he looked at debt; in social issues, he studied the family and literacy; in Constitutional law, he focused on judicial review; in foreign relations, he dealt with the Persian Gulf; in higher education, he concentrated on liberty; in religion, he reported on revival. In each area, Robertson looked for the specific information that would be most helpful in illuminating the whole subject. Not wanting to get lost in all the details, he attempted to grasp first what was most important.

Robertson is confident that he understands what is happening and can explain it. Experts know more and more about less and less; they are specialists. Robertson would rather know what is really essential to be able to cope with large tasks.

Robertson was born-again at a time when few public leaders were openly religious and few evangelicals were drawn toward government. Up until the mid-seventies he seemed to accept this state of affairs. His own burgeoning success at CBN coincided with his effort to understand why the impact of the church was so feeble and why government seemed so frustrated. This combination of a church without influence and government encumbered by problems of its own making is the state of affairs which he wants to change.

Robertson seems intent on getting government to focus more effectively on the obvious needs of America. Broadcasting gave him a means to bring change to America and to the world; it was a role of tremendous personal influence and responsibility. Television is very important to Americans, and Robertson's broadcasting impacted lives. CBN programs, always personable and entertaining, presented religion in easily comprehensible terms. By comparison, politics seemed impersonal and government bureaucracy inefficient. If religion can be brought down-to-earth, Robertson thought, why can't government be made more effective and approachable?

Clearly, television counts for the election and the presidency. Communication skills help to equip one to deal with substantive issues, events, institutions, budgetary processes, relations with Congress, the press, and interest groups. However, the hard and laborious effort to move government through its daily tasks generally does not take place on television.

Robertson thinks the Constitution restricts the president to an executive role in a federal system. He does not want the president to dominate the Congress, the Supreme Court, or state and local governments, but rather he would encourage each part of the government to make its unique contribution to the nation. In this, Robertson is a classic conservative, guarding against tyranny, defending liberty, wary of giving anyone too much power.

Robertson also believes that in a republic a president represents all the people and should be concerned for their welfare. The president, in short, is more than a chief administrator responsible for the operation of the executive branch. He is that, but if the presidency was simply a governmental position of limited authority and no more, then Robertson would not have left broadcasting. Instead, Robertson says, presidents must use all their talents and powers to give the entire nation a vision for the future and a sense of how individuals, the private sector, and government can each, separately and working together, better accomplish national purposes. In this, he has a broad view of the presidency. Robertson is persuaded that he understands what all Americans, including the government, must do to provide for America's welfare

Can Robertson be an effective president, handling pressure, building an effective management team, designing a workable agenda, establishing detailed public policy programs, delegating authority, waiting patiently while all the facts come in? These are all skills of a national chief executive. Can he also help to unify the nation in common tasks? When Robertson himself is asked if he has the necessary qualifications, he replies that no job anywhere completely prepares a person to be president. He has made the most of his previous experience and is prepared to be tested in a campaign. This grueling several-year process certainly weeds out most candidates, though effective leaders may not win. Robertson's ability to fight the political wars, to maintain his composure, to tread lightly to avoid offending too many power brokers or voters, will be known shortly, but governing competence cannot be fully demonstrated until one is president.

Source Notes
Chapter 1
Understanding the Man

1. "Robertson Starts Presidential Campaign as Protestors Strive to Shout Him Down," *Wall Street Journal*, October 2, 1987, pp. A1, A10; Pat Robertson, Transcripts, Speech in Boston, November 13, 1986; Freedom Council, Florida, June 15, 1986.

2. Americans for Robertson, Biography of Pat Robertson; Pat Robertson and Jamie Buckingham, *Shout It From the Housetops* (Plainfield, N.J.: Logos International, 1972); *TV Guide*, August 15, 1987, pp. 8, 9.

3. Robertson, Transcript, Gorman and Littleton, New Hampshire, May 28, 1987.

4. Robertson, Transcript, Marlin Maddoux, Interview, Dallas, March 11, 1987.

5. *Virginian-Pilot*, August 15, 1987.

6. Robertson, Transcript, Remarks to Virginia Press Association, July 12, 1986.

7. Robertson, Transcript, Interview, *Christian Monthly*, New Hampshire, May 1987.

8. Harry James and Frederick D. Williams, eds., *The Diary of James A. Garfield*, Vol. I (Lansing, Mich.: Michigan State University Press, 1967); Robert G. Caldwell, *James A. Garfield, Party Chieftain* (Hamden, Conn.: Archon Books, 1965), pp. 39–50; Vernon B. Hampton, *Religious Background of the White House* (Boston: Christopher Publishing House, 1932), pp. 58–71.

9. Ibid., p. 69.

10. Robertson, Transcript, State GOP and Press, Georgia, May 23, 1987; *Tulsa World*, September 30, 1987, p. A5.

11. Robertson, Transcripts, Hyatt Regency Press Conference, New Orleans, September 1986; Nieman Fellows, Harvard, Boston, November 13, 1986; Georgia State GOP.

12. Pat Robertson with Bob Slosser, *The Secret Kingdom* (Nashville: Thomas Nelson, 1982), pp. 13–15; *America's Dates With Destiny* (Nashville: Thomas Nelson, 1986), pp. 25–30.

13. Robertson, *Dates With Destiny*, p. 27.

14. Ibid., p. 35.

15. Pat Robertson and Jamie Buckingham, *Shout It From the Housetops* (Virginia Beach: CBN Press, 1986), pp. 155, 156.

16. Pat Robertson, "Perspective," Fall 1979; August 1980.

17. Ibid. Fall 1980.

18. "TV Ministries Feature More Than Requests for Donations," *Virginian-Pilot*, May 9, 1987, p. 3; Interview, Rev. David Geyerston, CBN, May 1987.

19. Interviews with David Poteet, Herbert Titus, Robert Skolrood, Summer 1987.

20. "700 Club" Transcript, June 28, 1987.

21. Cory SerVaas and Maynard Good Stoddard, "CBN's Pat Robertson: White House Next?" The *Saturday Evening Post*, March 1985.

22. "CBN's Pat Robertson: Headed for the White House?" *Conservative Digest*, August 1985; "Pat Robertson for President," *Christianity Today*, November 8, 1985, pp. 48–51; "Power, Glory, and Politics," *Time*, February 17, 1986; "Wild Cards for the White House," *U.S. News & World Report*, July 14, 1986, pp. 20–25; "Heaven Only Knows," *People*, August 11, 1986, pp. 27–31; "Robertson: Blending Charity and Politics," *Washington Post*, November 2, 1987, pp. A1, 26.

23. Robertson, Transcript of remarks at reception by Bunker Hunt, Dallas, Texas, August 1, 1986; Transcript, "A New Vision for America," Washington, D.C., September 17, 1986.

24. Robertson, Transcript, Associated Press Editorial Board, New York, November 18, 1986; Radio Interview, WEJC, North Carolina, undated; Marshall, Channel 8, Tampa, Florida, January 24, 1987; *Virginian-Pilot*, February 11, 1987, pp. A1, A2.

25. Press Clippings, July 3, 1987.

26. Robertson, Hyatt Regency, New Orleans; Marlin Maddoux; Georgia State GOP; "Robertson Libel Trial, Primaries Coincide," *Tulsa World*, September 24, 1987, p. A11; *Time*, September 2, 1987, p. 23; "Letters in Robertson Suit Fuel Combat Role Charge," *Los Angeles Times*, October 28, 1987, pp. 1, 18.

27. Robertson, Marshall, Channel 8.

28. Ibid.

29. Ibid.

30. Interview, John Whitehead, Rutherford Institute, Manassas, Virginia, May 28, 1987.

31. Ibid.

Chapter 2
What Kind of a President?

1. Robertson, Transcript, State GOP and Press, Georgia, May 23, 1987.

2. Robertson, Transcript, Economic Club Speech, Detroit, Michigan, September 22, 1986.

Source Notes

3. Robertson, Transcript, Gorman and Littleton, New Hampshire, May 28, 1987.

4. Robertson, "Perspective," February 1977.

5. Ibid., September 1977; December 1978.

6. Ibid., January 1978.

7. Ibid., October 1977; April 1978; March 1979.

8. Ibid., April 1979.

9. Ibid.

10. Ibid., April 1980; September 1980.

11. Ibid., January 1979; March 1979. Robertson, Transcript, Right to Life Interview, Concord, New Hampshire, May 26, 1987.

12. Robertson, Transcript, Radio Interview, New Hampshire, May 27, 1987.

13. Robertson, Right to Life Interview.

14. Robertson, Transcript, *Rocky Mountain News* Editorial Board, Denver, Colorado, June 11, 1987.

15. Pat Robertson and Jamie Buckingham, *Shout It From the Housetops* (Plainfield, N.J.: Logos International, 1972), p. 13.

16. Robertson, "700 Club" Transcript, May 10, 1984.

17. Robertson, Transcript, W. H. Fellowship, undated; "700 Club" Transcript, March 15, 21, 1984.

18. Robertson, Transcript, *Concord Monitor* Editorial Board, New Hampshire, May 27, 1987.

19. Robertson, Transcript of Interviews, Boston, undated 1987.

20. Robertson, "Perspective," June 1979; May 1980.

21. Robertson, Transcripts, *Pittsburgh Times*, Pennsylvania, January 24, 1987; *Salem Observer*, March 25, 1987; Associated Press Editorial Board, New York, November 18, 1986; *Christian Monthly*, New Hampshire, May 1987.

22. Robertson, Transcript, "Larry King Live," April 23, 1987.

23. Robertson, Transcripts, John Reese Interview, West Virginia, April 24, 1987; W. H. Fellowship.

24. Robertson, Transcripts, Yale Forum, New Haven, Connecticut, March 1987; Georgia State GOP.

25. Robertson, Marlin Maddoux, Interview, Dallas, March 11, 1987; *Concord Monitor* Board; Gorman and Littleton.

26. Robertson, AP Board; Yale Forum; *Concord Monitor* Board; Jewish Federation, undated.

27. Robertson, W. H. Fellowship.

28. Alan Gitelson, Margaret Conway, and Frank Feigert, *American*

Political Parties: Stability and Change (Boston: Houghton Mifflin Co., 1984); Stephen J. Wayne, *The Road to the White House: The Politics of Presidential Elections*, 3d edition (New York: St. Martin's Press, 1988).

29. Robertson, "Perspective," April 1977.
30. *Time*, February 11, 1986, pp. 62–69.

Chapter 3
The Economy: Barometer of the Presidency

1. Seymour Martin Lipset and William Schneider, "The Confidence Gap During the Reagan Years, 1981–1987," *Political Science Quarterly*, Vol. 102, No. 1, Spring 1987, p. 2.
2. Ibid., pp. 1–11.
3. Ibid.
4. Ibid., pp. 11–19.
5. Ibid., pp. 19–23.
6. Robertson, Transcript, Nieman Fellows, Harvard, Boston, November 13, 1986.
7. Peter G. Peterson, "The Morning After," *Atlantic Monthly*, October 1987, p. 50.
8. Ibid., pp. 46–49.
9. Ibid., p. 60.
10. Ibid., p. 68.
11. Robertson, Transcript, Remarks at the Tiger Bay Club, St. Petersburg, Florida, June 12, 1986.
12. Robertson, Transcript, Remarks at the Economic Club, Florida, June 11, 1986.
13. Ibid.
14. Robertson, Tiger Bay Club; Pat Robertson and Jamie Buckingham, *Shout it From the Housetops* (Virginia Beach: CBN Press, 1986), pp. 152, 153.
15. Robertson, Transcript, Pastors' Brunch, St. Petersburg, Florida, June 12, 1986.
16. Robertson, Transcript, "A New Vision for America," Washington, D.C., September 17, 1986.
17. Ibid.
18. Paul Morken, CBN University, 1986.
19. Robertson, Economic Club.
20. Robertson, Tiger Bay Club.
21. Robertson, Transcripts, National Association of Treasurers, Osage

Source Notes

Beach, Missouri, November 1986; Associated Press Editorial Board, New York, November 18, 1986.

23. Ibid.

24. Robertson, Association of Treasurers.

25. Robertson, Businessmen's Breakfast.

26. Robertson, Transcript, *Atlanta Journal* Editors, Georgia, April 13, 1987; *Pittsburgh Times*, Pennsylvania, January 24, 1987.

27. Robertson, AP Board.

28. Robertson, Transcript, W. H. Fellowship, undated, 1987.

29. Newspaper clipping, undated, by Ed Roberts, *Union Leader* Correspondent, Nashua, New Hampshire.

30. Robertson, Transcripts, AP Board; St. Louis Rotary, Jefferson City, Missouri, March, 12, 1987.

31. Robertson, Transcript, National Press Club, Washington, D.C., October 18, 1985.

32. Robertson, St. Louis Rotary; National Press Club.

33. Ibid.

34. Ibid.

35. Robertson, Businessmen's Breakfast; National Press Club.

36. Leviticus 25; Robertson, "Perspective," January 1981.

37. Ibid.

38. Ibid., September 1981.

39. Robertson, Transcript, Marlin Maddoux, and Fort Worth Media, Dallas, Texas, March 11, 1987.

40. Ibid.

41. Robertson, Transcripts, Interviews, Boston, Undated, 1987; Media Conference, Baton Rouge, Louisiana, September 8, 1986.

42. Robertson, Transcripts, W. H. Fellowship; Robertson, "700 Club," May 7, 1984.

43. Robertson, Transcript, Marlin Maddoux, and Fort Worth Media.

44. Robertson, "Perspective," January 1981; "700 Club" Transcript, May 7, 1984.

45. Robertson, "Perspective," March 1981.

46. Robertson, "Perspective," May, October 1977.

47. Robertson, Businessmen's Breakfast.

48. Robertson, "Perspective," January, 1981; April 1982.

49. Robertson, Transcripts, Jewish Federation, undated 1987; National Press Club, October 18, 1985.

50. Robertson, "Perspective," May 1980; Transcript, Tiger Bay Club.

51. Robertson, "Perspective," April 1980.

52. Robertson, Transcripts, Gorham Breakfast, New Hampshire, May 22, 1987; Tiger Bay Club.

53. Robertson, W. H. Fellowship.

54. Robertson, Transcripts, *Atlantic Monthly* Interview, October 20, 1986; *Pittsburgh Times*, Pennsylvania, January 24, 1987; State GOP and Press, Georgia, May 23, 1987; Jewish Federation; National Press Club; Robertson, "Perspective," May 1977.

55. Robertson, August 1978; Transcript, John Reese Interview, West Virginia, April 24, 1987.

56. Robertson, "Perspective," February 1978. Transcripts, Jewish Federation; National Press Club; State GOP, Virginia, December 6, 1986.

57. Robertson, *Atlantic Monthly*.

58. Ibid.

59. Ibid.

60. Robertson, Transcripts of Interviews, Boston; Gorham Breakfast; Press Conference, Lafayette, Louisiana, March 27, 1987.

61. Robertson, "Perspective," November 1977; Transcript, Economic Club Speech, Detroit, Michigan, September 22, 1986.

62. Ibid.; Robertson, "700 Club" Transcripts, August 14, 1985; March 3, 1986.

63. "Grand Tetons Offer Lesson in Economics," *Tulsa World*, August 26, 1987, p. A15.

64. "God and Money," *Time*, August 3, 1987, pp. 48–55.

Chapter 4
Responding to America's Social Crises

1. Pat Robertson and Jamie Buckingham, *Shout It From the Housetops* (Virginia Beach: CBN, 1986), p. 152.

2. Ibid., p. 153

3. Ibid.; Isaiah 58:6–11.

4. Robertson, Transcript, Pastor's Breakfast, February 18, 1987.

5. Robertson, *Shout It* (1986 edition), pp. 155, 161, 162.

Source Notes

6. Robertson, Transcripts, Yale Forum, New Haven, Connecticut, March, 1987; Luncheon, Laconia, New Hampshire, May 27, 1987; Press Conference, Midwest GOP, May 30, 1987; undated, May 1987.

7. Robertson, Transcripts, *Atlantic Monthly,* October 20, 1986; Midwest GOP, May 30, 1987.

8. Robertson, Pastor's Breakfast.

9. Robertson, undated, May 1987.

10. Robertson, *America's Dates With Destiny* (Nashville: Thomas Nelson, 1986), pp. 179, 180; Yale Forum.

11. E. D. Hirsch, Jr., *Cultural Literacy: What Every American Needs to Know* (Boston: Houghton Mifflin Co., 1987), pp. 1–8.

12. Ibid., pp. 1–33.

13. Ibid., pp. 12, 13.

14. Ibid., p. 87.

15. Ibid., p. 145.

16. Robertson, "700 Club" Transcript, July 13, 1984; Transcripts, Lunch interview, *Salem Observer,* Rochester, New Hampshire, March 25, 1987; State GOP and Press, Georgia, May 23, 1987; *Concord Monitor* Editorial Board, New Hampshire, May 27, 1987; Gorham Breakfast, New Hampshire, May 22, 1987; *Rocky Mountain News* Editorial Board, Denver, Colorado, June 11, 1987.

17. Hirsch, *Cultural Literacy,* p. 100.

18. Robertson, *Concord Monitor.*

19. Robertson, Laconia Luncheon.

20. Robertson, Transcript, Anti-Defamation League, Boston, November 13, 1986; *Salem Observer;* "700 Club" September 4, 1985.

21. Ibid.

22. Robertson, Transcripts, New York Academy of TV Arts and Sciences, March 1986; Gorham and Littleton, New Hampshire, May 28, 1987.

23. Robertson, Transcript, Tiger Bay Club, St. Petersburg, Florida, June 12, 1986; W. H. Fellowship, May 1987.

24. Robertson, Transcript, National Press Club, October 18, 1985.

25. Robertson, Interview with Karen, Louisiana, April 1987.

26. Robertson, Transcript, Marshall, Channel 8, Tampa, Florida, January 24, 1987; "Larry King Live," April 23, 1987; "Perspective," June 1977.

27. Robertson, "700 Club" Transcripts, September 17, 1985; October 11, 1985.

28. Robertson, "700 Club" Transcripts, November 21, 1984; January 11, 1985.

29. Robertson, Transcripts, New Hampshire, May 28, 1987; GOP of Virginia, Virginia, December 6, 1986; Georgia State GOP; Jewish Federation, undated 1987; *Denver Post* Editorial Board, Colorado, June 1987.

Chapter 5
Giving Families Support

1. Pat Robertson and Jamie Buckingham, *Shout It From the Housetops* (Virginia Beach: CBN, 1986), p. 28.
2. Robertson, Transcript, Pastor's Breakfast, February 18, 1987.
3. Robertson, Transcript, "The Wealth of Black Families," Conservative Political Action Committee (C-Pac), February 20, 1987.
4. Ibid.
5. Robertson, "700 Club" Transcript, August 13, 1985.
6. Robertson, Transcript, untitled, 1987.
7. Robertson, Transcripts, Speech in Boston, November 13, 1986; Gorham Breakfast, New Hampshire, May 22, 1987.
8. Robertson, Boston speech.
9. Robertson, Transcript, State GOP and Press, Georgia, May 23, 1987.
10. Robertson, C-Pac Speech.
11. Ibid.
12. Ibid.
13. Ibid.
14. Robertson, Transcripts, Lunch interview, *Salem Observer*, Rochester, New Hampshire, March 25, 1987; Pastors' Breakfast.
15. Ibid.
16. Robertson, Transcript, Marshall, Channel 8, Tampa, Florida, January 24, 1987; *Time* magazine interview, February 12, 1987.
17. Robertson, Georgia State GOP; *Atlanta Journal* Editors, Georgia, April 13, 1987.
18. Robertson, Transcript, A Women's Group in New Hampshire, undated.
19. Ibid.
20. Robertson, "Perspective," Fall 1981; August 1978; Transcripts, Georgia State GOP; "700 Club," July 17, 1984; August 15, 1985.
21. Robertson, Georgia State GOP.

Chapter 6
Endangered Liberty

1. Pat Robertson, Transcript, Freedom Council Rally, Michigan, July 29, 1986.

Source Notes

2. "Conservative Party Manifesto, British General Election Campaign of 1987," British Information Services, New York, p. 1.

3. Ibid., pp. 8, 9.

4. Ibid., p. 3.

5. Ibid., pp. 1, 21.

6. Walter Berns, *Taking the Constitution Seriously* (New York: Simon and Schuster, 1987), p. 31.

7. Pat Robertson, *America's Dates With Destiny* (Nashville: Thomas Nelson, 1986), pp. 18, 19.

8. Ibid., p. 18.

9. Allan Bloom, *The Closing of the American Mind* (New York: Simon and Schuster, 1987), p. 239.

10. Ibid., p. 169.

11. Robertson, *Dates With Destiny*, p. 68.

12. Robertson, Transcript of remarks at Freedom Council Rally, Florida, June 11, 1986.

13. Robertson, *Dates With Destiny*, pp. 69, 70; Kenneth Wald, *Religion and Politics in the United States* (New York: St. Martin's Press, 1987), pp. 35–60; Harry Jaffa, *Crisis of the House Divided: An Interpretation of the Issues in the Lincoln–Douglas Debates* (New York: Doubleday and Company, 1959), pp. 308–329.

14. Robertson, *Dates With Destiny*, p. 72.

15. Ibid., p. 150.

16. Ibid., p. 155.

17. Ibid., p. 152.

18. Ibid., p. 155.

19. Ibid., pp. 91, 92, 93. *See also* Walter Berns, pp. 11–63.

20. Robertson, *Dates With Destiny*, pp. 89, 90; Berns, pp. 12, 13.

21. Robertson, *Dates With Destiny*, p. 94.

22. Bloom, *Closing of the American Mind*, p. 33.

23. Ibid., p. 29.

24. Ibid., p. 158.

25. Ibid., pp. 51–55.

26. Ibid., p. 54.

27. Ibid., p. 60.

28. Ibid., pp. 54, 55.

29. Ibid., p. 53.

30. Ibid., p. 27.

31. Ibid.

32. Robertson, *Dates With Destiny*, pp. 173–184.

33. Ibid., p. 176.

34. Ibid., pp. 178, 179.

35. Ibid., pp. 179, 180.

36. Ibid., p. 270.

37. Bloom, *Closing of the American Mind*, p. 165.

38. Ibid., p. 166.

39. Ibid., pp. 25–43.

40. Ibid., pp. 150, 151.

41. Ibid., p. 156.

42. Ibid., p. 25.

43. Bloom gives extensive treatment to all these subjects and much more, Ibid., pp. 47–137.

44. Ibid., p. 25.

45. Ibid., p. 26.

46. Ibid., p. 29.

47. Ibid., p. 141.

48. Ibid., p. 147.

49. Ibid., pp. 147–152.

50. Ibid., p. 156.

51. Robertson, *Dates With Destiny*, p. 169.

52. Ibid., p. 167.

53. Ibid., pp. 167, 168.

54. Robertson, Transcript, Pastors' Breakfast, February 18, 1987; Bloom, *Closing of the American Mind*, p. 381.

Chapter 7
Law: The Backbone of Liberty

1. A. Bartlett Giamatti, "A Liberal Education and the New Coercion," a speech to freshmen at Yale University, August 31, 1981 (Transcript, Yale University).

2. Ibid., p. 3.

3. Ibid.

4. *Bowers v. Hardwick*,—U.S.—, 106 S.CT. 2841, 92 L.ED. 2D 140, 54 U.S.L.W. 4919 (June 30, 1986). Robertson, "Perspective," June 1977.

5. Robertson, "700 Club" Transcripts, January 11, 1985.

Source Notes

6. John Henry Cardinal Newman, *The Idea of a University* (New York: Image Books, 1959), p. 224.

7. Contrasting common law foundations with recent interpretations of law, *see* Herbert W. Titus, *God, Man and Law: The Biblical Principles*, Temp. Ed. 1982 (Unpublished teaching materials). Also, *see* Harold Berman, *The Interaction of Law and Religion* (Nashville: Abingdon Press, 1974).

8. For a defense of the tao (the way) against modern attacks, see C. S. Lewis, *The Abolition of Man* (New York: Macmillan Publishing Company, 1962).

9. Robertson, Transcript, Johns Hopkins University, October 28, 1986.

10. William Lee Miller, *The First Liberty: Religion and the American Republic* (New York: Alfred A. Knopf, 1986); Gary Glenn, "Did the First Amend ment Originally Limit or Expand Congress's Power Respecting Religion?" Paper presented at the American Political Science Association, Religion and Politics Section, Chicago, September 3–6, 1987.

11. Robertson, Transcript, speech, undated.

12. Robertson, Johns Hopkins University.

13. Ibid.

14. Robert Skolrood, Interview, June 11, 1987.

15. Skolrood, Letter dated July 1, 1987

16. Skolrood, Interview.

17. Ibid.

18. Ibid.

19. *Tulsa World*, August 27, 1987, p. C16; *Smith v. Hunt*, et al., No. 87-7216, the United States Court of Appeals for the Eleventh Circuit, August 26, 1987.

20. Robertson, Transcript, Jewish Federation, undated 1987.

21. Ibid.

22. Ibid.

23. Robertson, Transcripts, Yale Law School, New Haven, Connecticut, March 25, 1986; the University of Virginia Law School, April 16, 1986.

24. Ibid.

25. Ibid.

26. Ibid.

27. Ibid.

28. Ibid.

29. Robertson, Transcript, Off the Record Club, Washington, D.C., August 11, 1986.

Source Notes

30. Robertson, Yale Law School; the University of Virginia Law School.

31. Robertson, University of Virginia Law School.

32. Ibid.

33. *Stone v. Graham* (1980).

34. Robertson, *America's Dates With Destiny* (Nashville: Thomas Nelson Publisher, 1986), p. 195.

35. Robertson, Transcript, Tiger Bay Club, St. Petersburg, Florida, June 18, 1986.

36. *Washington Post,* July 14, 1986, pp. A10, 11; *Virginian-Pilot,* June 27, 1986, pp. A1, A3.

37. Memo from Herbert Titus to Pat Robertson, June 24, 1986; Interview with Herbert Titus, CBN, Spring 1987.

38. Abraham Lincoln, Opening Speech, Quincy, Roy Basher, ed., *The Collected Works of Abraham Lincoln,* Vol. 2, 1848–1855 (New Brunswick: Rutgers University Press, 1953), p. 333.

39. Basher, *Collected Works,* Lincoln, Speech at Springfield, Illinois, June 26, 1857, pp. 400–403; Herbert Titus, "The Supreme Court Isn't Supreme: The Constitution Is," *Washington Post,* July 14, 1986, p. A11.

40. Louis Fisher, "Constitutional Interpretation by Members of Congress," *North Carolina Law Review,* Vol. 63, 1985, pp. 707–747.

41. Joseph Sobran, "Pat Robertson's Severe Logic," *Charlotte Observer* clipping, undated 1987.

42. "Robertson's Law," *Virginian-Pilot,* June 28, 1986, p. A14.

43. Herbert Titus, "Robertson, Lincoln, and the Court," *Virginian-Pilot,* undated.

44. "Robertson Can't Say Oath," *Philadelphia Inquirer,* undated, Spring 1987.

45. Robertson, Transcripts, Associated Press Editorial Board, New York, November 18, 1986; *Atlantic Monthly,* October 20, 1986.

46. Robertson, Transcript, *Concord Monitor* Editorial Board, Concord New Hampshire, May 27, 1987.

47. Robertson, Yale Law School.

48. Ibid.

49. Herbert W.Titus, "The Law of Our Land," Manuscript, Spring 1987.

50. Robertson, Transcripts, Press Conference, New Orleans, Louisiana, September 1986; *Atlantic Monthly;* W. H. Fellowship.

51. Robertson, Transcript, Press Conference, Oral Roberts University, Tulsa, Oklahoma, November 1, 1985.

Chapter 8
Foreign Policy: What Robertson Would Do Differently

1. Robertson, Transcript, Gorham Breakfast, New Hampshire, May 28, 1987.

2. Robertson, Transcripts, Manuscript No. 79, location and date unknown, May 1987; Gorham Breakfast.

3. Robertson, "Dictatorships and Single Standards," *Policy Review*, The Heritage Foundation, Number 39, Winter 1987, reprint.

4. James H. Billington, "Realism and Vision in American Foreign Policy," *Foreign Affairs*, Vol. 65, No. 3, 1987, p. 630.

5. Ibid., pp. 630, 631, 644, 645.

6. Ibid., p. 647.

7. Ibid.

8. Ibid.

9. Robertson, Transcript, "Toward a Community of Democratic Nations," Council on Foreign Relations, March 8, 1987.

10. Ibid.

11. Ibid.

12. Ibid.

13. Ibid.

14. Robertson, Transcripts, John Reese Interview, West Virginia, April 24, 1987; "Toward a Community."

15. Robertson, "Toward a Community."

16. Robertson, Transcript of interviews, Boston, undated 1987.

17. Robertson, Boston, undated; "Perspective," April 1978.

18. Robertson, Transcript, Jewish Federation, undated 1987.

19. Robertson, Transcripts, National Press Club, October 18, 1985; Jewish Federation; "700 Club," September 10, 1985; "Dictatorships and Single Standards."

20. Robertson, Transcript, Press Conference, Lafayette, Louisiana, March 27, 1987.

21. Robertson, Transcript, State GOP and Press, Georgia, May 23, 1987.

22. Robertson, "700 Club" Transcripts, December 31, 1985; June 18, 1985; July 12, 1985; Radio interview, New Hampshire, May 27, 1987.

23. Robertson, National Press Club; "700 Club" Transcript, March 15, 1985.

24. Robertson, "700 Club" Transcript, June 4, 1984.

25. Robertson, "Perspective," December 1980.

26. Robertson, Transcript, W. H. Fellowship Continuation, undated.

27. Robertson, Georgia State GOP.

28. Robertson, "700 Club," April 23, 1985; January 3, 1984.

29. Ibid., November 26, 1984.

30. Robertson, Transcripts, Reese Interview; United Conservative Appeal, April 27, 1987; Georgia State GOP and Press; Interviews, Boston.

31. Robertson, Gorham Breakfast.

32. Robertson, Interviews, Boston.

33. Robertson, *Concord Monitor* Editorial Board, New Hampshire, May 27, 1987.

34. Robertson, "700 Club," March 10, 1986.

35. Robertson, "Dictatorships and Single Standards."

36. "700 Club," March 10, 1986.

37. Ibid.

38. Ibid., June 22, 1984.

39. Ibid., July 16, 1984.

40. Robertson, Transcripts, Rotary of St. Louis, Missouri, March 12, 1987; United Conservative Appeal.

41. Robertson, Gorham Breakfast; "700 Club," November 15, 1985.

42. Robertson, Transcript, Press Conference Midwest GOP, May 30, 1987.

43. Robertson, National Press Club; Economic Club Speech, Detroit, Michigan, September 22, 1986.

44. Robertson, "700 Club," November 21 and 23, 1983.

45. Ibid., April 22 and August 6, 1985.

46. Robertson, Radio interview, New Hampshire.

47. Robertson, Transcripts, *Atlantic Monthly*, October 20, 1986; United Conservative Appeal; Gorham Breakfast.

48. Ibid.

49. Robertson, Transcripts, *Concord Monitor*; Address at a home, New Hampshire, May 28, 1987.

50. Robertson, Transcript, Marlin Maddoux, Interview, Dallas, March 11, 1987; Press Conference Midwest GOP.

51. Robertson, Interviews, Boston: United Conservative Appeal; "700 Club," July 19, 1985.

52. Robertson, United Conservative Appeal.

53. Robertson, Yale Forum; United Conservative Appeal; Interviews, Boston; *Rocky Mountain News* Editorial Board, Denver, July 11, 1987.

54. Robertson, "Perspective," July 1977; March 1978; Transcript, New Hampshire.

55. Robertson, "Perspective," May 1978.

56. Robertson, "Perspective," January 1980.

57. Robertson, Gorham Breakfast.

58. Robertson, Transcripts, Interview, Marshall, Channel 8, Tampa, Florida, January 24, 1987; Reese Interview.

59. Robertson, Transcript, At a home, New Hampshire.

60. Robertson, Transcript, *Rocky Mountain News* Editorial Board.

61. Robertson, Transcript, Yale Forum, New Haven, Connecticut, March 1987.

62. Robertson, Transcript, Anti-Defamation League, Boston, November 13, 1986.

63. Ibid.

64. Robertson, Transcript, "The MacNeil-Lehrer News Hour," November 11, 1985.

65. "700 Club," November 18, 1983; February 10, 1984; December 2, 1983.

66. Robertson, "Perspective," September 1980; the *Jerusalem Post*, Friday, April 3, 1987.

67. "700 Club," August 5, 1985.

68. *Time*, August 3, 1987, p. 21. George F. Kennan, *American Diplomacy* (Chicago: University of Chicago Press, 1985), pp. 119, 120; *Foreign Affairs*, Vol. 25, No. 4 (July 1947), pp. 566–582.

69. Kennan, *American Diplomacy*, pp. 95 103.

70. Ibid., p. 95.

71. Ibid., pp. 95–103.

Chapter 9
Robertson's Principles for Success

1. Aaron Wildavsky, *Moses as a Political Leader* (Alabama: The University of Alabama Press, 1984), p. 4.

2. A. James Reichley, *Religion in American Public Life* (Washington, D.C.: The Brookings Institution, 1985).

3. Kenneth Wald, *Religion and Politics in the United States* (New York: St. Martin's Press, 1987), pp. 210, 211.

Source Notes

4. Dean Curry, "An Epistemological Analysis of American Evangelicalism's Engagement of Politics: The Limits of Sola Scriptura," 1986; Charles Dunn, ed., *American Political Theology* (New York: Prager, 1984).

5. Pat Robertson with Bob Slosser, *The Secret Kingdom* (Nashville: Thomas Nelson, 1982), p. 218.

6. Ibid., p. 198.

7. Ibid., pp. 47–57.

8. Robertson, Transcript, New Hampshire, Spring 1987

9. Robertson, *Secret Kingdom*, p. 51.

10. Robertson, Transcript, Remarks at the New York Academy of TV Arts and Sciences, March 19, 1986.

11. Robertson, *Secret Kingdom*, pp. 21–34.

12. Ibid., pp. 21, 22.

13. Ibid., pp. 13–17.

14. Ibid., pp. 35, 36.

15. Ibid., pp. 76–100.

16. Ibid., pp. 13–17, 100.

17. Ibid., pp. 103–120.

18. Ibid., pp. 116, 117; Transcript, *Concord Monitor* Editorial Board, New Hampshire, May 27, 1987.

19. Robertson, *Secret Kingdom*, pp. 119, 120.

20. Ibid., pp. 104–106.

21. Ibid.

22. Ibid., pp. 121–136.

23. Ibid., p. 199.

24. Robertson, Transcript, New Hampshire, Spring 1987.

25. Robertson, *Secret Kingdom*, pp. 137–143.

26. Ibid., pp. 145–155.

27. Ibid., pp. 156–166.

28. Ibid., pp. 167–179.

29. Ibid., pp. 180–197.

30. Ibid., p. 199; *Shout It*, pp. 152, 153.

31. Robertson, *Secret Kingdom*, pp. 201–204.

32. Ibid., pp. 202, 203.

33. Ibid., p. 200.

34. Ibid., p. 201; Robertson, Transcript, Yale Forum, New Haven, March 1987.

35. Robertson, *Secret Kingdom*, pp. 171–173.

36. Ibid., pp. 203, 204.

37. Ibid., pp. 137–210; Transcript, Interview with Judy Forton, Channel 9, Manchester, New Hampshire, November 1986.

38. Hubert Morken, "Prophetic Politics: Three Models," *The Drew Gateway*, Fall 1986, pp. 25–41.

39. Robertson, *Secret Kingdom*, pp. 211, 212.

Chapter 10
What Kind of Revival for America?

1. Peter Grose, *A Changing Israel* (New York: Random House; Vintage Books, 1985), p. 23; Yael Yishai, *Land or Peace: Whither Israel?* (Stanford: Hoover Institution Press, 1987), pp. 100–141, 185, 186, 202–207.

2. Grose, *A Changing Israel*, p. 21.

3. Ibid., p. 35, 42.

4. Ibid., p. 43.

5. Ibid., p. 127.

6. Ibid., p. 29.

7. Ibid., p. 105–129.

8. Robertson, Transcript, Associated Press Editorial Board, New York, November 18, 1986.

9. Robertson, Transcript, "A New Vision for America," Washington, D.C., September 17, 1986.

10. Jean Jacques Rousseau, *The Creed of a Priest of Savoy* (New York: Frederick Ungar Publishing Co., 1957).

11. Pat Robertson, *America's Dates With Destiny* (Nashville: Thomas Nelson Publisher, 1986), pp. 15–21.

12. "700 Club" Videotape, July 7, 8, 9, 10, 1986

13. Robertson, Transcript, Oral Roberts University Commencement Address, May 1986.

14. Ibid., Zechariah 4:10.

15. Robertson, Transcript, National Religious Broadcasters, Washington, D.C., February 5, 1986.

16. Pat Robertson and Jamie Buckingham, *Shout It From the Housetops* (Plainfield, N.J.: Logos International, 1972), p. 40.

17. Robertson, Transcript, Interview at Harvard, Boston, Massachusetts, November 13, 1986.

18. Robertson, *Shout It* (1972 edition), p. 58.

19. Robertson, AP Board.

20. Robertson, *Shout It* (1972 edition), p. 120.

21. Interviews at CBN, May and June 1986.

22. "700 Club" Transcript, July 4, 1984.

23. Robertson, *Dates With Destiny*, pp. 73–85.

24. Robertson, "A New Vision for America."

25. "Meet the Press," Transcript, Vol. 85 (Washington, D.C., Kelly Press, December 15, 1985), p. 4; Robertson, Transcript, Nieman Fellows, Boston, Massachusetts, November 13, 1986.

26. Ibid.

27. Robertson, Transcript of Press Conference, Hyatt Regency, New Orleans, September 1986.

28. Robertson, "Perspective," August 1979.

29. Robertson, *Dates With Destiny*, pp. 29, 30; Isaiah 59:19.

30. Robertson, *Dates With Destiny*, pp. 29, 30.

31. Robertson, Nieman Fellows; "700 Club" Transcript, April 29, 1987; AP Board; *Dates With Destiny*, pp. 49–59, 129–144; *Shout It* (1986 edition), p 163.

32. Robertson, Nieman Fellows.

33. "700 Club" Video, July 7, 8, 9, 10, 1986.

34. "700 Club" Transcript, August 6, 1985.

35. Robertson, Transcript, United Conservative Appeal, April 27, 1987.

36. Robertson, Transcript, Freedom Council Luncheon, New Orleans Louisiana, September 1986.

37. Robertson, *Shout It* (1986 edition), p. 119.

38. Ibid., p. 158.

39. "700 Club" Transcript, November 13, 1984.

Chapter 11
Prayer: Robertson Depends on It

1. Robertson, Transcript, Off the Record Club, Washington, D.C., August 11, 1986.

2. "Does God Communicate Guidance?" *Virginian-Pilot*, December 27, 1986.

3. Transcript, Oral Roberts University Law School Press Conference, Tulsa, Oklahoma, November 1, 1985.

4. Robertson, Transcript, Interviews, Tampa, Florida, January 24, 1987.

Source Notes

5. Pat Robertson and William Proctor, *Beyond Reason* (New York: William Morrow; Bantam Books, 1986), p. 6.

6. Pat Robertson and Jamie Buckingham, *Shout It From the Housetops*, (Plainfield, N.J.: Logos International, 1972), pp. 105, 106.

7. Pat Robertson, *Answers to 200 of Life's Most Probing Questions* (Nashville: Thomas Nelson 1984), p. 105.

8. Ibid.; Robertson, *Shout It* (1972 edition), pp. 60, 61

9. Robertson, *Shout It* (1972 edition), pp. 84–86.

10. Ibid., pp. 218–233.

11. Robertson, Transcript, Reception by Bunker Hunt, Dallas, August 1, 1986.

12. Robertson, Off the Record Club.

13. Ibid.

14. Robertson, *Shout It* (1972 edition), pp. 20–23; Robertson, *Beyond Reason*, p. 81.

15. Pat Robertson, "Perspective," August 1980 (Virginia Beach: CBN), p. 1; "700 Club" Transcript, June 22, 1984.

16. Robertson, "Perspective," February 1977, p. 1.

17. Ibid., p. 2.

18. Robertson, Off the Record Club.

19. Interview on "Good Morning, America," New York, American Broadcasting Company.

20. Robertson, "700 Club" Transcript, April 23, 1985.

21. Ibid., December 2, 1983.

22. Ibid., September 18, 1985.

23. Ibid., June 5, 1985.

24. Interview on "The MacNeil-Lehrer News Hour," November 12, 1985.

25. Robertson, Transcript of remarks at the Pastors' Brunch, St. Petersburg, Florida, June 12, 1986; Transcript 79, undated.

26. Robertson, Off the Record Club. A work relating modernity to prayer is Jacques Ellul, *Prayer and Modern Man* (New York: Seabury Press, 1973); Acts 2; 1 Corinthians 12–14.

27. Robertson, *Shout It* (1972 edition), p. 189.

28. "Allison Blasts Robertson's Visit," *Tulsa World*, September 26, 1986, Section A, p. 2.

29. Robertson, Transcript, Atlanta Journalists, Atlanta, April 13, 1987; Remarks at the Freedom Council Rally, Florida, June 11, 1986.

30. Interview on "Face the Nation," p. 2; Robertson, Transcript, Jewish Federation, undated, 1987; *Shout It* (1972 edition), pp. 47–50; *Answers*, pp. 98–102.

31. Robertson, Transcript of interview with the *Pittsburgh Times*, Pennsylvania, January 24, 1987.

32. Robertson, Atlanta journalists; Virginia GOP Convention, Staunton, Virginia, December 6, 1986.

33. Interview with Herbert Titus, Provost, CBN University, Virginia Beach, Virginia, June 15, 1987.

34. Robertson, Transcript, Associated Press Editorial Board, New York, November 18, 1986.

35. Robertson, "Perspective," September-October 1978.

36. Robertson, *Shout It* (1972 edition), pp. 139, 140; Pat Robertson with Bob Slosser, *The Secret Kingdom* (Nashville: Thomas Nelson, 1982), pp. 13, 14.

Chapter 12
Prophecy: Robertson Defends It

1. *Eternity*, September 1987, pp. 11–13.

2. Pat Robertson and Jamie Buckingham, *Shout It From the Housetops* (Plainfield, N.J.: Logos International, 1972), p. 42.

3. Ibid., pp. 8–17.

4. Ibid., pp. 8–11.

5. Ibid., p. 10.

6. Ibid., pp. 51, 52.

7. Ibid., p. 86; Romans 5:5 KJV

8. Pat Robertson with Bob Slosser, *The Secret Kingdom* (Nashville: Thomas Nelson, 1982), p. 208; II Timothy 1:7; Kenneth Wald, Dennis Owen, and Samuel Hill, "Evangelical Politics and Status Issues," paper presented at American Political Science Association, September 3–6, 1987.

9. Robertson, *Answers to 200 of Life's Most Probing Questions* (Nashville: Thomas Nelson, 1984), pp. 27–34.

10. "700 Club" Transcript, September 3, 1985.

11. Ibid., December 30, 1985.

12. Robertson, *Answers*, pp. 27–34.

13. "700 Club" Transcript, May 8, 1985.

14. "700 Club" Transcript, December 30, 1983; July 10, 1984; January 1, 1985.

15. Ibid., December 30, 1983.

16. Ibid., January 1, 1985.

17. Ibid., December 13, 1983.

18. Robertson, "Perspective," May 1981.

19. *National Geographic*, Vol. 165, No. 2, February 1984, p. 145.

20. Ibid., p. 153.

21. Pat Robertson, "Perspective," May 1981.

22. Ibid., December 1977

23. Ibid., March 1977.

24. Robertson, Transcript of *Concord Monitor* Editorial Board, Concord, New Hampshire, May 27, 1987; Hyatt Regency Press, September 1986.

25. Ibid., February 1980; Robertson, *Shout It* (1972 edition), p. 190.

26. Robertson, "Perspective," February 1980.

27. Ibid., and February 1982.

28. "700 Club," Transcript, November 7, 1983.

29. David G. Gyertson, "God's Work Stands: An Historical Perspective of CBN University," unpublished manuscript; Robertson, *Secret Kingdom*, pp. 13, 14; *America's Dates With Destiny* (Nashville: Thomas Nelson, 1986), pp. 25–48; *Shout It* (1986 edition), p. 150.

30. Robertson, Transcript of Press Conference, LaFayette, Louisiana, March 27, 1987.

31. "700 Club" Transcript, January 7, 1985.

32. Robertson, Transcript of Freedom Council, Baton Rouge, Louisiana, September 1986.

33. "700 Club" Transcript, January 1, 1986.

34. "700 Club," November 13, 1984. Robertson, Transcript, "Face the Nation," Washington, D.C., August 17, 1986.

35. Robertson, *Shout It*, p. 60.

Chapter 13
Robertson Meets the Press

1. William F. Buckley, Jr., "Christ-Hunting," National Review, October 10, 1986, p. 62.

2. Joseph G. Gray, Interview, CBN, June 18, 1987.

3. Ibid.

4. Ibid.

5. Ibid.

6. Ibid.

7. Robertson, Transcripts, Marlin Maddoux, Interview, Dallas, March 11, 1987; Nieman Fellows, Harvard, Boston, November 13, 1986.

8. Robertson, Transcript, *Pittsburgh Times*, Pennsylvania, January 24, 1987.

9. Robertson, Transcript, Interview by Frank Ralch, *Christian Monthly*, Merrimack Valley, New Hampshire, May 1987.

10. Robertson, Transcript, United Conservative Appeal, April 27, 1987.

11. S. Robert Lichter, Stanley Rothman, and Linda Lichter, *The Media Elite* (Bethesda: Adler and Adler, 1986), pp. 294–297.

12. Ibid.

13. Ibid.

14. Transcript, "Larry King Live," April 4, 1987.

15. Ibid.

16. *New York Times*, July 25, 1987, p. A9.

17. Transcript, "Larry King Live."

18. Ibid.

19. Ibid.

20. Ibid.

21. "Robertson, Jackson May Be the Survivors," *Tulsa World*, October 6, 1987, p. A7.

22. "Robertson Forsook a Young Man's Joys for Faith That Has Led From a Pulpit Toward Presidency," *Wall Street Journal*, October 6, 1987, p. 60.

23. "Painfully, Robertson Corrects Record," *Washington Post*, October 8, 1987, pp. A1, A18.

24. "Robertson Blasts Reports as Invasion of Privacy," *Tulsa World*, October 9, 1987, p. A7.

25. Ibid.

26. Transcript, "Nightline," ABC, October 8, 1987.

27. Ibid.

28. Ibid.

29. Ibid.

30. Ibid.

31. Interviews with Michael Patrick, News Director, CBN News, and Dr. Herbert Titus, CBN School of Law, October 14, 1987.

32. "700 Club" Transcript, October 9, 1987.

33. "Why Is It Anybody's Business?" *Virginian-Pilot*, October 14, 1987, p. A9.

34. Ibid.

35. "Out, Pat," *Richmond News Leader*, October 8, 1987.

36. Cartoon, *Bloom County*, *Albany Sun Times Union*, April 12, 1987.

Chapter 14
Public Responses

1. "Robertson Campaign Persists Amid Setbacks," *Washington Post*, March 31, 1987, p. A8.

2. Ibid.; Marc Nuttle, Oral Roberts University Address, April 5, 1987.

3. Press Release, Annual Meeting National Executive Council, American Jewish Committee, October 31, 1986.

4. Ibid.

5. Ibid.

6. *The Watchman*, North Carolina, December 19, 1986, p. 6B.

7. Theodore Ellenoff, President, and David M. Gordes, Executive Vice-President, American Jewish Committee, Letters to the Editor, *Wall Street Journal*, December 2, 1986.

8. "Anti-Semitism, Extremism and the Farm Crisis," a Background Memorandum, Dr. Ellen Isler and Rabbi A. James Rudin, The American Jewish Committee.

9. Robertson, Transcript, Anti-Defamation League, Boston, November 13, 1986; "Pat Robertson and the Jewish vote," *Boston Jewish Times*, November 20, 1986.

10. Robertson, Anti-Defamation League.

11. Ibid.

12. Ibid.

13. Ibid.

14. Ibid.

15. Robertson, Transcript, Jewish Federation, undated 1987.

16. *New England Church Life*, Vol. 6, No. 9, November 1986, pp. 1, 7.

17. "Pat Robertson for President?" *Port Folio Magazine*, November 4, 1986.

18. "Reagan's Heir?" *Wanderer*, St. Paul, Minnesota, April 2, 1987.

19. Robertson, Transcript, Press Conference, Lafayette, Louisiana, March 27, 1987.

20. Robertson, Transcript, John Reese Interview, West Virginia, April 24, 1987.

21. "700 Club" Transcript, June 6, 1987.

22. Robertson, Reese Interview.

23. "Is Jesse Jackson Good for Blacks?" *Virginian-Pilot*, June 28, 1987, pp. C1, C2; Roger Hatch, "Jesse Jackson and Operation Push: A Case Study in the Relationship of Religion and Politics," 1983, p. 9; Charles Prysby and Lee Bernick, "The Impact of the Jackson Candidacy on the Democratic Party in the South," paper presented in Charleston, South Carolina, March 6, 7, 1986.

24. William Raspberry, "Why Is Jesse Jackson Running for President?" *Tulsa World*, June 6, 1986.

25. Robertson, Transcript, Speech in Boston, November 13, 1986; Marlin Maddoux, Interview, Dallas, March 11, 1987.

26. "Young Republicans Cheer Loudest for North," *Washington Post*, July 13, 1987, p. A8.

27. "Conservative Coalition Swamps Bush in Michigan," *Human Events*, March 7, 1987, pp. 200, 201.

28. "Cultural Conservatism, Republicanism, and the Republican Party," the author writing under a pseudonym, held a high position in the Reagan Administration; *Essays on Our Times*, Vol. 3, No. 1, Paul Weyrich, Publisher, March 1987, pp. 3–12.

29. David Lawrence and Richard Fleisher, "Puzzles and Confusions: Political Realignment in the 1980's," *Political Science Quarterly*, Vol. 102, No. 1, Spring 1987, pp. 79–92.

30. "The Next President," *Wall Street Journal*, May 22, 1987, pp. 1, 8.

31. *State*, Columbia, South Carolina, March 15, 1987; "If GOP Right Unites, Bush May Lose Lead," *Christian Science Monitor* March 5, 1987, pp. 3, 6.

32. Ibid.

Chapter 15
The Surprising Campaigner

1. Marc Nuttle, Lecture on Political Strategy, Oral Roberts University, Tulsa, Oklahoma, April 15, 1987; Michael Nelson, ed., *The Election of 1984* (Washington, D.C., Congressional Quarterly, Inc., 1985), pp. 27–82.

2. Nuttle, ORU.

3. Richard Goldstein, "The Christian Right: Will It Bring Political

Pentecost to America?" *Liberty: A Magazine of Religious Freedom*, Vol. 81, No. 6, November 1986, pp. 5–7.

4. Pat Robertson and Jamie Buckingham, *Shout It From the Housetops* (Plainfield, N.J.: Logos International, 1972), p. 179; Pat Robertson, *Shout It From the Housetops* (Virginia Beach: CBN Press, 1986), p. 106.

5. Goldstein, "The Christian Right," pp. 5–7.

6. "Pat Robertson: What Would He Do If He Were President?" *Charisma*, May 1986, p. 33.

7. Newspaper clipping, Bristol, Connecticut, undated, summer 1987.

8. Robertson, Transcript, Press Conference, Lansing, Michigan, July 30, 1986.

9. Chuck Colson, "Dear Pat: Winning Isn't Everything," *Christianity Today*, November 21, 1986.

10. Robertson, Transcript, Freedom Council, Baton Rouge, Louisiana, September 8, 1986.

11. Robertson, Transcript, *Rocky Mountain News* Editorial Board, Denver, Colorado, June 11, 1987.

12. Ibid.

13. Robertson, Transcript, GOP of Virginia, December 6, 1986. Comments made by Rev. Ed Dobson at Calvin College, Conference on Evangelicals in Politics in the 1980s, Fall 1986.

14. "Robertson Tests the Candidate Voice," *New York Times*, February 12, 1987.

15. *Valley News*, White River Junction, Vermont, April 20, 1987.

16. Robertson, Transcript, Pastors' breakfast, location unknown, February 18, 1987.

17. Ibid.

18. "The Mission of Bow-Tie Bob," *New Business*, Sarasota, Florida, March 1987.

19. "Catholic Aide to Robertson Puts Religious Differences Aside," *Atlanta Journal*, March 19, 1987.

20. "Robertson Campaigner Went from Shyness to Activism," *Fort Worth Star-Telegraph*, Fort Worth, Texas, December 7, 1986.

21. "Robertson for President Organizes," *News Examiner*, Gallatin, Tennessee, April 10, 1987.

22. *News Record*, Virginia, March 5, 1987; "Scripture Reading Helps Robertson Rally Iowans," *The Des Moines Register*, Iowa, February 22, 1987.

23. Robertson, Transcript, Pastors' Breakfast and Bloomington Lunch, February 18, 1987.

Source Notes

24. "Who's Ahead in the '88 Money Race," *Fortune*, June 8, 1987, p. 62; "Reports Show Bush Is Most Fiscally Fit Candidate," *USA Today*, July 16, 1987, p. 4A; "2 in Campaign Faulted on Funds," *New York Times*, July 16, 1987, p. A25; *Eagle and Beacon*, Wichita, Kansas, May 17, 1987, pp. 1A, 8A.

25. James L. Guth and John C. Green, "The GOP and the Christian Right: The Case of Pat Robertson's Campaign Contributors;" Paper presented at the 1987 Midwest Political Science Association, Chicago, Illinois, April 9–11, 1987; The *Washington Post*, April 15, 1987, p. A14; Robertson, Transcripts, *Atlanta Journal* Editors, April 13, 1987.

26. Ibid.

27. Ibid.; "Kemp's Strength in Minnesota Threatened," *Tulsa World*, September 29, 1987, p. A8.

28. "Rev. Pat Robertson's Candidacy Is Still Alive—and Kicking," *In These Times*, Chicago, Illinois, March 25, 1987.

29. "Robertson Bid Relying on Caucuses and Fervor," *New York Times*, July 7, 1987, p. A12.

30. Robertson, Transcripts, Bloomington; *Human Events*, Washington, D.C., April 7, 1987; *Concord Monitor* Editorial Board, New Hampshire, May 27, 1987.

31. "Don Gibson Emerging From Shadows to Position of Strength," *Sunday-Post/Courier*, Charleston, South Carolina, April 12, 1987.

32. Robertson, *Concord Monitor* Board.

33. Jack Germond and Jules Witcover, "Bush May Be Headed for Trap," *Tulsa World*, August 21, 1987, p. A12.

34. Ibid.

35. Ibid; "Bush–Robertson Fight Spreads South," *Washington Post*, October 9, 1987, pp. A4, 5.

36. "Pat Robertson Leads Straw Poll at Iowa GOP Gathering," *Tulsa World*, September 13, 1987, p. A3; *Time* magazine, September 28, 1987, pp. 22, 23.

37. "Bush Wins Florida Straw Poll; Robertson Is Second," *Tulsa World*, November 15, 1987, p. A11; "Robertson Backers Sweep Up in Illinois Straw Poll," *USA Today*, November 2, 1987; "Robertson Nips Bush in Maine Straw Poll," *Los Angeles Times*, November 8, 1987, p. 26.

38. Guth and Green, "The GOP and the Christian Right."

39. Robertson, Transcript, Gorham Breakfast, New Hampshire, May 28, 1987; *Tampa Tribune*, April 1, 1987.

40. "Swapping the Pulpit for the White House," UPI, *Daily News*, New York, April 11, 1987.

41. William F. Buckley, Jr., "Who Are the Conservatives Backing for President?" *Tulsa World*, April 22, 1987.

42. Robertson, Transcript, Press Conference, Midwest GOP, May 30, 1987.

43. Robertson, Transcript, Home Interview, New Hampshire, May 28, 1987; Steve Kelly Radio Interview, Denver, Colorado, June 11, 1987.

44. Koinonia: *Christians in Government*, Vol. 4, No. 3, July 1987.

45. Robertson, Transcript, Interview by Frank Ralch, *Christian Monthly*, Merrimack Valley, New Hampshire, May 1987.

46. Robertson, Gorham Breakfast.

47. Robertson, Transcript, Associated Press Editorial Board, New York, November 18, 1986.

48. Robertson, *Atlanta Journal* Editors.